Teach Yourself

Microsoft®
Word 2000
VISUALLY™

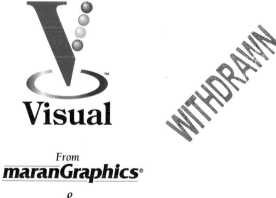

Visual

From
maranGraphics®

&

Hungry Minds™

Best-Selling Books • Digital Downloads • e-books • Answer Networks •
e-Newsletters • Branded Web Sites • e-learning

New York, NY ✦ Cleveland, OH ✦ Indianapolis, IN

Teach Yourself Microsoft® Word 2000 VISUALLY™

Published by
Hungry Minds, Inc.
909 Third Avenue
New York, NY 10022
www.hungryminds.com

Library of Congress Control Number: 99-62448

ISBN: 0-7645-6055-7

Printed in the United States of America

10 9 8 7

1K/SS/QR/QS/MG

Distributed in the United States by Hungry Minds, Inc.
Distributed by CDG Books Canada Inc. for Canada; by Transworld Publishers Limited in the United Kingdom; by IDG Norge Books for Norway; by IDG Sweden Books for Sweden; by IDG Books Australia Publishing Corporation Pty. Ltd. for Australia and New Zealand; by TransQuest Publishers Pte Ltd. for Singapore, Malaysia, Thailand, Indonesia, and Hong Kong; by Gotop Information Inc. for Taiwan; by ICG Muse, Inc. for Japan; by Intersoft for South Africa; by Eyrolles for France; by International Thomson Publishing for Germany, Austria and Switzerland; by Distribuidora Cuspide for Argentina; by LR International for Brazil; by Galileo Libros for Chile; by Ediciones ZETA S.C.R. Ltda. for Peru; by WS Computer Publishing Corporation, Inc. for the Philippines; by Contemporanea de Ediciones for Venezuela; by Express Computer Distributors for the Caribbean and West Indies; by Micronesia Media Distributor, Inc. for Micronesia; by Chips Computadoras S.A. de C.V. for Mexico; by Editorial Norma de Panama S.A. for Panama; by American Bookshops for Finland. For U.S. corporate orders, please call maranGraphics at 800-469-6616 or fax 905-890-9434.
For general information on Hungry Minds' products and services, please contact our Customer Care Department within the U.S. at 800-762-2974, outside the U.S. at 317-572-3993 or fax 317-572-4002.
For sales inquiries and reseller information, including discounts, premium and bulk quantity sales, and foreign-language translations, please contact our Customer Care Department at 800-434-3422, fax 317-572-4002, or write to Hungry Minds, Inc., Attn: Customer Care Department, 10475 Crosspoint Boulevard, Indianapolis, IN 46256.
For information on licensing foreign or domestic rights, please contact our Sub-Rights Customer Care Department at 212-844-5000.
For information on using Hungry Minds' products and services in the classroom or for ordering examination copies, please contact our Educational Sales Department at 800-434-2086 or fax 317-572-4005.
For press review copies, author interviews, or other publicity information, please contact our Public Relations department at 317-572-3168 or fax 317-572-4168.
For authorization to photocopy items for corporate, personal, or educational use, please contact maranGraphics at the address above.

Trademark Acknowledgments

Permissions

©**1999 maranGraphics, Inc.**
The 3-D illustrations are the copyright of maranGraphics, Inc.

 is a trademark of
Hungry Minds™ Hungry Minds, Inc.

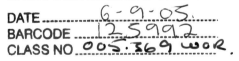

U.S. Corporate Sales	**U.S. Trade Sales**
Contact maranGraphics at (800) 469-6616 or fax (905) 890-9434.	Contact Hungry Minds at (800) 434-3422 or fax (317) 572-4002.

Some comments from our readers...

"I have to praise you and your company on the fine products you turn out. I have twelve of the *Teach Yourself VISUALLY* and *Simplified* books in my house. They were instrumental in helping me pass a difficult computer course. Thank you for creating books that are easy to follow."
  —*Gordon Justin (Brielle, NJ)*

"I commend your efforts and your success. I teach in an outreach program for the Dr. Eugene Clark Library in Lockhart, TX. Your *Teach Yourself VISUALLY* books are incredible and I use them in my computer classes. All my students love them!"
  —*Michele Schalin (Lockhart, TX)*

"Thank you so much for helping people like me learn about computers. The Maran family is just what the doctor ordered. Thank you, thank you, thank you."
  —*Carol Moten (New Kensington, PA)*

"I would like to take this time to compliment maranGraphics on creating such great books. Thank you for making it clear. Keep up the good work."
  —*Kirk Santoro (Burbank, CA)*

"I write to extend my thanks and appreciation for your books. They are clear, easy to follow, and straight to the point. Keep up the good work!"
  —*Seward Kollie (Dakar, Senegal)*

"What fantastic teaching books you have produced! Congratulations to you and your staff. You deserve the Nobel prize in Education in the Software category. Thanks for helping me to understand computers."
  —*Bruno Tonon (Melbourne, Australia)*

"Over time, I have bought a number of your 'Read Less-Learn More' books. For me, they are THE way to learn anything easily."
  —*José A. Mazón (Cuba, NY)*

"I was introduced to maranGraphics about four years ago and YOU ARE THE GREATEST THING THAT EVER HAPPENED TO INTRODUCTORY COMPUTER BOOKS!"
  —*Glenn Nettleton (Huntsville, AL)*

"Compliments To The Chef!! Your books are extraordinary! Or, simply put, Extra-Ordinary, meaning way above the rest! THANK YOU THANK YOU THANK YOU! for creating these."
  —*Christine J. Manfrin (Castle Rock, CO)*

"I'm a grandma who was pushed by an 11-year-old grandson to join the computer age. I found myself hopelessly confused and frustrated until I discovered the Visual series. I'm no expert by any means now, but I'm a lot further along than I would have been otherwise. Thank you!"
  —*Carol Louthain (Logansport, IN)*

"Thank you, thank you, thank you...for making it so easy for me to break into this high-tech world. I now own four of your books. I recommend them to anyone who is a beginner like myself. Now... if you could just do one for programming VCR's, it would make my day!"
  —*Gay O'Donnell (Calgary, Alberta, Canada)*

"You're marvelous! I am greatly in your debt."
  —*Patrick Baird (Lacey, WA)*

maranGraphics is a family-run business
located near Toronto, Canada.

At **maranGraphics**, we believe in producing great computer books—one book at a time.

Each maranGraphics book uses the award-winning communication process that we have been developing over the last 25 years. Using this process, we organize screen shots, text and illustrations in a way that makes it easy for you to learn new concepts and tasks.

We spend hours deciding the best way to perform each task, so you don't have to! Our clear, easy-to-follow screen shots and instructions walk you through each task from beginning to end.

Our detailed illustrations go hand-in-hand with the text to help reinforce the information. Each illustration is a labor of love—some take up to a week to draw!

We want to thank you for purchasing what we feel are the best computer books money can buy. We hope you enjoy using this book as much as we enjoyed creating it!

Sincerely,
The Maran Family

Please visit us on the Web at:
www.maran.com

CREDITS

Authors:
Ruth Maran
Kelleigh Wing

Copy Editor:
Roxanne Van Damme

Project Manager:
Judy Maran

**Editing &
Screen Captures:**
Raquel Scott
Janice Boyer
Michelle Kirchner
James Menzies
Frances Lea
Emmet Mellow

Layout Designer:
Treena Lees

Illustrators:
Russ Marini
Jamie Bell
Peter Grecco
Sean Johannesen
Steven Schaerer

**Screen Artist &
Revisions:**
Jimmy Tam

Indexer:
Raquel Scott

Post Production:
Robert Maran

Editorial Support:
Michael Roney

ACKNOWLEDGMENTS

maranGraphics™

Thanks to the dedicated staff of maranGraphics, including
Jamie Bell, Cathy Benn, Janice Boyer, Francisco Ferreira,
Peter Grecco, Jenn Hillman, Sean Johannesen, Michelle Kirchner,
Wanda Lawrie, Frances Lea, Treena Lees, Jill Maran, Judy Maran,
Maxine Maran, Robert Maran, Sherry Maran, Russ Marini,
Emmet Mellow, James Menzies, Stacey Morrison, Roben Ponce,
Steven Schaerer, Raquel Scott, Jimmy Tam, Roxanne Van Damme,
Paul Whitehead and Kelleigh Wing.

Finally, to Richard Maran who originated the easy-to-use
graphic format of this guide. Thank you for your
inspiration and guidance.

TABLE OF CONTENTS

Chapter 1

Getting Started

Chapter 2

Save and Open Documents

Chapter 3

Change Display of Documents

Chapter 4

Edit Text

TABLE OF CONTENTS

Chapter 5

Format Text

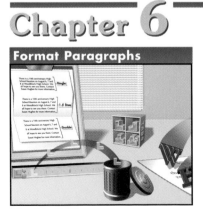

Chapter 6

Format Paragraphs

Chapter 7

Format Pages

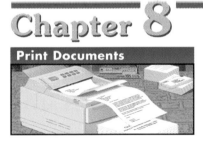

Chapter 8

Print Documents

Chapter 9

Work With Multiple Documents

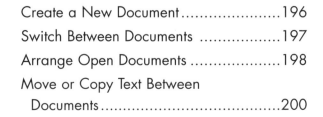

TABLE OF CONTENTS

Chapter 10

Work With Tables

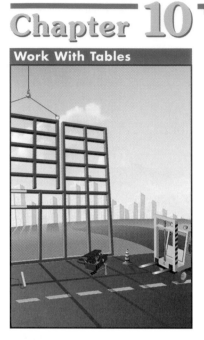

Chapter 11

Work With Graphics

Chapter 12
Time-Saving Features

Chapter 13
Mail Merge

Chapter 14
Word and the Internet

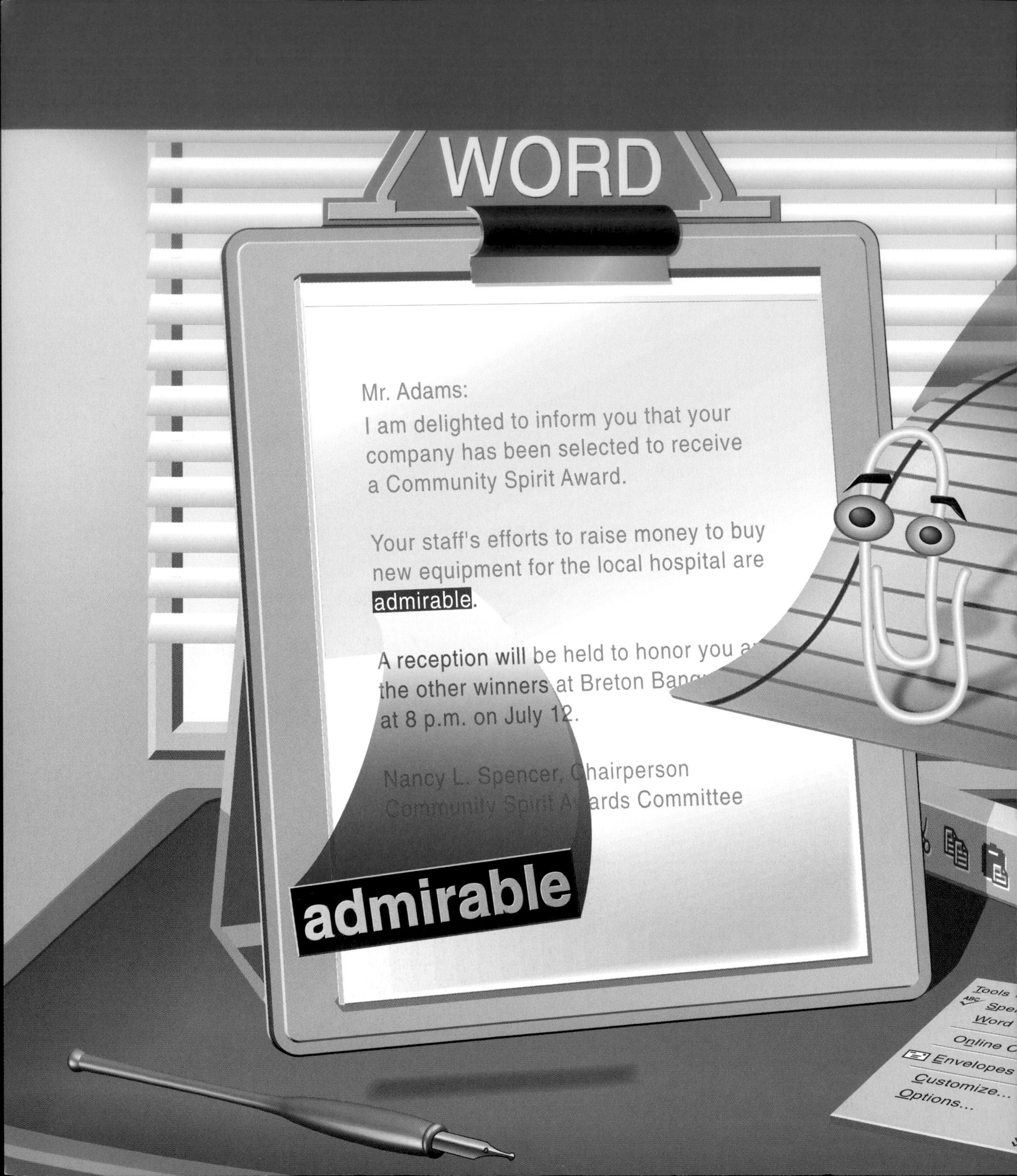

CHAPTER 1

Getting Started

Are you ready to begin using Microsoft Word 2000? This chapter will help you get started.

d Grammar... F7

ration

abels...

100%

INTRODUCTION TO WORD

Word lets you efficiently produce professional-looking documents, such as letters, reports, essays and newsletters.

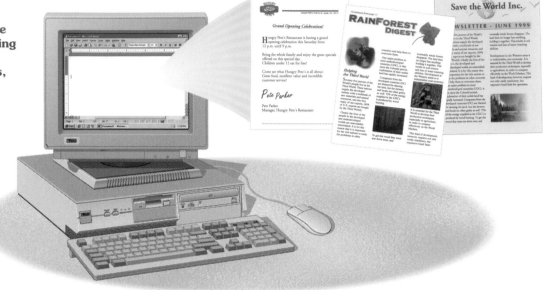

Edit Documents

Word offers many features that help you edit text in a document. You can add, delete and rearrange text. You can also check your document for spelling and grammar errors and use Word's built-in thesaurus to find more suitable words.

Format Documents

You can format a document to enhance the appearance of the document. You can use various fonts, styles and colors to emphasize important text. You can also center text on a page, adjust the spacing between lines of text, change the margins and create newspaper columns.

Print Documents

You can produce a paper copy of a document you create. Before printing, you can preview how the document will appear on a printed page. You can also print envelopes and mailing labels.

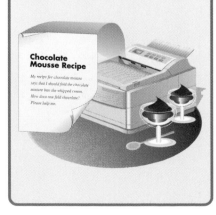

Create Tables

You can create tables to neatly display columns of information in a document. You can use one of Word's ready-to-use designs to instantly enhance the appearance of a table you create.

Add Graphics

Word comes with many types of graphics that you can use to make a document more interesting and entertaining. You can add graphics such as AutoShapes, text effects and clip art images.

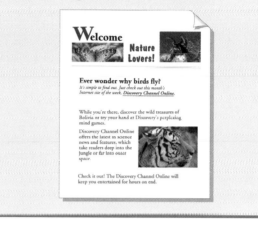

Mail Merge

You can quickly produce personalized letters and mailing labels for each person on a mailing list. This is useful if you often send the same document, such as an announcement or advertisement, to many people.

Word and the Internet

You can save a document as a Web page. This lets you place the document on the Internet for other people to view. You can also add a hyperlink to a document to connect the document to a Web page.

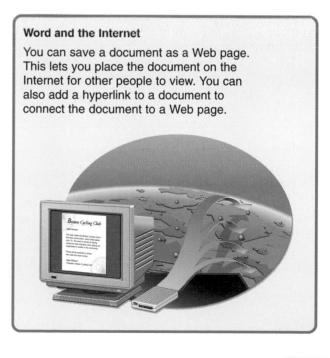

USING THE MOUSE

A mouse is a handheld device that lets you select and move items on your screen.

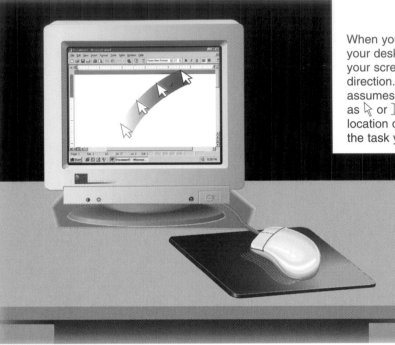

When you move the mouse on your desk, the mouse pointer on your screen moves in the same direction. The mouse pointer assumes different shapes, such as ⟍ or I, depending on its location on your screen and the task you are performing.

Resting your hand on the mouse, use your thumb and two rightmost fingers to move the mouse on your desk. Use your two remaining fingers to press the mouse buttons.

MOUSE ACTIONS

Click

Press and release the left mouse button.

Double-click

Quickly press and release the left mouse button twice.

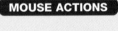

Right-click

Press and release the right mouse button.

Drag

Position the mouse pointer (⟍) over an object on your screen and then press and hold down the left mouse button. Still holding down the button, move the mouse to where you want to place the object and then release the button.

When you start Word, a blank document appears on your screen. You can type text into this document.

START WORD

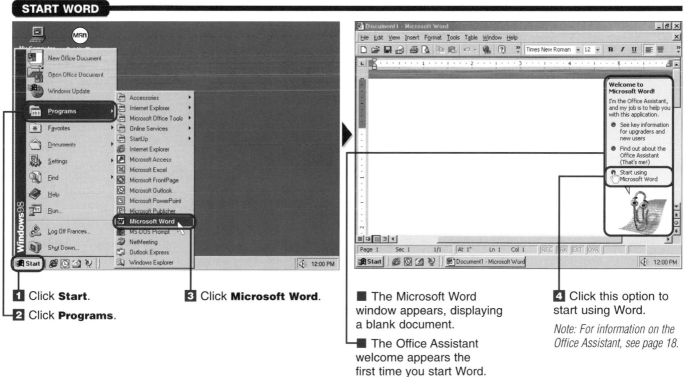

1 Click **Start**.

2 Click **Programs**.

3 Click **Microsoft Word**.

■ The Microsoft Word window appears, displaying a blank document.

■ The Office Assistant welcome appears the first time you start Word.

4 Click this option to start using Word.

Note: For information on the Office Assistant, see page 18.

THE WORD SCREEN

The Word screen
displays several items
to help you perform
tasks efficiently.

Standard Toolbar

Contains buttons
to help you select
common commands,
such as Save and
Print.

Insertion Point

The flashing line
on the screen that
indicates where
the text you type
will appear.

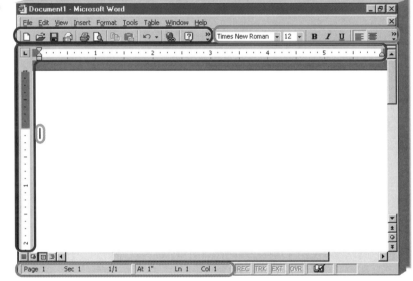

Formatting Toolbar

Contains buttons to
help you select
common formatting
commands, such as
Bold and Underline.

Ruler

Allows you to
change margin
and tab settings
for the document.

Status Bar

Provides information
about the area of the
document displayed
on the screen and
the position of the
insertion point.

Page 1

The page displayed
on the screen.

At 1"

The distance from
the top of the page
to the insertion point.

Sec 1

The section of the
document displayed
on the screen.

Ln 1

The number of lines
from the top margin
to the insertion point.

1/1

The page displayed
on the screen and the
total number of pages
in the document.

Col 1

The number of
characters from
the left margin to
the insertion point,
including spaces.

SELECT COMMANDS USING TOOLBARS

A toolbar contains buttons that you can use to select commands. Each command performs a different task.

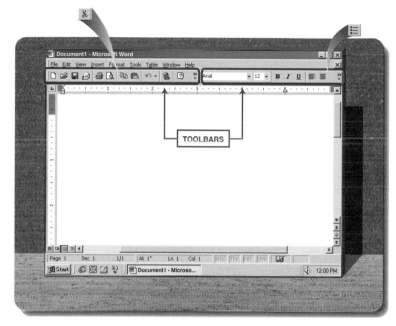

TOOLBARS

When you first start Word, the most commonly used buttons appear on each toolbar. As you work with Word, the toolbars automatically change to remove buttons you rarely use and display the buttons you use most often.

SELECT COMMANDS USING TOOLBARS

1 To display the name of a toolbar button, position the mouse ⌖ over the button.

■ After a few seconds, the name of the button appears in a yellow box. The button name can help you determine the task the button performs.

2 A toolbar may not be able to display all of its buttons. Click ⏩ to display additional buttons for the toolbar.

■ Additional buttons for the toolbar appear.

3 To use a toolbar button to select a command, click the button.

SELECT COMMANDS USING MENUS

You can select a command from a menu to perform a task. Each command performs a different task.

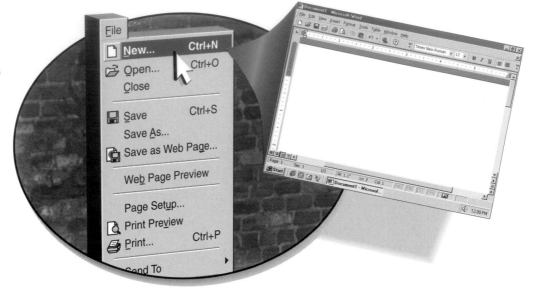

SELECT COMMANDS USING MENUS

1 Click the name of the menu you want to display.

■ A short version of the menu appears, displaying the most commonly used commands.

2 To expand the menu and display all the commands, position the mouse ⌖ over ✕.

Note: If you do not perform step 2, the expanded menu will automatically appear after a few seconds.

How can I make a command appear on the short version of a menu?

When you select a command from an expanded menu, the command is automatically added to the short version of the menu. The next time you display the short version of the menu, the command you selected will appear.

Expanded Menu

Short Menu

■ The expanded menu appears, displaying all the commands.

3 Click the command you want to use.

Note: A dimmed command is currently not available.

■ To close a menu without selecting a command, click outside the menu.

■ A dialog box appears if the command you selected displays three dots (...).

4 When you finish selecting options in the dialog box, click **OK** to confirm your changes.

■ To close the dialog box without selecting any options, click **Cancel**.

Word allows you to type text into your document quickly and easily.

■ The text you type will appear where the insertion point flashes on your screen.

1 Type the text for your document.

■ When the text you type reaches the end of a line, Word automatically wraps the text to the next line. You only need to press the **Enter** key when you want to start a new paragraph.

Note: In this example, the font of text was changed to Arial to make the document easier to read. To change the font of text, see page 96.

Can I enter text anywhere in my document?

Word's Click and Type feature allows you to enter text anywhere in your document. Double-click the location where you want to enter text and then type the text. The Click and Type feature is only available in the Print Layout and Web Layout views. For more information on the views, see page 44.

SPELLING ERRORS

■ Word automatically underlines spelling errors in red and grammar errors in green. The underlines will not appear when you print your document. To correct spelling and grammar errors, see pages 74 to 77.

■ Word automatically corrects common spelling errors as you type, such as recieve (receive) and nwe (new).

ENTER TEXT AUTOMATICALLY

■ Word's AutoText feature helps you quickly enter common words and phrases.

■ When you type the first few characters of a common word or phrase, a yellow box appears, displaying the text.

1 To insert the text, press the `Enter` key.

■ To ignore the text, continue typing.

Note: For more information on the AutoText feature, see pages 86 to 89.

Before performing many tasks in Word, you must select the text you want to work with. Selected text appears highlighted on your screen.

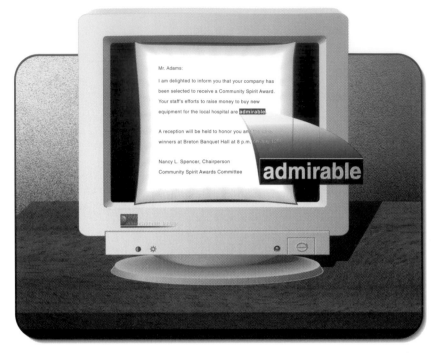

admirable

SELECT TEXT

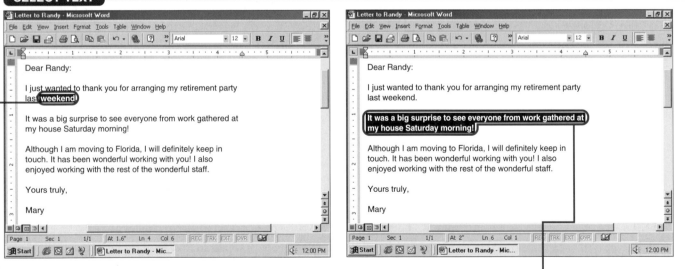

SELECT A WORD

1 Double-click the word you want to select.

■ To deselect text, click outside the selected area.

SELECT A SENTENCE

1 Press and hold down the `Ctrl` key.

2 Still holding down the `Ctrl` key, click the sentence you want to select.

?

How do I select all the text in my document?

To quickly select all the text in your document, press and hold down the **Ctrl** key as you press the **A** key.

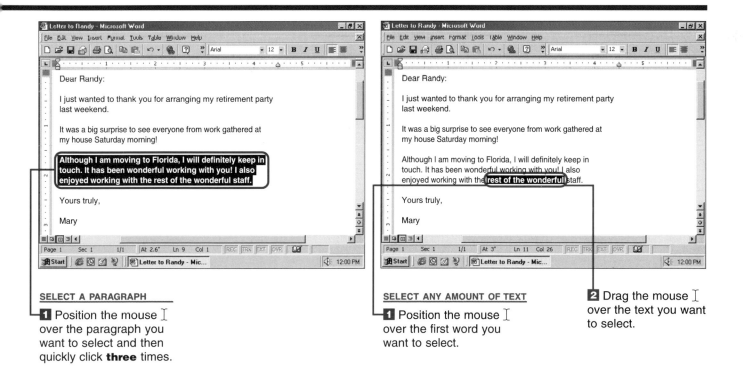

SELECT A PARAGRAPH

1 Position the mouse I over the paragraph you want to select and then quickly click **three** times.

SELECT ANY AMOUNT OF TEXT

1 Position the mouse I over the first word you want to select.

2 Drag the mouse I over the text you want to select.

MOVE THROUGH A DOCUMENT

You can easily move to another location in your document.

If you create a long document, your computer screen may not be able to display all the text at once. You must scroll through your document to view other parts of the document.

MOVE THROUGH A DOCUMENT

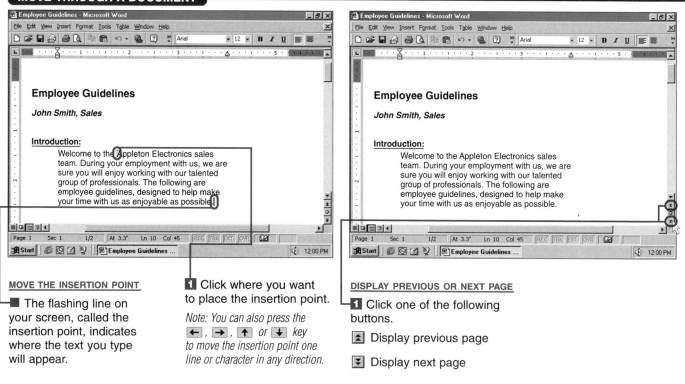

MOVE THE INSERTION POINT

■ The flashing line on your screen, called the insertion point, indicates where the text you type will appear.

1 Click where you want to place the insertion point.

Note: You can also press the ← , → , ↑ *or* ↓ *key to move the insertion point one line or character in any direction.*

DISPLAY PREVIOUS OR NEXT PAGE

1 Click one of the following buttons.

⬆ Display previous page

⬇ Display next page

How do I use a wheeled mouse to scroll through my document?

A wheeled mouse has a wheel between the left and right mouse buttons. Moving this wheel lets you quickly scroll through your document. The Microsoft IntelliMouse is a popular example of a wheeled mouse.

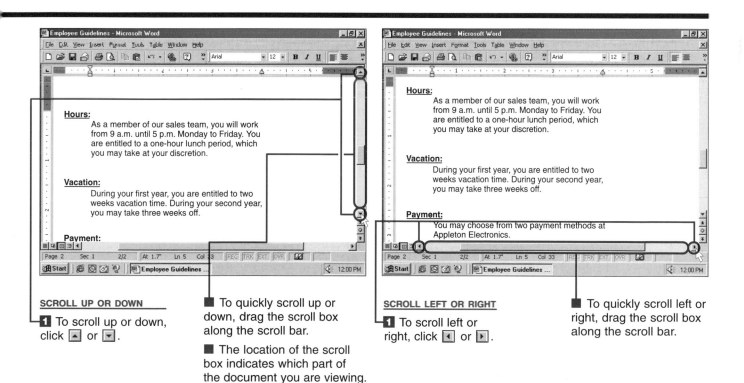

SCROLL UP OR DOWN

■1 To scroll up or down, click ▲ or ▼.

■ To quickly scroll up or down, drag the scroll box along the scroll bar.

■ The location of the scroll box indicates which part of the document you are viewing. To view the middle of the document, drag the scroll box halfway down the scroll bar.

SCROLL LEFT OR RIGHT

■1 To scroll left or right, click ◄ or ►.

■ To quickly scroll left or right, drag the scroll box along the scroll bar.

GETTING HELP

If you do not know how to perform a task, you can ask the Office Assistant for help.

USING THE OFFICE ASSISTANT

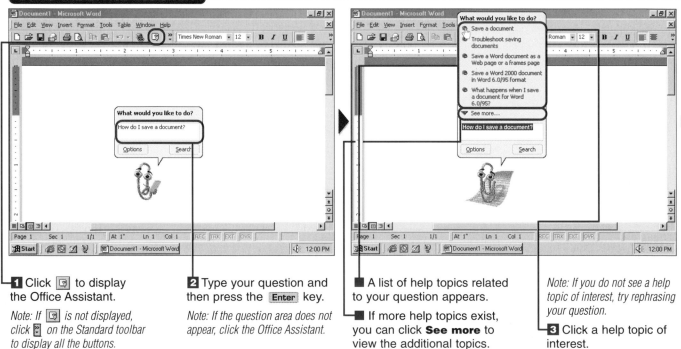

1 Click 🔘 to display the Office Assistant.

Note: If 🔘 is not displayed, click 🔘 on the Standard toolbar to display all the buttons.

2 Type your question and then press the **Enter** key.

Note: If the question area does not appear, click the Office Assistant.

■ A list of help topics related to your question appears.

■ If more help topics exist, you can click **See more** to view the additional topics.

Note: If you do not see a help topic of interest, try rephrasing your question.

3 Click a help topic of interest.

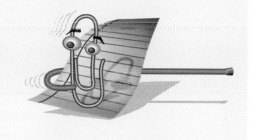

Can I move the Office Assistant?

If the Office Assistant covers information on your screen, you may need to move the Office Assistant. Position the mouse over the Office Assistant and then drag it to a new location.

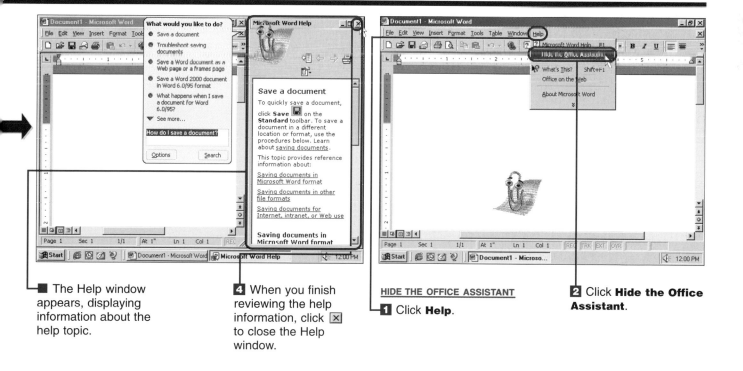

■ The Help window appears, displaying information about the help topic.

4 When you finish reviewing the help information, click ☒ to close the Help window.

HIDE THE OFFICE ASSISTANT

1 Click **Help**.

2 Click **Hide the Office Assistant**.

GETTING HELP

You can use Word's
help index to locate
help topics of interest.

USING THE HELP INDEX

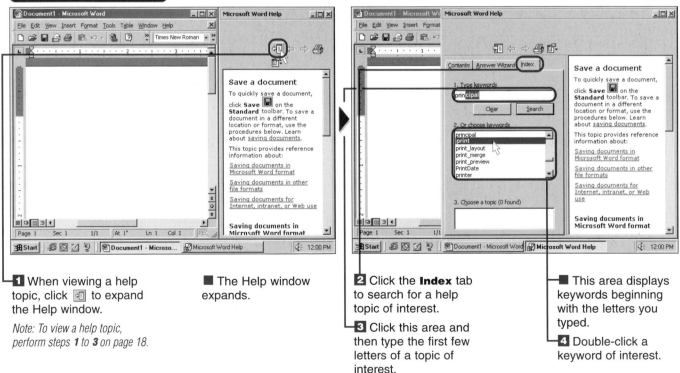

1 When viewing a help
topic, click 🔲 to expand
the Help window.

*Note: To view a help topic,
perform steps 1 to 3 on page 18.*

■ The Help window
expands.

2 Click the **Index** tab
to search for a help
topic of interest.

3 Click this area and
then type the first few
letters of a topic of
interest.

■ This area displays
keywords beginning
with the letters you
typed.

4 Double-click a
keyword of interest.

CITY OF WESTMINSTER COLLEGE
MAIDA VALE LEARNING CENTRE

DATE................ 6 - 9 - 05 ....
BARCODE .... 125992 ....
CLASS NO ....

Why do some words in the Help window appear in blue?

You can click a word or phrase that appears in blue with an underline to display a related help topic.

You can click a word or phrase that appears in blue without an underline to display a definition of the text. To hide the definition, click anywhere on your screen.

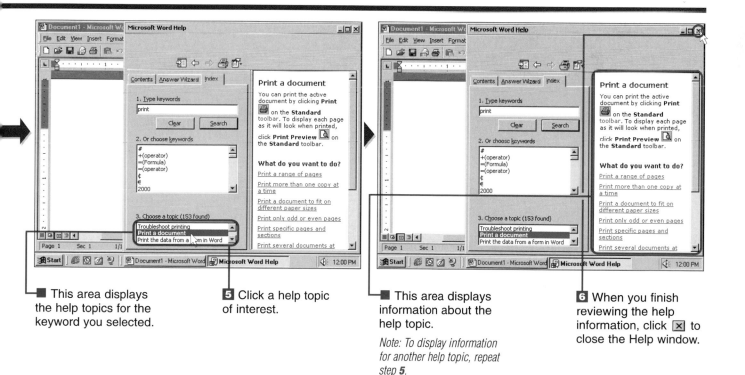

■ This area displays the help topics for the keyword you selected.

5 Click a help topic of interest.

■ This area displays information about the help topic.

Note: To display information for another help topic, repeat step 5.

6 When you finish reviewing the help information, click ⊠ to close the Help window.

CHAPTER 2

Save and Open Documents

Are you wondering how to save, close or open a Word document? Learn how in this chapter.

Meeting

Sales Meeting

12:00 PM

SAVE A DOCUMENT

You can save your
document to store it
for future use. This
allows you to later
review and edit the
document.

SAVE A DOCUMENT

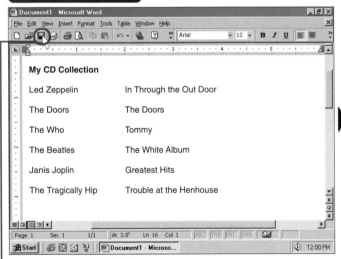

My CD Collection

Led Zeppelin	In Through the Out Door
The Doors	The Doors
The Who	Tommy
The Beatles	The White Album
Janis Joplin	Greatest Hits
The Tragically Hip	Trouble at the Henhouse

1 Click 🔲 to save
your document.

*Note: If 🔲 is not displayed,
click ⟩⟩ on the Standard toolbar
to display all the buttons.*

■ The Save As dialog
box appears.

*Note: If you previously saved
your document, the Save As
dialog box will not appear
since you have already named
the document.*

2 Type a name for the
document.

24

What are the commonly used folders I can access?

History
Provides access to folders and documents you recently used.

My Documents
Provides a convenient place to store a document.

Desktop
Lets you store a document on the Windows desktop.

Favorites
Provides a place to store a document you will frequently access.

Web Folders
Can help you store a document on the Web.

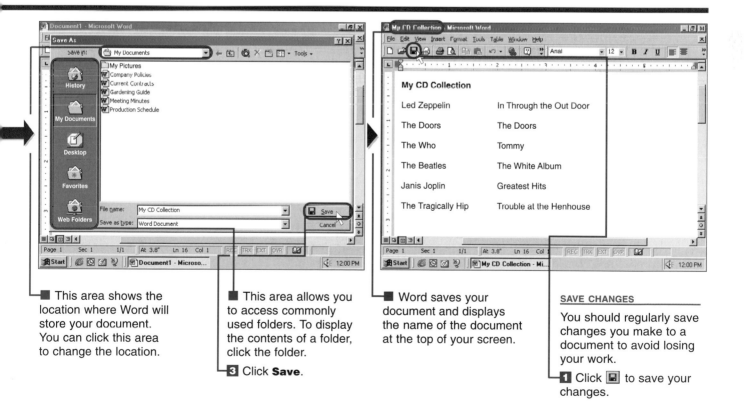

■ This area shows the location where Word will store your document. You can click this area to change the location.

■ This area allows you to access commonly used folders. To display the contents of a folder, click the folder.

3 Click **Save**.

■ Word saves your document and displays the name of the document at the top of your screen.

SAVE CHANGES

You should regularly save changes you make to a document to avoid losing your work.

1 Click 🖫 to save your changes.

SAVE A DOCUMENT IN A DIFFERENT FORMAT

You can save a Word document in a different format. This is useful if you need to share a document with a colleague who does not use Word 2000.

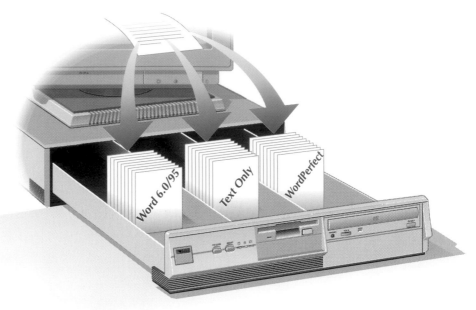

SAVE A DOCUMENT IN A DIFFERENT FORMAT

1 Click **File**.

2 Click **Save As**.

■ The Save As dialog box appears.

3 Type a name for your document.

Why does a dialog box appear when I save my document In a different format?

A dialog box appears if Word needs to install software before saving the document in the new format. Insert the CD-ROM disc you used to install Word into your CD-ROM drive. Then click **Yes** to install the software.

> **Microsoft Word**
>
> Microsoft Word can't export in the specified format. This feature is not currently installed. Would you like to install it now?
>
> [Yes]   [No]

4 Click this area to select the format you want to use to save the document.

5 Click the format you want to use.

6 Click **Save** to save your document.

■ A dialog box may appear, indicating that some of the formatting in your document may be lost when you save the document in the new format.

7 Click **Yes** to continue.

■ Word saves your document in the new format. You can now open and work with the document in another program.

CLOSE A DOCUMENT

When you finish
working with a
document, you can
close the document
to remove it from
your screen.

When you close a
document, you do not
exit the Word program.
You can continue to work
with other documents.

CLOSE A DOCUMENT

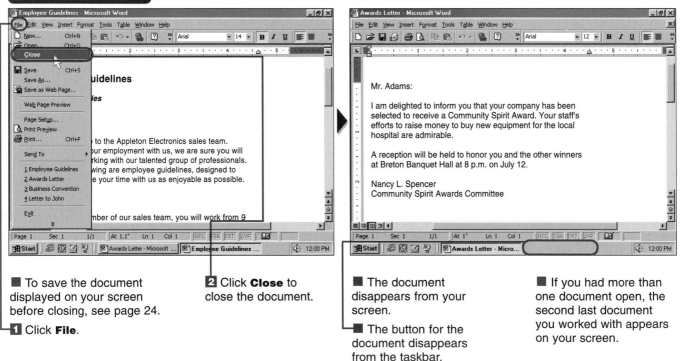

■ To save the document
displayed on your screen
before closing, see page 24.

1 Click **File**.

2 Click **Close** to
close the document.

■ The document
disappears from your
screen.

■ The button for the
document disappears
from the taskbar.

■ If you had more than
one document open, the
second last document
you worked with appears
on your screen.

When you finish using Word, you can exit the program.

You should always exit all programs before turning off your computer.

EXIT WORD

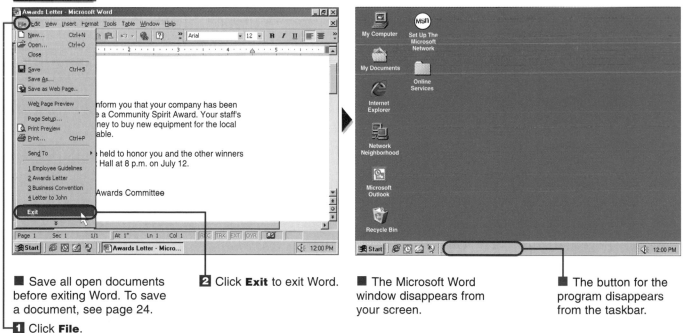

■ Save all open documents before exiting Word. To save a document, see page 24.

1 Click **File**.

2 Click **Exit** to exit Word.

■ The Microsoft Word window disappears from your screen.

■ The button for the program disappears from the taskbar.

OPEN A DOCUMENT

You can open a saved
document and display
it on your screen. This
allows you to review
and make changes to
the document.

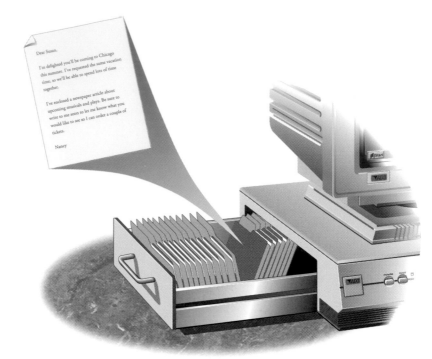

OPEN A DOCUMENT

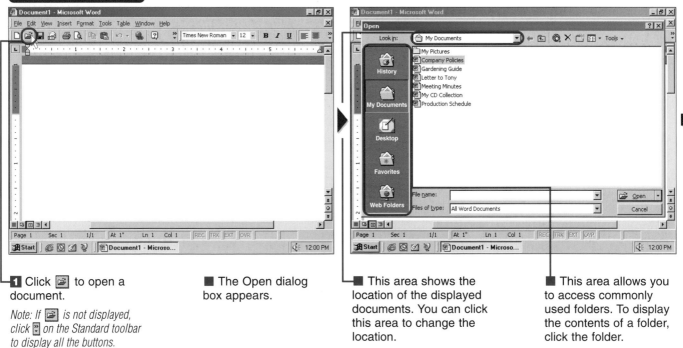

1 Click 📝 to open a
document.

*Note: If 📝 is not displayed,
click 💬 on the Standard toolbar
to display all the buttons.*

■ The Open dialog
box appears.

■ This area shows the
location of the displayed
documents. You can click
this area to change the
location.

■ This area allows you
to access commonly
used folders. To display
the contents of a folder,
click the folder.

*Note: For information on
the commonly used folders,
see the top of page 25.*

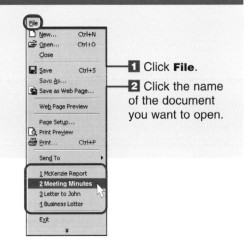

?

Can I quickly open a document I recently worked with?

Word remembers the names of the last four documents you worked with. You can quickly open one of these documents.

1 Click **File**.

2 Click the name of the document you want to open.

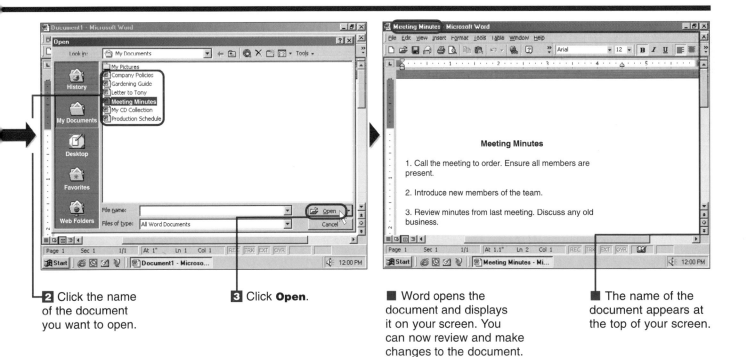

2 Click the name of the document you want to open.

3 Click **Open**.

■ Word opens the document and displays it on your screen. You can now review and make changes to the document.

■ The name of the document appears at the top of your screen.

OPEN A DOCUMENT IN A DIFFERENT FORMAT

You can use Word to open and work with a document that was created in another program. This helps you work with colleagues who use different word processing programs.

OPEN A DOCUMENT IN A DIFFERENT FORMAT

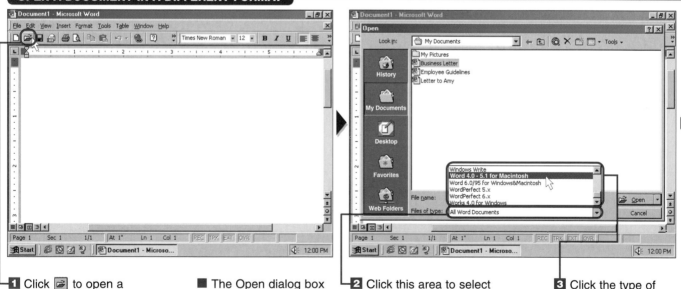

1 Click 📂 to open a document.

Note: If 📂 is not displayed, click 📷 on the Standard toolbar to display all the buttons.

■ The Open dialog box appears.

2 Click this area to select the type of document you want to open.

3 Click the type of document you want to open.

*Note: If you do not know the type of document you want to open, click **All Files**.*

What types of documents can I open using Word?

You can open documents created in many different programs, such as WordPerfect, Write, Word for Macintosh and older versions of Word for Windows.

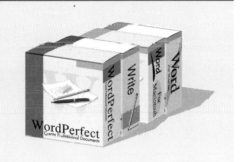

■ This area shows the location of the displayed documents. You can click this area to change the location.

4 Click the name of the document you want to open.

5 Click **Open**.

Note: A dialog box may appear if Word needs to install software before opening the document. To install the software, see the top of page 27.

■ Word opens the document and displays it on your screen. You can now review and make changes to the document.

■ The name of the document appears at the top of your screen.

FIND A DOCUMENT

If you cannot remember
the name or location of
a document you want to
work with, you can search
for the document.

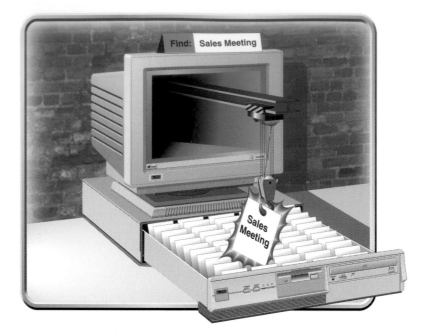

FIND A DOCUMENT

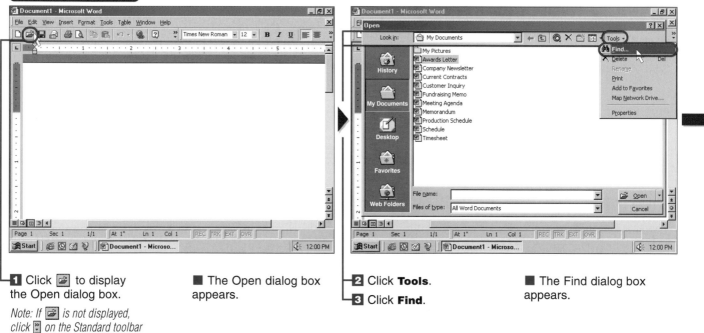

1 Click 🖼 to display
the Open dialog box.

*Note: If 🖼 is not displayed,
click 🖺 on the Standard toolbar
to display all the buttons.*

■ The Open dialog box
appears.

2 Click **Tools**.

3 Click **Find**.

■ The Find dialog box
appears.

How can I search for a document?

When searching for a document, you must specify a property for the search. Common properties include the document contents, creation date, file name and number of pages. After you specify a property, you can specify a condition and value for the search.

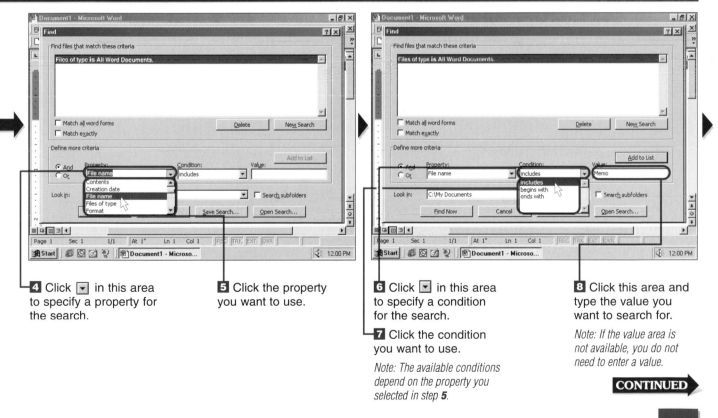

4 Click ▼ in this area to specify a property for the search.

5 Click the property you want to use.

6 Click ▼ in this area to specify a condition for the search.

7 Click the condition you want to use.

Note: The available conditions depend on the property you selected in step 5.

8 Click this area and type the value you want to search for.

Note: If the value area is not available, you do not need to enter a value.

CONTINUED

You can specify the
location where you want
to search for a document.

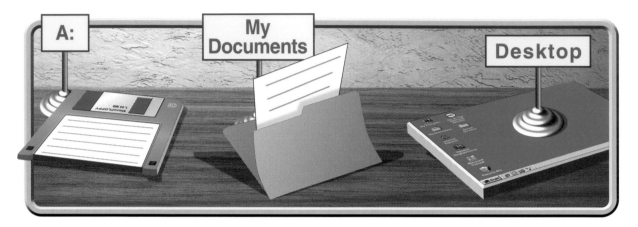

FIND A DOCUMENT (CONTINUED)

9 Click ▼ in this area to specify where you want to search for the document.

10 Click the location you want to search.

11 To search the contents of all the folders in the location you specified, click **Search subfolders** (☐ changes to ☑).

12 Click **Add to List** to confirm the search criteria you specified.

■ The search criteria you specified appears in this area.

*Note: Word automatically adds the criteria **Files of type is All Word Documents** to the list of search criteria for you.*

13 Click **Find Now** to start the search.

When I started the search, why did a dialog box appear, asking if I want to install FindFast?

FindFast is a feature that can help speed up your searches. To install FindFast, insert the CD-ROM disc you used to install Word into your CD-ROM drive. Then click **Yes** to install FindFast.

Microsoft Office

This operation would be considerably faster if FindFast were installed. Would you like to install FindFast now to speed this operation up in the future?

Yes   No

■ The Open dialog box reappears.

■ This area displays the names of the documents Word found.

14 To open a document, click the name of the document.

15 Click **Open**.

■ Word opens the document and displays it on your screen. You can now review and make changes to the document.

PROTECT A DOCUMENT

You can prevent other
people from opening
or making changes to a
document by protecting
it with a password.

PROTECT A DOCUMENT

1 Click **Tools**.

2 Click **Options**.

■ The Options dialog
box appears.

3 Click the **Save** tab.

?

What password should I use to protect my document?

When choosing a password, you should not use words that people can easily associate with you, such as your name or favorite sport. The most effective passwords connect two words or numbers with a special character (example: **blue@123**). A password can contain up to 15 characters, including letters, numbers and symbols.

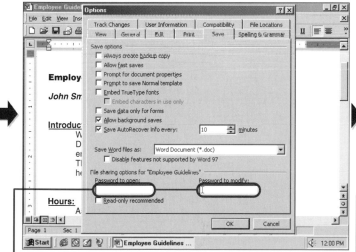

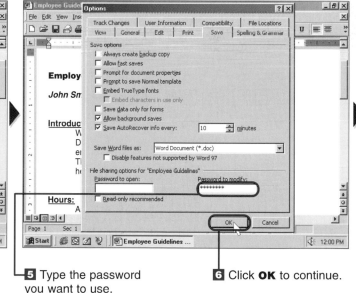

4 Click the box for the type of password you want to enter.

Password to open

Prevents people from opening the document without entering the correct password.

Password to modify

Prevents people from making changes to the document without entering the correct password.

5 Type the password you want to use.

6 Click **OK** to continue.

CONTINUED

PROTECT A DOCUMENT

After you protect a document with a password, Word will ask you to enter the password each time you open the document.

You should write down your password and keep it in a safe place. If you forget the password, you may not be able to open the document.

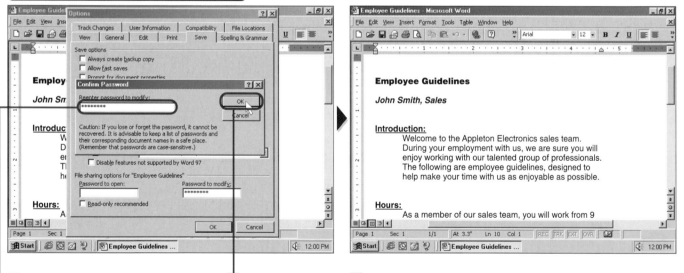

■ The Confirm Password dialog box appears, asking you to confirm the password you entered.

7 Type the password again to confirm the password.

8 Click **OK**.

9 Save the document to save your changes. To save a document, see page 24.

■ To unprotect a document, perform steps **1** to **6** starting on page 38, except delete the existing password in step **5**. Then perform step **9**.

I typed the correct password, but Word will not open my document. What is wrong?

Passwords in Word are case sensitive. If you do not enter the correct uppercase and lowercase letters, Word will not accept the password. For example, if your password is **Car**, you cannot enter **car** or **CAR** to open the document.

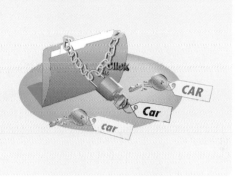

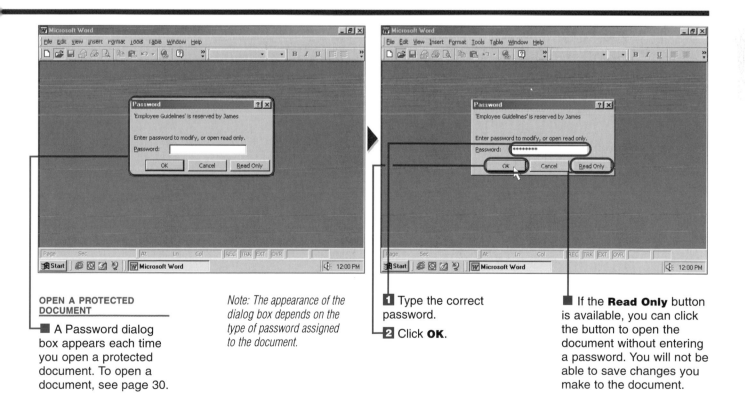

OPEN A PROTECTED DOCUMENT

■ A Password dialog box appears each time you open a protected document. To open a document, see page 30.

Note: The appearance of the dialog box depends on the type of password assigned to the document.

1 Type the correct password.

2 Click **OK**.

■ If the **Read Only** button is available, you can click the button to open the document without entering a password. You will not be able to save changes you make to the document.

Dear Susan,

I'm delighted you'll be coming to Chicago this
summer. I've requested the same vacation time,
so we'll be able to spend lots of time together.
In the three years I've been living in Chicago, I've
really grown to love the city. I know all the best places
I'll be a great tour guide during your visit!

ee years I've be

I've really grow

be a great tour

Change Display of Documents

Would you like to change the way your document appears on your screen? In this chapter you will learn how to display your document in a different view, zoom in or out, display or hide a toolbar and more.

CHANGE THE VIEW

Word offers four ways to view your document. You can choose the view that best suits your needs.

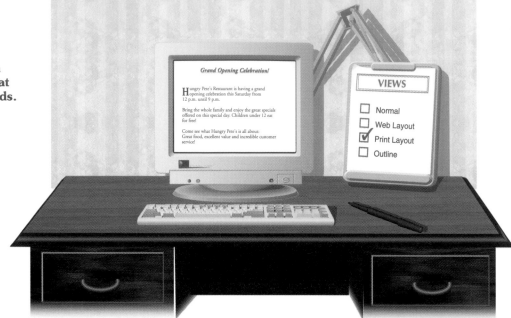

CHANGE THE VIEW

■ When you first start Word, the document appears in the Print Layout view.

1 To change the view, click one of the following buttons.

   ▤ Normal

   ▣ Web Layout

   ▣ Print Layout

   ▤ Outline

■ The document appears in the new view.

THE FOUR VIEWS

Normal View

This view simplifies your document so you can quickly enter, edit and format text. The Normal view does not display margins, headers, footers or page numbers.

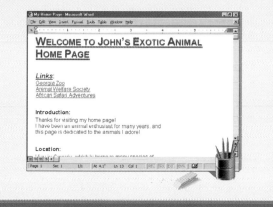

Web Layout View

This view displays your document as it will appear on the Web. The Web Layout view is useful when you are using Word to create a Web page.

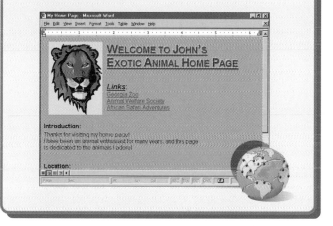

Print Layout View

This view displays your document as it will appear on a printed page. The Print Layout view displays margins, headers, footers and page numbers.

Outline View

This view helps you review and work with the structure of your document. The Outline view lets you collapse a document to see only the main headings or expand a document to see all the main headings and text. This view is useful when working with long documents.

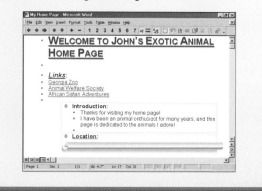

DISPLAY OR HIDE THE RULER

You can display or hide the ruler at any time. The ruler helps you position text in a document.

When you first start Word, the ruler appears on your screen. Hiding the ruler provides a larger and less cluttered working area.

You cannot display or hide the ruler in the Outline view. For more information on the views, see page 44.

DISPLAY OR HIDE THE RULER

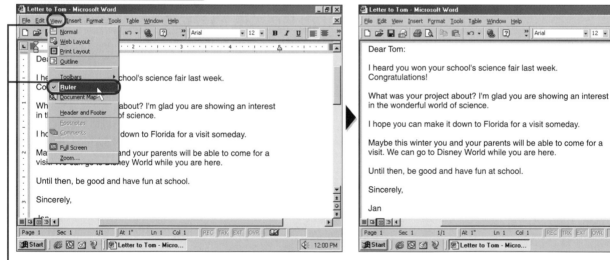

1 Click **View**.

2 Click **Ruler**. A check mark (✔) beside **Ruler** indicates the ruler is currently displayed.

Note: If Ruler does not appear on the menu, position the mouse ⍭ over the bottom of the menu to display all the menu commands.

■ Word displays or hides the ruler.

Word offers several toolbars that you can display or hide at any time. Each toolbar contains buttons that help you quickly perform common tasks.

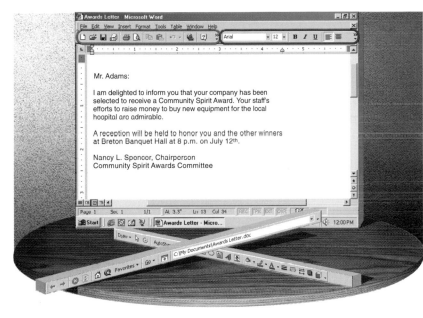

When you first start Word, the Standard and Formatting toolbars appear on your screen.

Standard

Formatting

DISPLAY OR HIDE A TOOLBAR

■1 To display or hide a toolbar, click **View**.

■2 Click **Toolbars**.

■ A list of toolbars appears. A check mark (✔) beside a toolbar name tells you the toolbar is currently displayed.

■3 Click the name of the toolbar you want to display or hide.

■ Word displays or hides the toolbar you selected.

SIZE A TOOLBAR

You can increase the size of a toolbar to display more buttons on the toolbar. This is useful when a toolbar appears on the same row as another toolbar and cannot display all of its buttons.

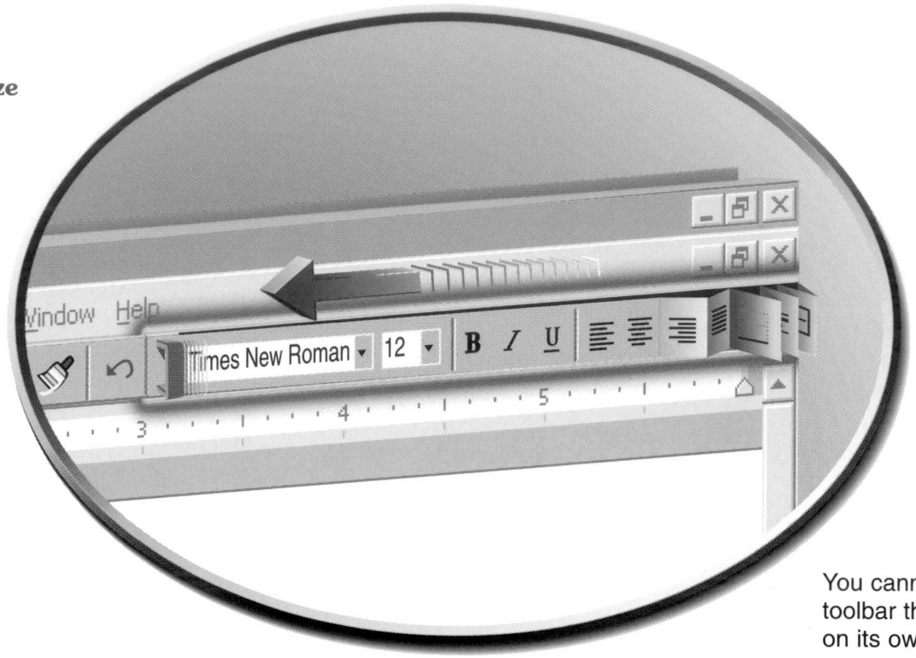

You cannot size a toolbar that appears on its own row.

SIZE A TOOLBAR

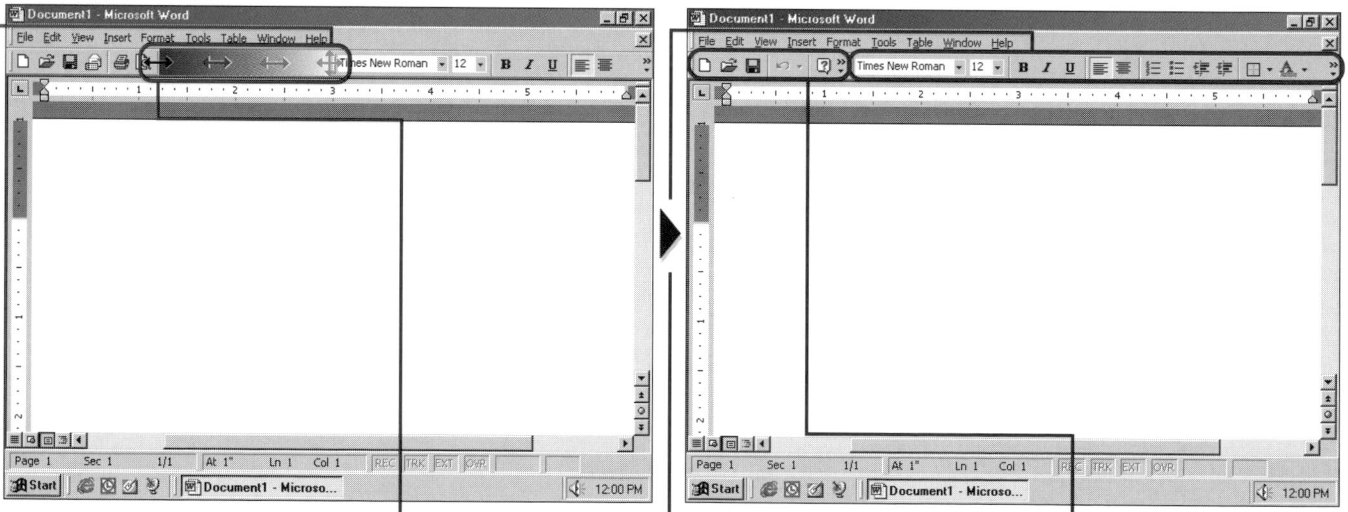

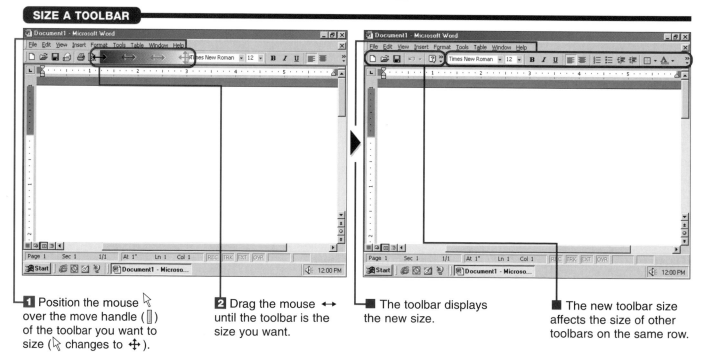

1 Position the mouse ↖ over the move handle (▯) of the toolbar you want to size (↖ changes to ✥).

2 Drag the mouse ↔ until the toolbar is the size you want.

■ The toolbar displays the new size.

■ The new toolbar size affects the size of other toolbars on the same row.

You can move a
toolbar to the top,
bottom, right or
left edge of your
screen.

Moving a toolbar to its
own row allows you to
display more buttons
on the toolbar.

MOVE A TOOLBAR

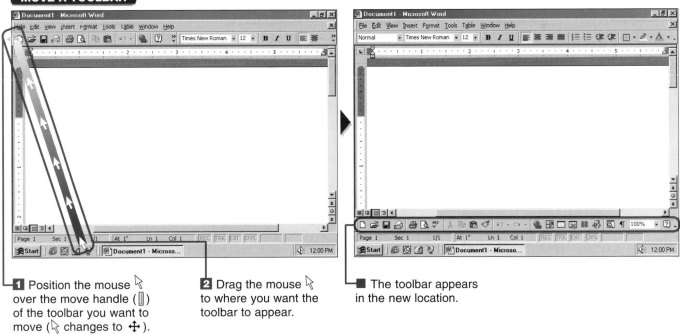

1 Position the mouse ⬉
over the move handle (▯)
of the toolbar you want to
move (⬉ changes to ✛).

2 Drag the mouse ⬉
to where you want the
toolbar to appear.

■ The toolbar appears
in the new location.

Word allows you to enlarge or reduce the display of text on your screen.

Changing the zoom setting will not affect the way text appears on a printed page.

ZOOM IN OR OUT

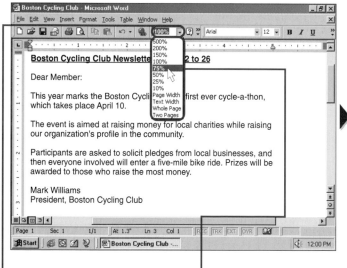

1 Click ▾ in this area to display a list of zoom settings.

Note: If the Zoom area is not displayed, click ⁐ on the Standard toolbar to display all the buttons.

2 Click the zoom setting you want to use.

■ The document appears in the new zoom setting. You can edit the document as usual.

■ To return to the normal zoom setting, repeat steps **1** and **2**, except select **100%** in step **2**.

You can display a larger working area by hiding parts of the Word screen. This is useful when reviewing and editing long documents.

DISPLAY FULL SCREEN

1 Click **View**.

2 Click **Full Screen**.

Note: If Full Screen does not appear on the menu, position the mouse ⤢ over the bottom of the menu to display all the menu commands.

■ Word hides parts of the screen to display a larger working area.

■ To once again display the hidden parts of the screen, click **Close Full Screen**.

DISPLAY OR HIDE FORMATTING MARKS

You can display formatting marks in your document. Formatting marks can help you edit your document and check for errors such as extra spaces between words.

Memo

Peter:¶
¶
Don't·forget·to·attend·tonight's·board·
meeting.·There·will·be·some·important·
topics·up·for·discussion.¶
¶
James

Formatting Marks

Formatting marks will not appear when you print your document.

DISPLAY OR HIDE FORMATTING MARKS

1 Click ¶ to display the formatting marks in your document.

Note: If ¶ is not displayed, click » on the Standard toolbar to display all the buttons.

■ The formatting marks appear in your document.

■ Examples of formatting marks include the following.

¶ Paragraph

▪ Space

→ Tab

■ To once again hide the formatting marks, repeat step **1**.

You can split your
document into separate
sections. This allows you
to display different areas
of a long document at
the same time.

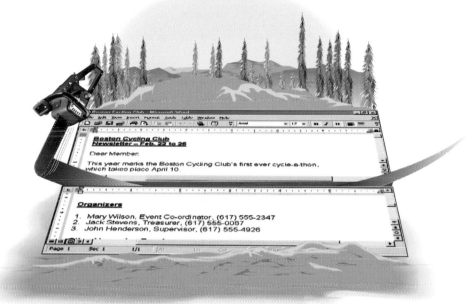

SPLIT A DOCUMENT

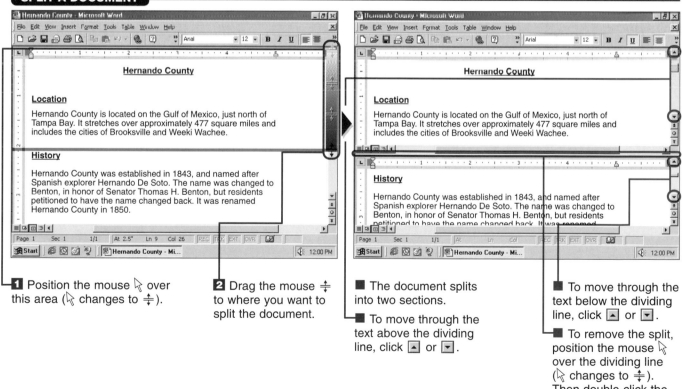

1 Position the mouse ⊾ over
this area (⊾ changes to ⇕).

2 Drag the mouse ⇕
to where you want to
split the document.

■ The document splits
into two sections.

■ To move through the
text above the dividing
line, click ▲ or ▼.

■ To move through the
text below the dividing
line, click ▲ or ▼.

■ To remove the split,
position the mouse ⊾
over the dividing line
(⊾ changes to ⇕).
Then double-click the
dividing line.

USING THE DOCUMENT MAP

You can use the Document Map to move through a document. The Document Map displays an outline of the document on your screen.

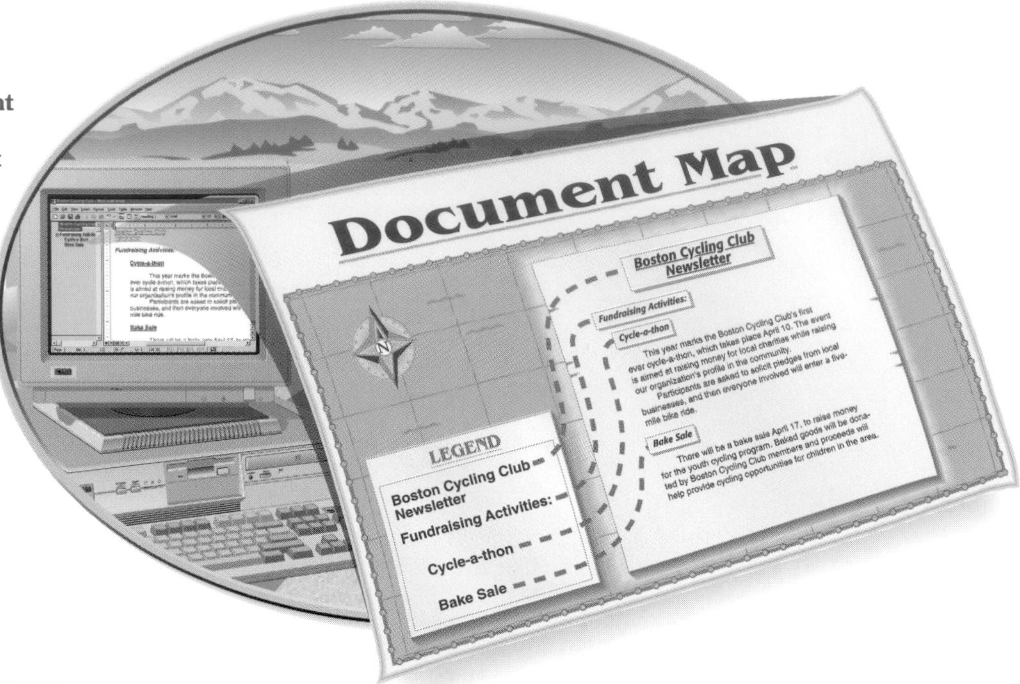

USING THE DOCUMENT MAP

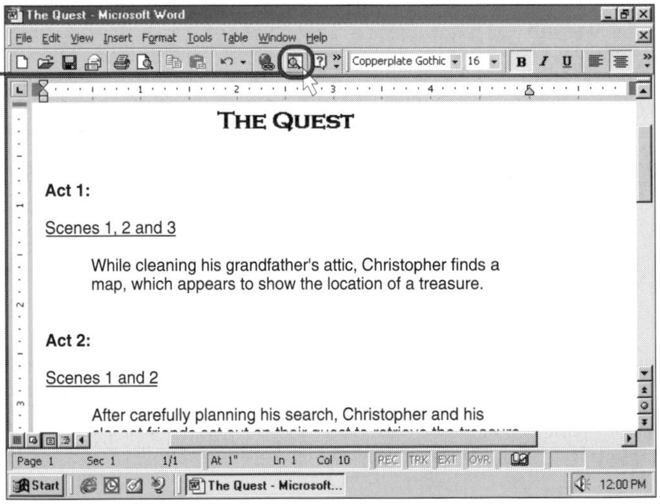

1 Click the Document Map button to display the Document Map.

Note: If the Document Map button is not displayed, click the More Buttons button on the Standard toolbar to display all the buttons.

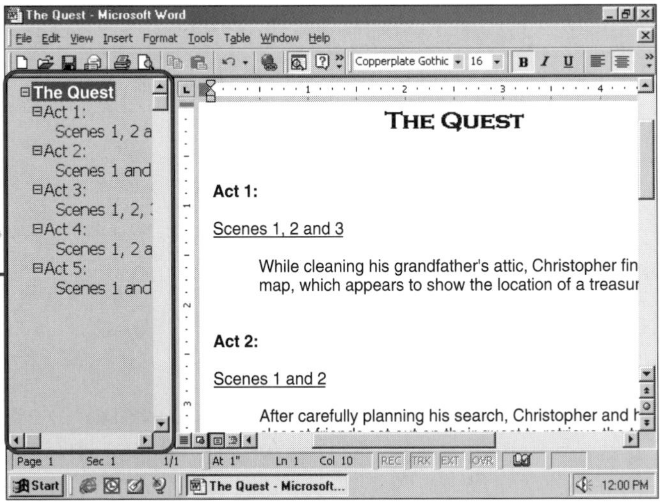

■ The Document Map appears, showing the headings in your document.

Note: If Word does not find any headings in your document, the Document Map is blank.

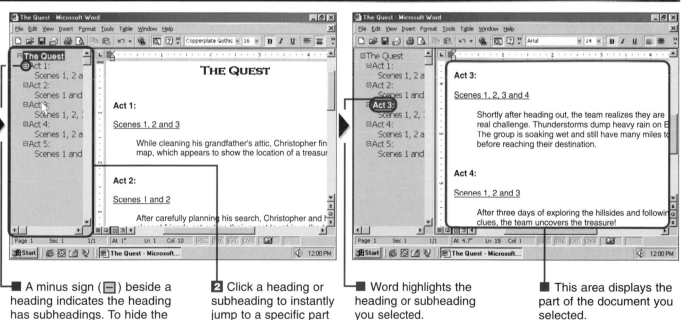

Why doesn't the Document Map display any headings?

If Word does not find any headings in your document, the Document Map is blank. If you want to be able to use the Document Map to move through a document, you should format the headings in your document using styles. For information on styles, see pages 114 to 119.

■ A minus sign (⊟) beside a heading indicates the heading has subheadings. To hide the subheadings, click the minus sign (⊟ changes to ⊞).

Note: To once again display the subheadings, click the plus sign (⊞).

2 Click a heading or subheading to instantly jump to a specific part of your document.

■ Word highlights the heading or subheading you selected.

■ This area displays the part of the document you selected.

■ To hide the Document Map, repeat step **1**.

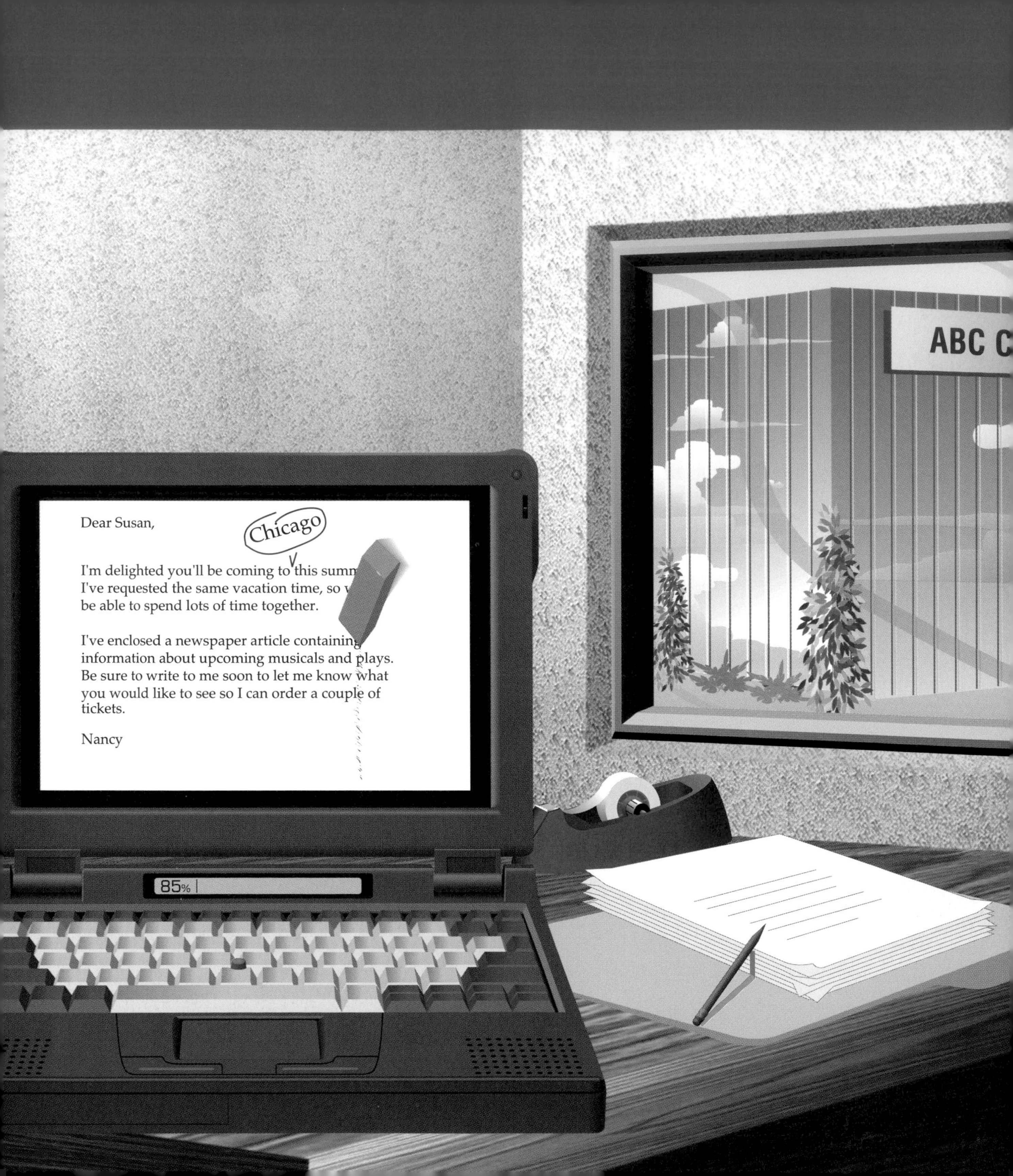

Dear Susan,

Chicago

I'm delighted you'll be coming to this summ
I've requested the same vacation time, so w
be able to spend lots of time together.

I've enclosed a newspaper article containing
information about upcoming musicals and plays.
Be sure to write to me soon to let me know what
you would like to see so I can order a couple of
tickets.

Nancy

CHAPTER 4

Edit Text

Do you want to edit the text in your document or check your document for spelling and grammar errors? This chapter teaches you how.

INSERT AND DELETE TEXT

Word lets you add new text to your document and remove text you no longer need.

INSERT TEXT

Dear John:

How are things going in Florida?

I'm sorry I haven't written to you in a while, but things have been hectic here in St. Louis. My business is taking off and Mary and I are now the proud parents of a baby girl named Jessica.

Will you be coming to St. Louis for a visit anytime soon?

If so, let me know so we can make plans.

I look forward to seeing you.

Your pal,

Mike

Dear John:

How are things going in Florida?

I'm sorry I haven't written to you in a while, but things have been hectic here in St. Louis. My business is taking off and Mary and I are now the proud parents of a baby girl named Jessica.

Will you be coming to St. Louis for a visit anytime soon?

If so, let me know in advance so we can make plans.

I look forward to seeing you.

Your pal,

Mike

1 Click where you want to insert the new text.

■ The text you type will appear where the insertion point flashes on your screen.

Note: You can press the ←, →, ↑ or ↓ key to move the insertion point.

2 Type the text you want to insert. To insert a blank space, press the **Spacebar**.

■ The words to the right of the new text move forward.

Why does the existing text in my document disappear when I insert new text?

When **OVR** appears in **bold** at the bottom of your screen, the Overtype feature is on. When this feature is on, the text you type will replace the existing text in your document. To turn off the Overtype feature, press the Insert key.

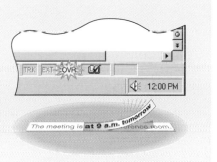

DELETE TEXT

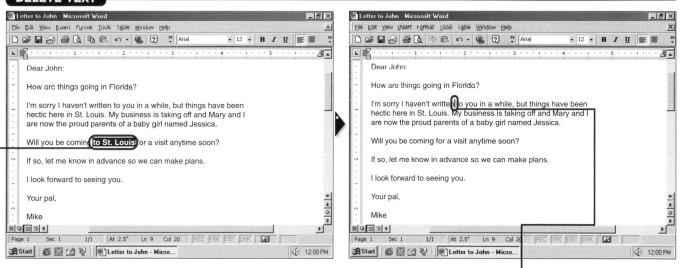

1 Select the text you want to delete. To select text, see page 14.

2 Press the Delete key to remove the text.

■ The text disappears. The remaining text moves to fill any empty spaces.

DELETE ONE CHARACTER

1 Click to the right of the character you want to delete.

2 Press the ◆Backspace key to delete the character to the left of the flashing insertion point.

INSERT THE DATE AND TIME

You can insert the current date and time into your document. Word can automatically update the date and time each time you open or print the document.

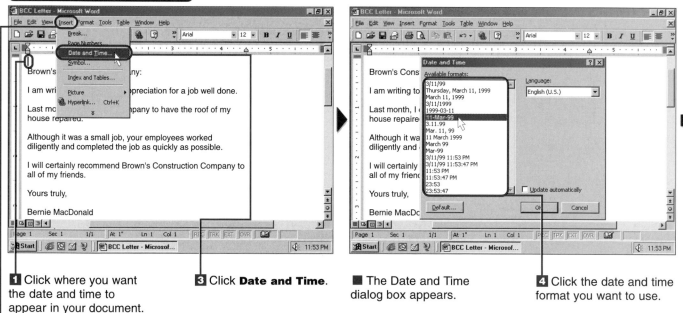

1 Click where you want the date and time to appear in your document.

2 Click **Insert**.

3 Click **Date and Time**.

■ The Date and Time dialog box appears.

4 Click the date and time format you want to use.

Why did Word insert the wrong date and time into my document?

Word uses your computer's built-in clock to determine the current date and time. If Word inserts the wrong date and time into your document, you must change the date and time set in your computer. To change the date and time set in your computer, refer to your Windows manual.

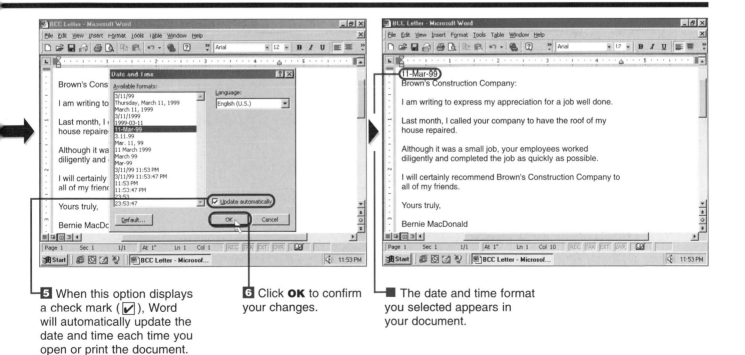

5 When this option displays a check mark (✓), Word will automatically update the date and time each time you open or print the document. You can click the option to add (✓) or remove (☐) the check mark.

6 Click **OK** to confirm your changes.

■ The date and time format you selected appears in your document.

MOVE OR COPY TEXT

You can move or copy text to a new location in your document by dragging and dropping the text. This method is useful when moving or copying text short distances in your document.

marks the Boston Cycling C...
...akes place April 10.

...e event is aimed at raising money for local c...
...munity profile of the **Boston Cycling Club**.

Participants are asked to solicit pledges from local...
...hen everyone involved will enter a five-mile bike...

...ark Williams
...ident **Boston Cycling Club**

USING DRAG AND DROP

1 Select the text you want to move or copy. To select text, see page 14.

2 Position the mouse I over the selected text (I changes to ↖).

What is the difference between moving and copying text?

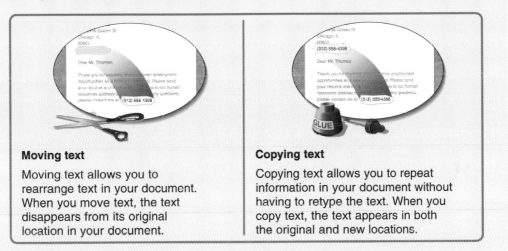

Moving text

Moving text allows you to rearrange text in your document. When you move text, the text disappears from its original location in your document.

Copying text

Copying text allows you to repeat information in your document without having to retype the text. When you copy text, the text appears in both the original and new locations.

3 To move the text, drag the mouse to where you want to place the text.

■ To copy the text, press and hold down the Ctrl key as you drag the mouse to where you want to place the text.

■ The text will appear where you position the dotted insertion point on your screen.

■ The text appears in the new location.

■ To immediately cancel the move or copy, click.

Note: If is not displayed, click on the Standard toolbar to display all the buttons.

MOVE OR COPY TEXT

You can move or copy text to a new location in your document by using toolbar buttons. This method is useful when moving or copying text long distances in your document.

USING THE TOOLBAR BUTTONS

1 Select the text you want to move or copy. To select text, see page 14.

2 Click one of the following buttons.

✂ Move text

🖹 Copy text

Note: If the button you want is not displayed, click ⯯ on the Standard toolbar to display all the buttons.

3 Click the location where you want to place the text.

4 Click 🖹 to place the text in the new location.

Note: If 🖹 is not displayed, click ⯯ on the Standard toolbar to display all the buttons.

■ The text appears in the new location.

Can copying text help me edit my document?

If you plan to make major changes to a paragraph, you may want to copy the paragraph before you begin. This gives you two copies of the paragraph–the original paragraph and a paragraph with all the changes.

There is a **10th** anniversary High School Reunion on August 8, 9 and 10 at **Woodblock** High School. We all hope to see you there. **Contact Susan Hughes** for more information.

There is an **11th** anniversary High School Reunion on August 8, 9 and 10 at **Brown** High School. We all hope to see you there. **Call Bob Maki** for more information.

Boston Cycling Club - Microsoft Word

File Edit View Insert Format Tools Table Window Help

Arial 12 B I U

Newsletter - Feb. 22 to 26
Mark Williams
President, Boston Cycling Club

Dear Boston Cycling Club Member:

This year marks the Boston Cycling Cl... which takes place April 10.

Clipboard (3 of 12)
Paste All

The event is aimed at raising money for local charities while raising our organization's profile in the community.

We hope to see you there!

Participants are asked to solicit pledges from local businesses, and then everyone involved will enter a five-mile bike ride.

Page 1 Sec 1 1/1 At 3.8" Ln 16 Col 1 REC TRK EXT OVR

Start Boston Cycling Club -... 12:00 PM

Boston Cycling Club - Microsoft Word

File Edit View Insert Format Tools Table Window Help

Arial 12 B I U

Newsletter - Feb. 22 to 26
Mark Williams
President, Boston Cycling Club

Dear Boston Cycling Club Member:

This year marks the Boston Cycling Cl... which takes place April 10.

Clipboard (3 of 12)
Paste All

The event is aimed at raising money for local charities while raising our organization's profile in the community.

Participants are asked to solicit pledges from local businesses, and then everyone involved will enter a five-mile bike ride.

We hope to see you there!

Page 1 Sec 1 1/1 At 3.8" Ln 16 Col 26 REC TR EXT OV

Start Boston Cycling Club -... 12:00 PM

USING THE CLIPBOARD TOOLBAR

■ The Clipboard toolbar may appear when you move or copy text using the toolbar buttons. Each icon on the toolbar represents text you have selected to move or copy.

Note: To display the Clipboard toolbar, see page 47.

1 To see the text an icon represents, position the mouse ⌖ over the icon. A yellow box appears, displaying the first few words.

2 To place the text in your document, click the location where you want the text to appear.

3 Click the icon to place the text in your document.

■ The text appears in your document.

4 Click ✕ to close the Clipboard toolbar.

Word remembers the last changes you made to your document. If you regret these changes, you can cancel them by using the Undo feature.

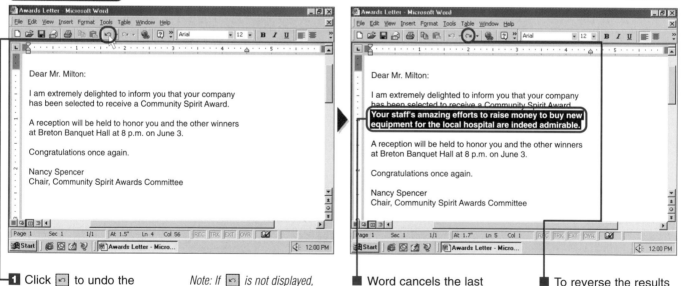

The Undo feature can cancel your last editing and formatting changes.

UNDO CHANGES

1 Click 🔄 to undo the last change you made to your document.

Note: If 🔄 is not displayed, click 🔽 on the Standard toolbar to display all the buttons.

■ Word cancels the last change you made to your document.

■ You can repeat step **1** to cancel previous changes you made.

■ To reverse the results of using the Undo feature, click 🔄.

Note: If 🔄 is not displayed, click 🔽 on the Standard toolbar to display all the buttons.

COUNT WORDS IN A DOCUMENT

You can quickly count the number of words in your document.

Dear Susan:

Trafalgar High School celebrates its 50ᵗʰ anniversary this year. We will be celebrating on September 11 with an Open House, followed by a buffet dinner.

Please bring your school photos and memorabilia for our display table.

Word Count

3 8 1

When you count the number of words in your document, Word also displays the number of pages, characters, paragraphs and lines in the document.

COUNT WORDS IN A DOCUMENT

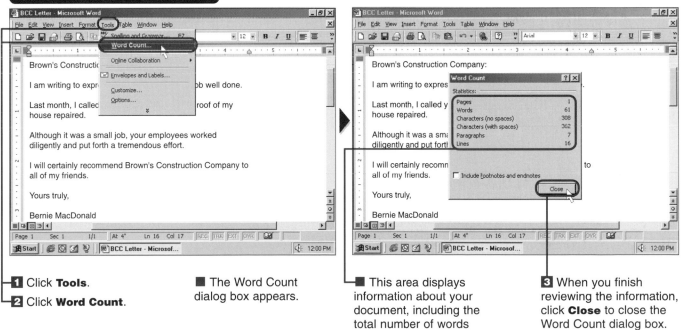

1 Click **Tools**.

2 Click **Word Count**.

■ The Word Count dialog box appears.

■ This area displays information about your document, including the total number of words in the document.

3 When you finish reviewing the information, click **Close** to close the Word Count dialog box.

FIND TEXT

You can use the Find feature to locate a word or phrase in your document.

FIND TEXT

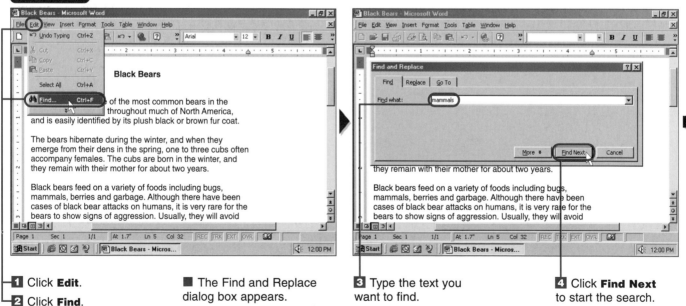

1 Click **Edit**.

2 Click **Find**.

■ The Find and Replace dialog box appears.

3 Type the text you want to find.

4 Click **Find Next** to start the search.

? Can I search for part of a word?

When you search for text in your document, Word will find the text even if the text is part of a larger word. For example, if you search for **place**, Word will also find **place**s, **place**ment and common**place**.

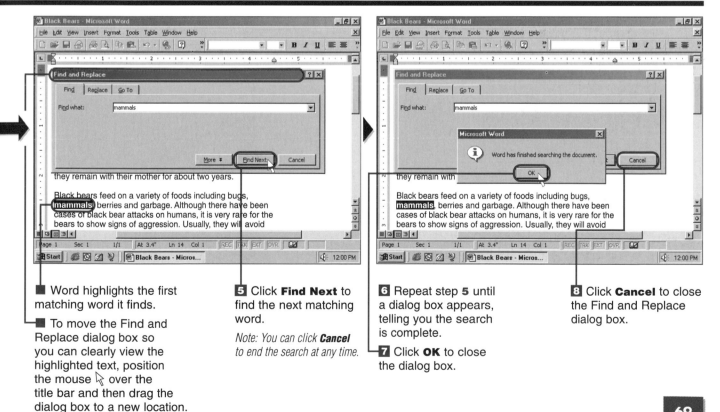

■ Word highlights the first matching word it finds.

■ To move the Find and Replace dialog box so you can clearly view the highlighted text, position the mouse ⓚ over the title bar and then drag the dialog box to a new location.

5 Click **Find Next** to find the next matching word.

*Note: You can click **Cancel** to end the search at any time.*

6 Repeat step **5** until a dialog box appears, telling you the search is complete.

7 Click **OK** to close the dialog box.

8 Click **Cancel** to close the Find and Replace dialog box.

Word provides several advanced search options to help you find the text you want.

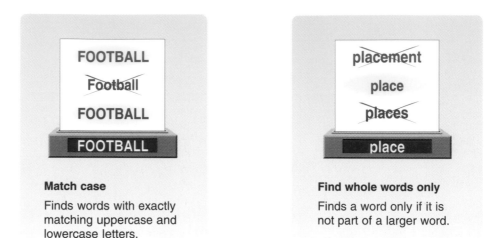

Match case

Finds words with exactly matching uppercase and lowercase letters.

Find whole words only

Finds a word only if it is not part of a larger word.

FIND TEXT (USING ADVANCED SEARCH OPTIONS)

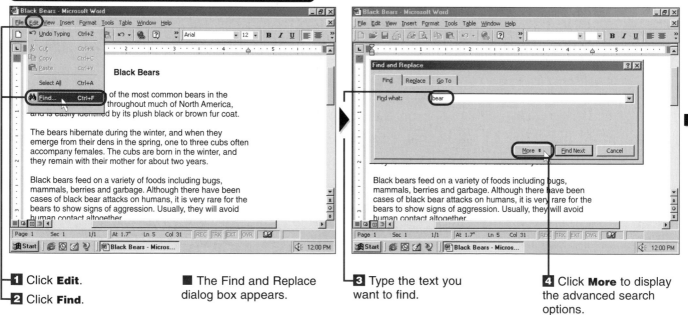

1 Click **Edit**.

2 Click **Find**.

■ The Find and Replace dialog box appears.

3 Type the text you want to find.

4 Click **More** to display the advanced search options.

Use wildcards

Uses wildcard characters to find text. The asterisk (*) wildcard represents many characters. The question mark (?) wildcard represents a single character.

Sounds like

Finds words that sound the same but are spelled differently.

Find all word forms

Finds all forms of the word. This option is not installed by default. Word will ask you to install this option the first time you use the option.

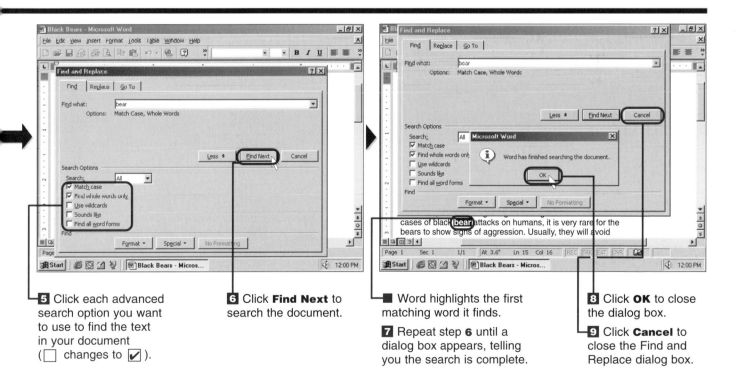

5 Click each advanced search option you want to use to find the text in your document (☐ changes to ☑).

6 Click **Find Next** to search the document.

■ Word highlights the first matching word it finds.

7 Repeat step **6** until a dialog box appears, telling you the search is complete.

8 Click **OK** to close the dialog box.

9 Click **Cancel** to close the Find and Replace dialog box.

REPLACE TEXT

The Replace feature can locate and replace every occurrence of a word or phrase in your document. This is useful if you have frequently misspelled a name.

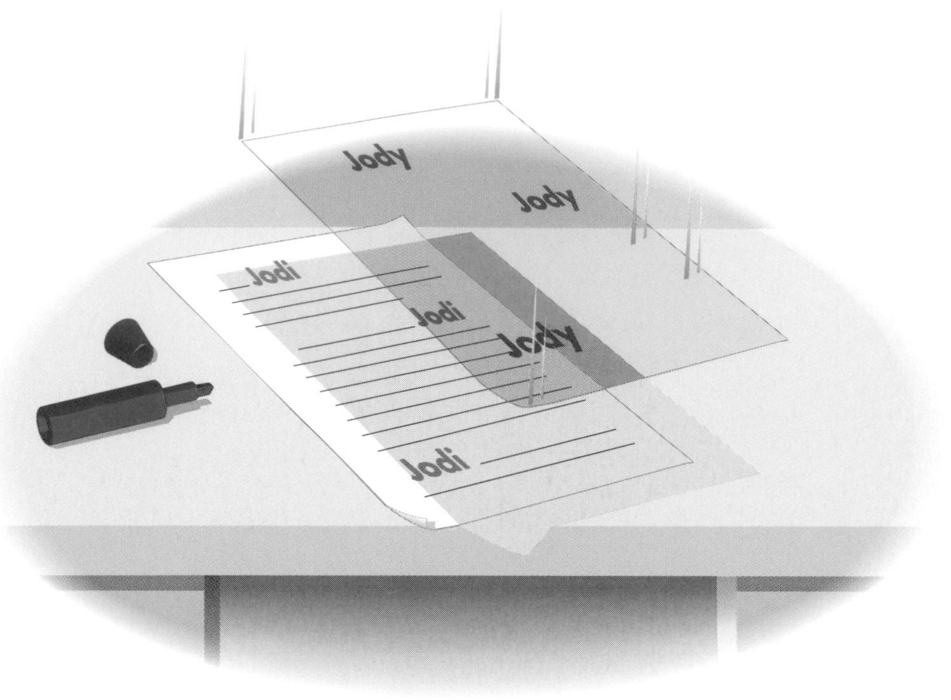

REPLACE TEXT

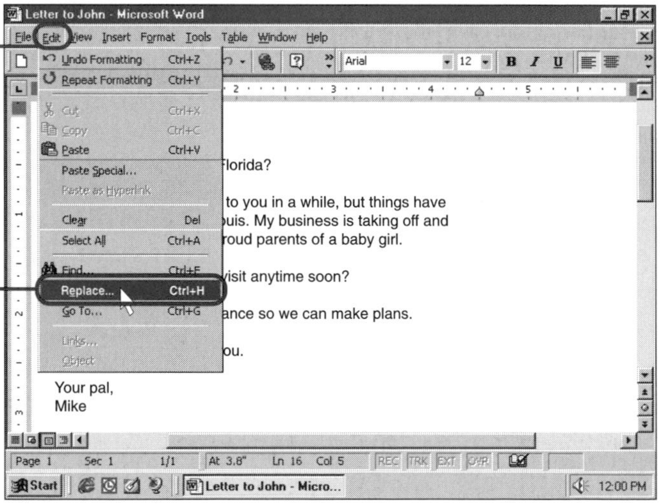

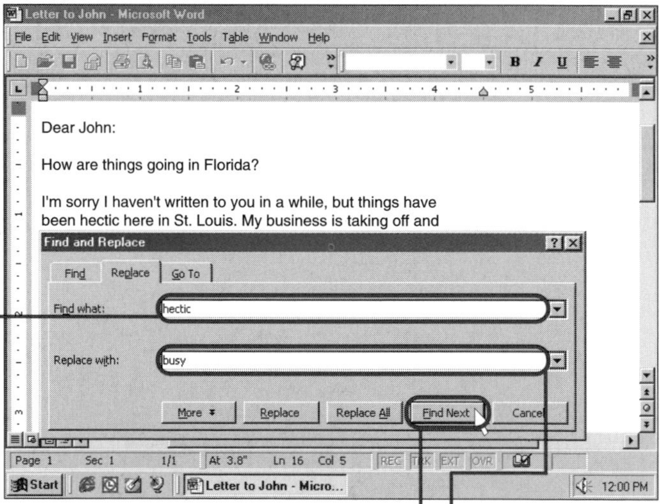

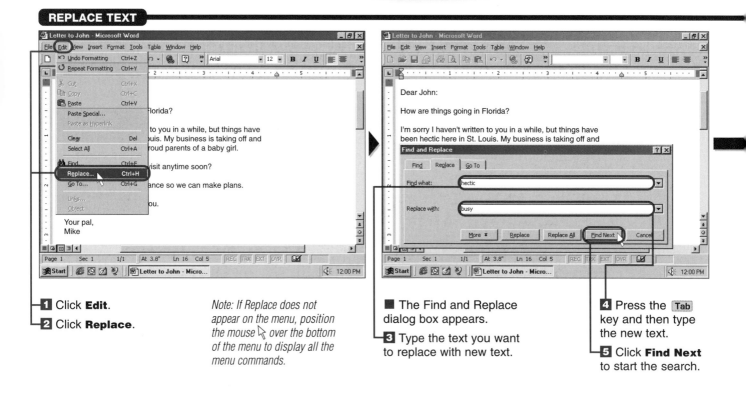

1 Click **Edit**.

2 Click **Replace**.

Note: If Replace does not appear on the menu, position the mouse over the bottom of the menu to display all the menu commands.

■ The Find and Replace dialog box appears.

3 Type the text you want to replace with new text.

4 Press the Tab key and then type the new text.

5 Click **Find Next** to start the search.

Can I use the Replace feature to quickly enter text?

The Replace feature is useful when you have to type a long word or phrase, such as **University of Massachusetts**, many times in a document.

You can type a short form of the word or phrase, such as **UM**, throughout your document and then have Word replace the short form with the full word or phrase.

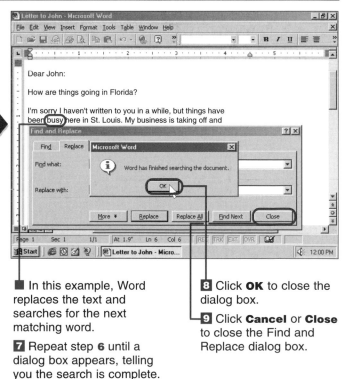

■ Word highlights the first matching word it finds.

6 Click one of these options.

Replace - Replace the word

Replace All - Replace the word and all other matching words in the document

Find Next - Ignore the word

*Note: To end the search at any time, click **Cancel**.*

■ In this example, Word replaces the text and searches for the next matching word.

7 Repeat step **6** until a dialog box appears, telling you the search is complete.

8 Click **OK** to close the dialog box.

9 Click **Cancel** or **Close** to close the Find and Replace dialog box.

CHECK SPELLING AND GRAMMAR

Word automatically checks your document for spelling and grammar errors as you type. You can correct the errors that Word finds.

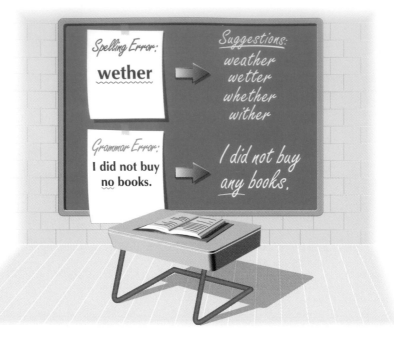

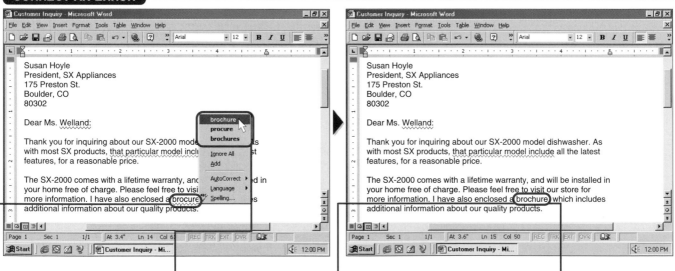

■ Word automatically underlines spelling errors in red and grammar errors in green.

1 Right-click an error in your document.

■ A menu appears with suggestions to correct the error.

2 Click the suggestion you want to use.

Note: If Word does not display a suggestion you want to use, click outside the menu to close the menu.

■ The suggestion you selected replaces the error in your document.

■ The red or green underline disappears.

Why did Word underline a correctly spelled word?

Word compares every word in your document to words in its dictionary. If a word in your document does not exist in Word's dictionary, the word is considered misspelled.

IGNORE AN ERROR

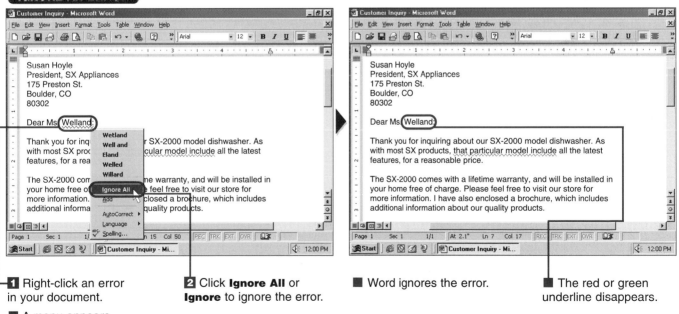

1 Right-click an error in your document.

■ A menu appears with suggestions to correct the error.

2 Click **Ignore All** or **Ignore** to ignore the error.

■ Word ignores the error.

■ The red or green underline disappears.

CHECK SPELLING AND GRAMMAR

You can find and correct all the spelling and grammar errors in your document at once.

CORRECT ENTIRE DOCUMENT

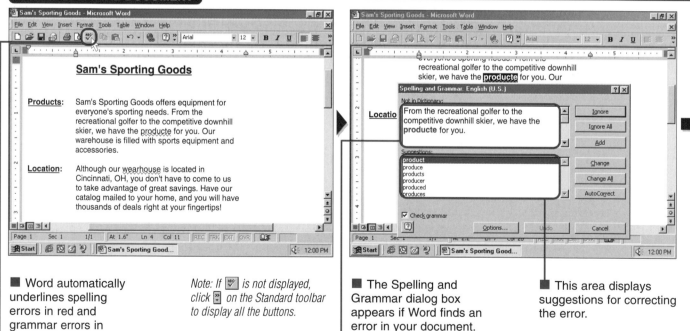

■ Word automatically underlines spelling errors in red and grammar errors in green.

1 Click 📝 to correct your entire document.

Note: If 📝 is not displayed, click 🔼 on the Standard toolbar to display all the buttons.

■ The Spelling and Grammar dialog box appears if Word finds an error in your document.

■ This area displays the spelling or grammar error.

■ This area displays suggestions for correcting the error.

?

Can Word automatically correct my typing mistakes?

Word's AutoCorrect feature automatically corrects common spelling errors as you type. For more information on the AutoCorrect feature, see page 84.

adn	and
aiot	a lot
comittee	committee
don;t	don't
nwe	new
occurence	occurrence
recieve	receive
seperate	separate
teh	the

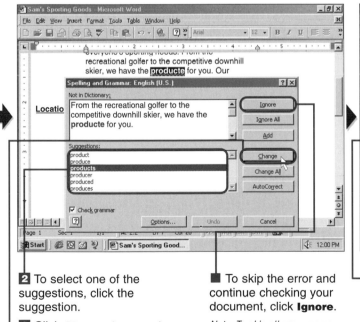

2 To select one of the suggestions, click the suggestion.

3 Click **Change** to correct the error in your document.

■ To skip the error and continue checking your document, click **Ignore**.

*Note: To skip all occurrences of the error, click **Ignore All** or **Ignore Rule**. The appearance of the button depends on whether Word found a spelling or grammar error.*

4 Correct or ignore spelling and grammar errors until this dialog box appears, telling you the spelling and grammar check is complete.

5 Click **OK** to close the dialog box.

TURN OFF SPELLING AND GRAMMAR CHECK

You can turn off Word's automatic spelling and grammar check features. This is useful if you are distracted by the red and green underlines Word uses to indicate errors in your documents.

Mr. Peterson:

I am delited to inform you that your company has been selected to receive a Community Spirit Award. Your staff's efforts to raise money to buy,, new equipment for the local hosipital are admirable.

A reception will be held to honor you and the other winners at Breton Banqeut Hall at 8 p.m. on July 12.

Nancy L. Spencer, Chairperson
Community Spirit Awards Committee

TURN OFF SPELLING AND GRAMMAR CHECK

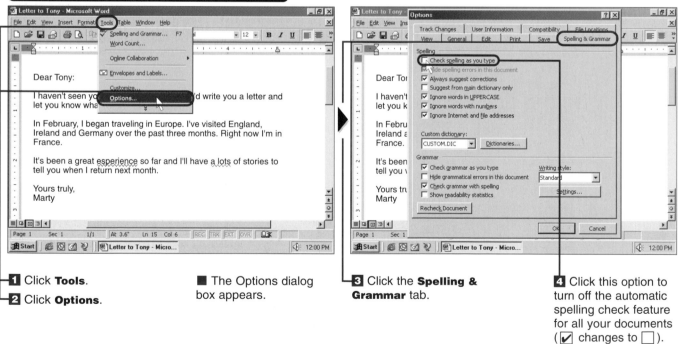

1 Click **Tools**.

2 Click **Options**.

■ The Options dialog box appears.

3 Click the **Spelling & Grammar** tab.

4 Click this option to turn off the automatic spelling check feature for all your documents (☑ changes to ☐).

How can I find errors in my documents after I turn off the automatic spelling and grammar check features?

You can check for spelling and grammar errors in your documents at any time. For information, see page 76.

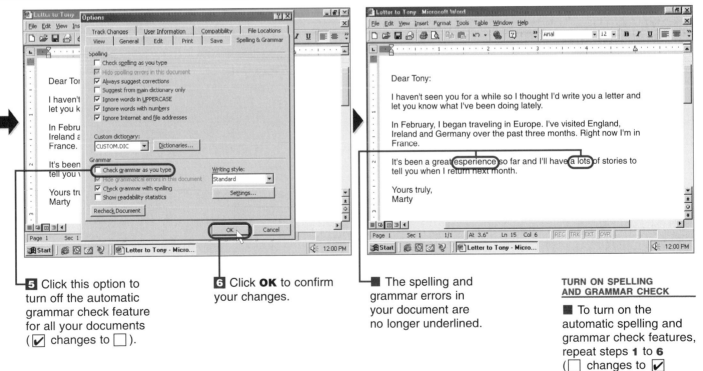

5 Click this option to turn off the automatic grammar check feature for all your documents (☑ changes to ☐).

6 Click **OK** to confirm your changes.

■ The spelling and grammar errors in your document are no longer underlined.

TURN ON SPELLING AND GRAMMAR CHECK

■ To turn on the automatic spelling and grammar check features, repeat steps **1** to **6** (☐ changes to ☑ in steps **4** and **5**).

USING THE THESAURUS

You can use the Thesaurus feature to replace a word in your document with a word that is more suitable.

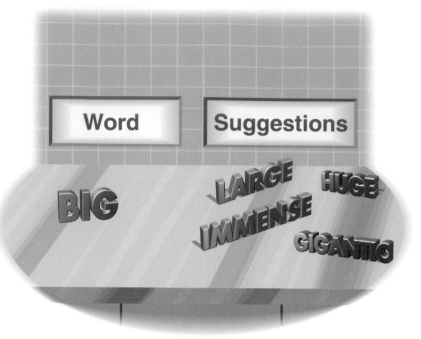

USING THE THESAURUS

1 Click the word you want to replace with another word.

2 Click **Tools**.

3 Click **Language**.

Note: If Language does not appear on the menu, position the mouse ⌖ over the bottom of the menu to display all the menu commands.

4 Click **Thesaurus**.

■ The Thesaurus dialog box appears.

5 Click the correct meaning of the word.

■ This area displays words that share the meaning you selected.

How can the thesaurus help me?

Many people use the thesaurus to replace a word that appears repeatedly in a document. Replacing repeatedly used words can help add variety to your writing. Using the thesaurus included with Word is faster and more convenient than searching through a printed thesaurus.

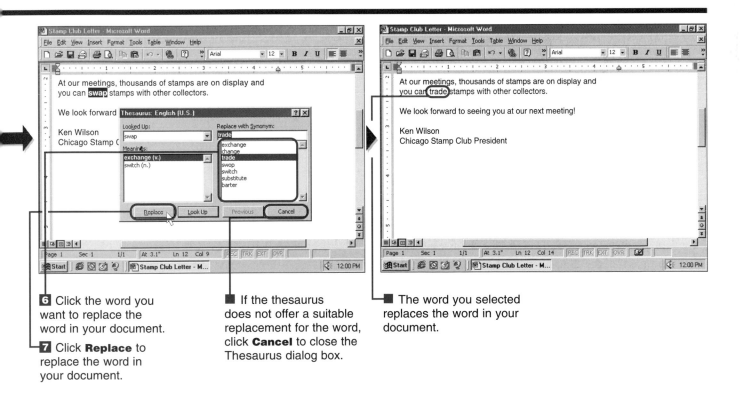

6 Click the word you want to replace the word in your document.

7 Click **Replace** to replace the word in your document.

■ If the thesaurus does not offer a suitable replacement for the word, click **Cancel** to close the Thesaurus dialog box.

■ The word you selected replaces the word in your document.

INSERT SYMBOLS

You can insert symbols that do not appear on your keyboard into your document.

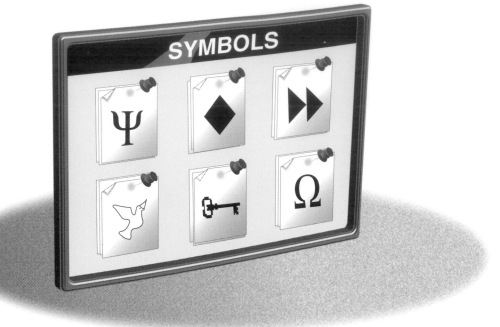

INSERT SYMBOLS

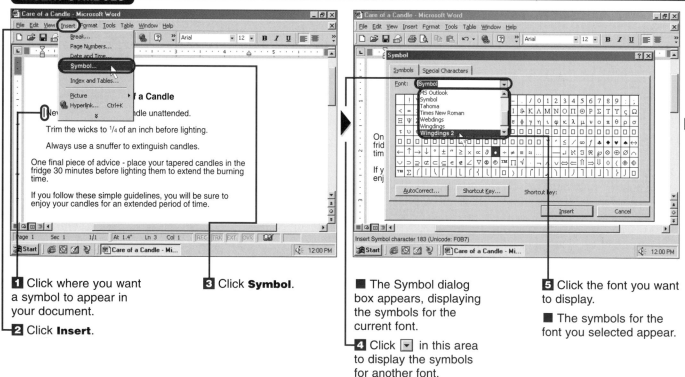

1 Click where you want a symbol to appear in your document.

2 Click **Insert**.

3 Click **Symbol**.

■ The Symbol dialog box appears, displaying the symbols for the current font.

4 Click ▾ in this area to display the symbols for another font.

5 Click the font you want to display.

■ The symbols for the font you selected appear.

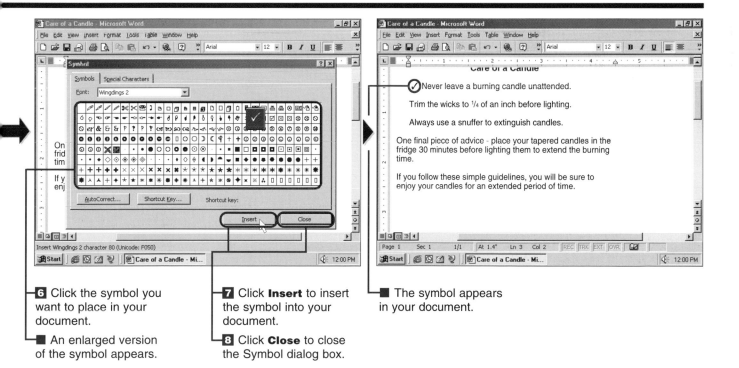

How can I quickly enter symbols into my document?

If you type one of the following sets of characters, Word automatically replaces the characters with a symbol. This allows you to quickly enter symbols that are not available on your keyboard.

(c)	⟶ Ⓒ
(r)	⟶ Ⓡ
(tm)	⟶ TM
:(	⟶ ☹
:)	⟶ ☺
:|	⟶ ☺
<--	⟶ ←
-->	⟶ →
<==	⟶ ⬅
==>	⟶ ➡
<=>	⟶ ⬌

6 Click the symbol you want to place in your document.

■ An enlarged version of the symbol appears.

7 Click **Insert** to insert the symbol into your document.

8 Click **Close** to close the Symbol dialog box.

■ The symbol appears in your document.

USING AUTOCORRECT

Word automatically corrects hundreds of typing, spelling and grammar errors as you type. You can create an AutoCorrect entry to add your own words and phrases to the list of errors that Word corrects.

(c)	©
(tm)	TM
accordingto	according to
ahve	have
can;t	can't
i	I
may of been	may have been
recieve	receive
seperate	separate
teh	the

USING AUTOCORRECT

1 Type the text you want Word to automatically place in your documents.

2 Select the text. To select text, see page 14.

3 Click **Tools**.

4 Click **AutoCorrect**.

Note: If AutoCorrect does not appear on the menu, position the mouse ⇖ over the bottom of the menu to display all the menu commands.

■ The AutoCorrect dialog box appears.

■ This area displays a list of the AutoCorrect entries included with Word.

■ This area displays the text you selected in step **2**.

What types of AutoCorrect entries can I create?

You can create AutoCorrect entries for typing, spelling and grammar errors you often make. You can also create AutoCorrect entries to quickly enter words and phrases you frequently use, such as your name.

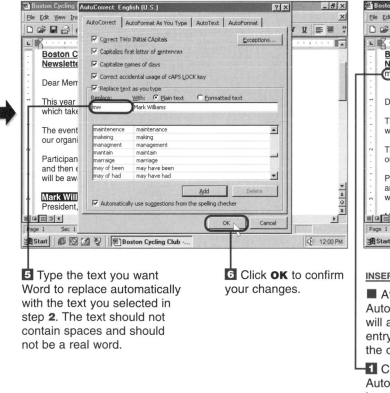

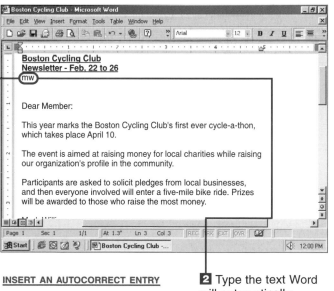

5 Type the text you want Word to replace automatically with the text you selected in step **2**. The text should not contain spaces and should not be a real word.

6 Click **OK** to confirm your changes.

INSERT AN AUTOCORRECT ENTRY

■ After you create an AutoCorrect entry, Word will automatically insert the entry each time you type the corresponding text.

1 Click where you want the AutoCorrect entry to appear in your document.

2 Type the text Word will automatically replace.

3 Press the **Spacebar** and the AutoCorrect entry replaces the text you typed.

You can use the AutoText feature to store text you frequently use. This lets you avoid typing the same information over and over again.

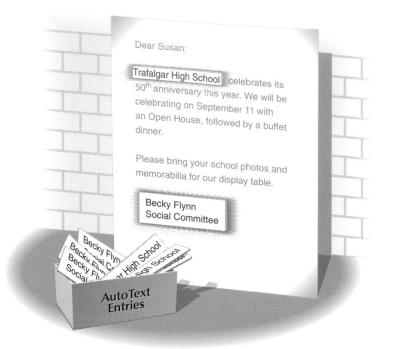

CREATE AN AUTOTEXT ENTRY

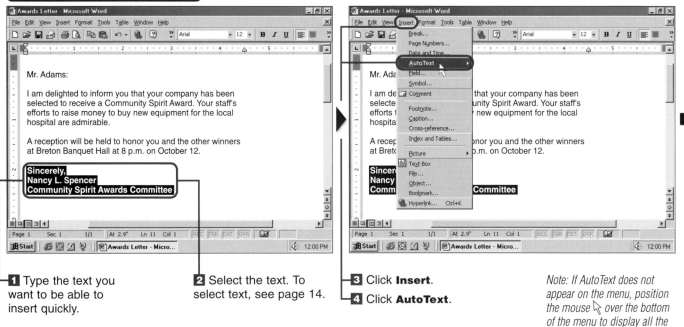

1 Type the text you want to be able to insert quickly.

2 Select the text. To select text, see page 14.

3 Click **Insert**.

4 Click **AutoText**.

Note: If AutoText does not appear on the menu, position the mouse ⌖ over the bottom of the menu to display all the menu commands.

What types of AutoText entries can I create?

You can create an AutoText entry for information you plan to use often, such as a mailing address, product name, legal disclaimer or closing remark. Word will store any formatting you apply to the text, such as bold or underline. To format text, see pages 94 to 107.

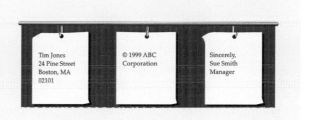

Tim Jones
24 Pine Street
Boston, MA
02101

© 1999 ABC
Corporation

Sincerely,
Sue Smith
Manager

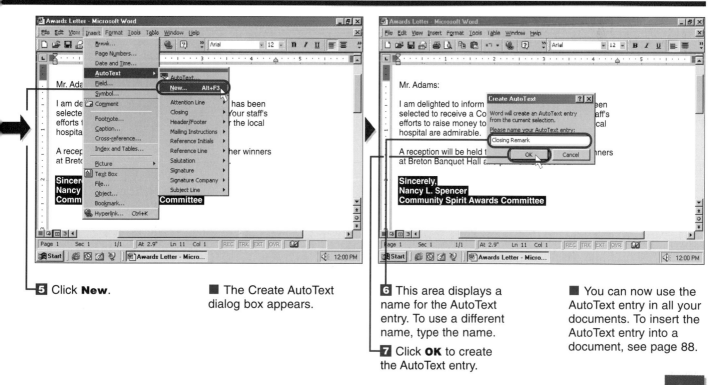

5 Click **New**.

■ The Create AutoText dialog box appears.

6 This area displays a name for the AutoText entry. To use a different name, type the name.

7 Click **OK** to create the AutoText entry.

■ You can now use the AutoText entry in all your documents. To insert the AutoText entry into a document, see page 88.

USING AUTOTEXT

After you create an
AutoText entry, you
can insert the text
into a document.

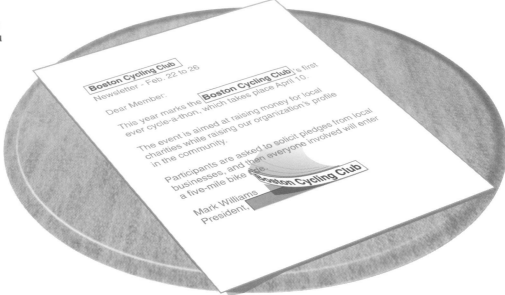

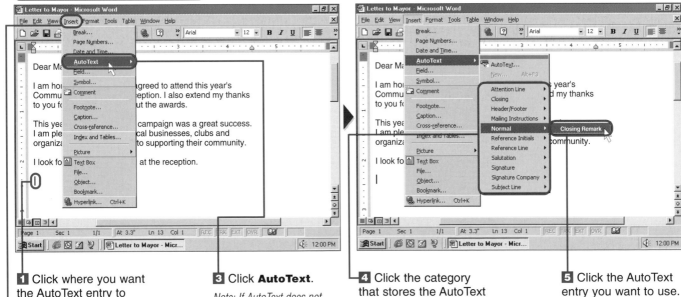

1 Click where you want
the AutoText entry to
appear in your document.

2 Click **Insert**.

3 Click **AutoText**.

*Note: If AutoText does not
appear on the menu, position
the mouse ⤷ over the bottom
of the menu to display all the
menu commands.*

4 Click the category
that stores the AutoText
entry you want to use.

*Note: The Normal category
stores most AutoText entries
you have created.*

5 Click the AutoText
entry you want to use.

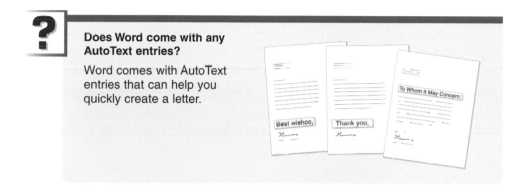

Does Word come with any AutoText entries?

Word comes with AutoText entries that can help you quickly create a letter.

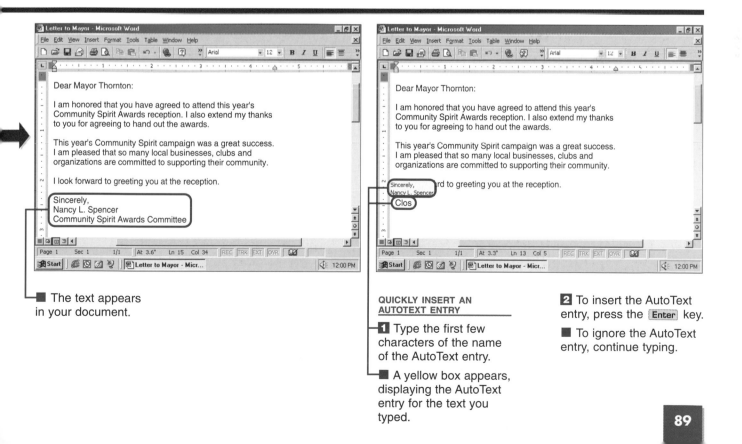

■ The text appears in your document.

QUICKLY INSERT AN AUTOTEXT ENTRY

1 Type the first few characters of the name of the AutoText entry.

■ A yellow box appears, displaying the AutoText entry for the text you typed.

2 To insert the AutoText entry, press the Enter key.

■ To ignore the AutoText entry, continue typing.

ADD A COMMENT

You can add a comment
to text in your document.
A comment can provide
a note, explanation or
reminder about information
you need to verify later.

ADD A COMMENT

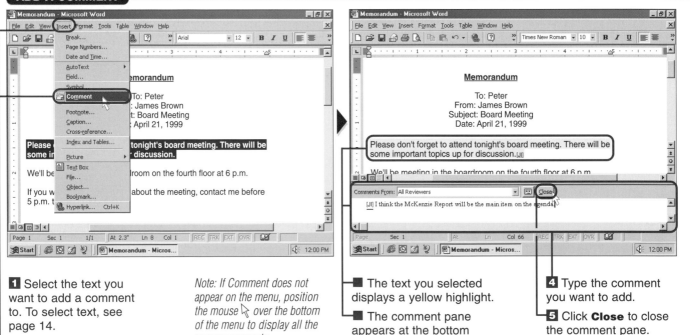

1 Select the text you
want to add a comment
to. To select text, see
page 14.

2 Click **Insert**.

3 Click **Comment**.

*Note: If Comment does not
appear on the menu, position
the mouse ⟋ over the bottom
of the menu to display all the
menu commands.*

■ The text you selected
displays a yellow highlight.

■ The comment pane
appears at the bottom
of your screen.

4 Type the comment
you want to add.

5 Click **Close** to close
the comment pane.

90

Can I display all the comments in my document at once?

Yes. Displaying all the comments in your document at once allows you to review and edit the comments.

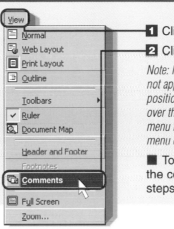

1 Click **View**.

2 Click **Comments**.

Note: If Comments does not appear on the menu, position the mouse ▷ over the bottom of the menu to display all the menu commands.

■ To once again hide the comments, repeat steps **1** and **2**.

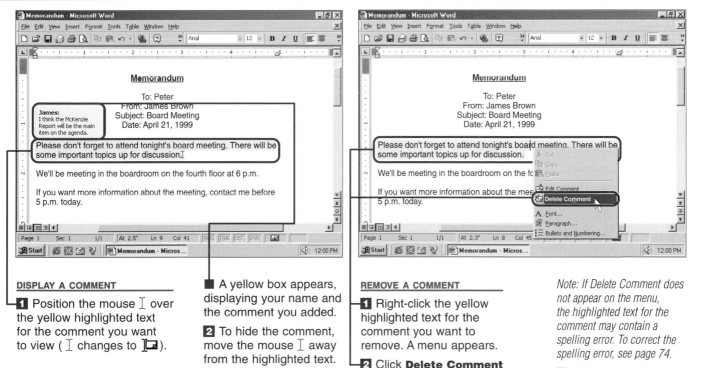

DISPLAY A COMMENT

1 Position the mouse I over the yellow highlighted text for the comment you want to view (I changes to 🖽).

■ A yellow box appears, displaying your name and the comment you added.

2 To hide the comment, move the mouse I away from the highlighted text.

REMOVE A COMMENT

1 Right-click the yellow highlighted text for the comment you want to remove. A menu appears.

2 Click **Delete Comment** to remove the comment.

Note: If Delete Comment does not appear on the menu, the highlighted text for the comment may contain a spelling error. To correct the spelling error, see page 74.

■ Word removes the yellow highlight from the text.

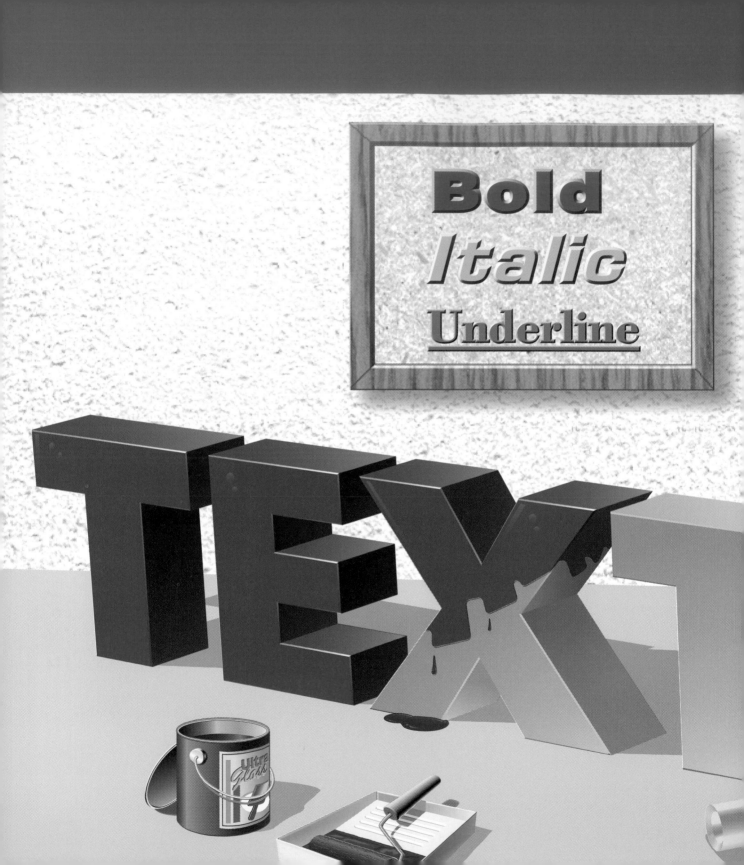

CHAPTER 5

Format Text

Would you like to emphasize information in your document and enhance the appearance of text? Read this chapter to learn how.

DEAR MRS. GLEDHILL:

There is a 10th anniversary High

School Reunion on Augus

and 8 at Woodbloc

School. For

plea

You can change the case of text in your document without retyping the text. Word offers five case styles you can choose from.

CHANGE CASE OF TEXT

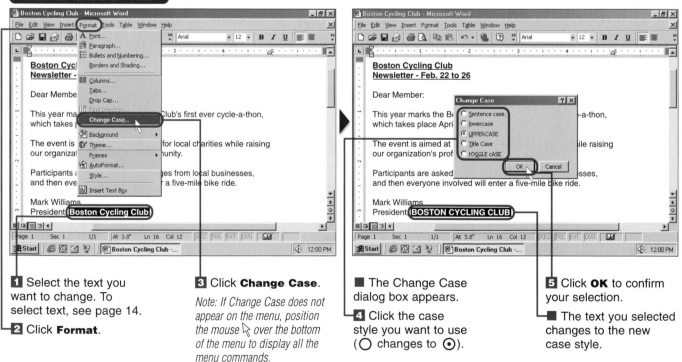

1 Select the text you want to change. To select text, see page 14.

2 Click **Format**.

3 Click **Change Case**.

Note: If Change Case does not appear on the menu, position the mouse ⌖ over the bottom of the menu to display all the menu commands.

■ The Change Case dialog box appears.

4 Click the case style you want to use (○ changes to ⊙).

5 Click **OK** to confirm your selection.

■ The text you selected changes to the new case style.

You can use the
Bold, Italic and
Underline features
to emphasize text
in your document.

BOLD, ITALICIZE OR UNDERLINE TEXT

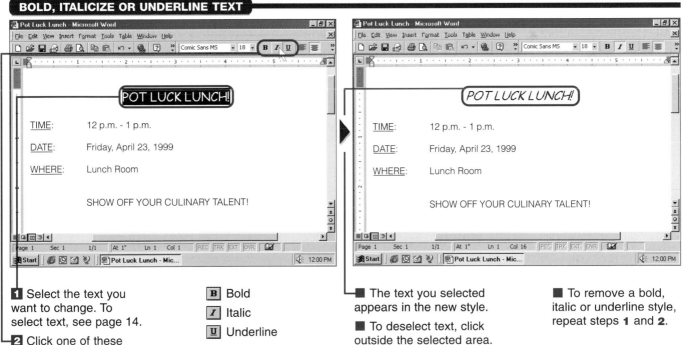

1 Select the text you
want to change. To
select text, see page 14.

2 Click one of these
buttons.

B Bold

I Italic

U Underline

*Note: If the button you want is
not displayed, click ⊞ on the
Formatting toolbar to display
all the buttons.*

■ The text you selected
appears in the new style.

■ To deselect text, click
outside the selected area.

■ To remove a bold,
italic or underline style,
repeat steps **1** and **2**.

CHANGE FONT OF TEXT

You can enhance the appearance of your document by changing the design, or font, of the text.

1 Select the text you want to change. To select text, see page 14.

2 Click ☐ in this area to display a list of the available fonts.

Note: If the Font area is not displayed, click ☒ on the Formatting toolbar to display all the buttons.

3 Click the font you want to use.

■ The text you selected changes to the new font.

■ To deselect text, click outside the selected area.

CHANGE SIZE OF TEXT

You can increase
or decrease the
size of text in
your document.

8 point
12 point
14 point
18 point
24 point

Word measures the size of text
in points. There are approximately
72 points in one inch.

Larger text is easier to
read, but smaller text
allows you to fit more
information on a page.

CHANGE SIZE OF TEXT

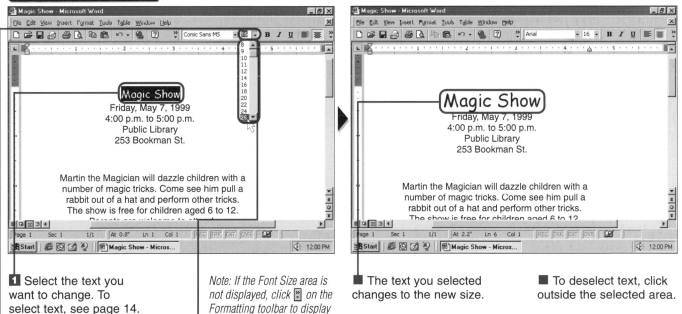

1 Select the text you
want to change. To
select text, see page 14.

2 Click ▾ in this area
to display a list of the
available sizes.

*Note: If the Font Size area is
not displayed, click ▸ on the
Formatting toolbar to display
all the buttons.*

3 Click the size you
want to use.

■ The text you selected
changes to the new size.

■ To deselect text, click
outside the selected area.

CHANGE COLOR OF TEXT

You can change the color of text to draw attention to headings or important information in your document.

1 Select the text you want to change to a different color. To select text, see page 14.

2 Click ⋅ in this area to select a color.

Note: If ▲⋅ is not displayed, click ❯❯ on the Formatting toolbar to display all the buttons.

3 Click the color you want to use.

■ The text appears in the color you selected.

■ To deselect text, click outside the selected area.

■ To remove a color from text, repeat steps **1** to **3**, except select **Automatic** in step **3**.

98

You can highlight text you want to stand out in your document. Highlighting text is useful for marking information you want to review or verify later.

DEAR MRS. GLEDHILL:

There is a 10th anniversary High School Reunion on August 6, 7 and 8 at Woodblock High School. For more information, please contact Susan Hughes at (954) 555-1234.

We hope to see you there!

HIGHLIGHT TEXT

1 Select the text you want to highlight. To select text, see page 14.

2 Click ▪ in this area to select a highlight color.

Note: If ✐▪ is not displayed, click ❯ on the Formatting toolbar to display all the buttons.

3 Click the highlight color you want to use.

■ The text appears highlighted in the color you selected.

■ To remove a highlight, repeat steps **1** to **3**, except select **None** in step **3**.

CHANGE ALIGNMENT OF TEXT

You can enhance
the appearance of
your document by
aligning text in
different ways.

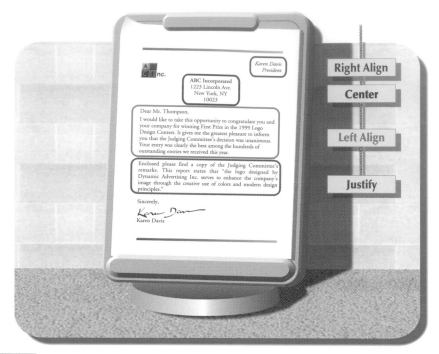

Right Align

Center

Left Align

Justify

CHANGE ALIGNMENT OF TEXT

Susan Hoyle
President, SX Appliances
175 Preston St.
Boulder, CO
80302

Dear Ms. Jones:

Thank you for inquiring about our SX-2000 model dishwasher. As
with most SX products, this particular model includes all the latest
features, for a reasonable price.

The SX-2000 comes with a lifetime warranty, and will be installed in
your home free of charge. Please feel free to visit our store for
more information. I have also enclosed a brochure, which includes
additional information about our quality products.

Susan Hoyle
President, SX Appliances
175 Preston St.
Boulder, CO
80302

Dear Ms. Jones:

Thank you for inquiring about our SX-2000 model dishwasher. As
with most SX products, this particular model includes all the latest
features, for a reasonable price.

The SX-2000 comes with a lifetime warranty, and will be installed in
your home free of charge. Please feel free to visit our store for
more information. I have also enclosed a brochure, which includes
additional information about our quality products.

USING TOOLBAR BUTTONS

1 Select the text you
want to align differently.
To select text, see
page 14.

2 Click one of these
buttons.

📄 Left align

📄 Center

📄 Right align

📄 Justify

*Note: If the button you want is
not displayed, click* 》 *on the
Formatting toolbar to display
all the buttons.*

■ The text displays
the new alignment.

■ To deselect text, click
outside the selected area.

? Can I use different alignments within a single line of text?

You can use the Click and Type feature to vary the alignment within a single line of text. For example, you can left align your name and right align the date on the same line.

USING CLICK AND TYPE

1 Click 📧 to display the document in the Print Layout view.

2 Position the mouse I where you want the text to appear. The appearance of the mouse I indicates how Word will align the text.

I⁼ Left align

I Center

⁼I Right align

Note: If the appearance of the mouse I does not change, click where you want to add the text.

3 Double-click the location to position the insertion point.

4 Type the text you want to add.

COPY FORMATTING

You can make
one area of text
in your document
look exactly like
another.

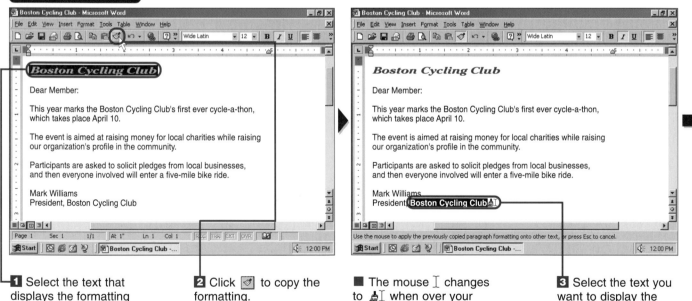

1 Select the text that
displays the formatting
you want to copy. To
select text, see page 14.

2 Click 🖌 to copy the
formatting.

*Note: If 🖌 is not displayed,
click ⟩ on the Standard toolbar
to display all the buttons.*

■ The mouse I changes
to 🖌I when over your
document.

3 Select the text you
want to display the
formatting.

Why would I want to copy the formatting of text?

You may want to copy the formatting of text to make all the headings or important words in your document look the same. This will give your document a consistent appearance.

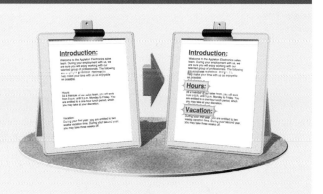

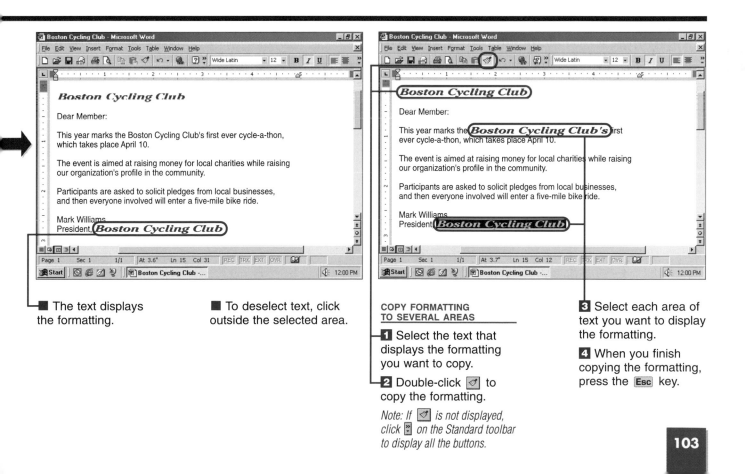

■ The text displays the formatting.

■ To deselect text, click outside the selected area.

COPY FORMATTING TO SEVERAL AREAS

1 Select the text that displays the formatting you want to copy.

2 Double-click 🖋 to copy the formatting.

Note: If 🖋 is not displayed, click 🔽 on the Standard toolbar to display all the buttons.

3 Select each area of text you want to display the formatting.

4 When you finish copying the formatting, press the Esc key.

CHANGE APPEARANCE OF TEXT

You can make text in your document look more attractive by using various fonts, styles, sizes, colors, underlines and special effects.

1 Select the text you want to change. To select text, see page 14.

2 Click **Format**.

3 Click **Font**.

■ The Font dialog box appears.

4 Click the **Font** tab.

5 To select a font for the text, click the font you want to use.

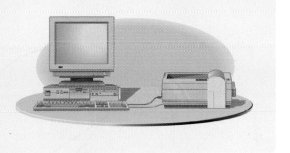

What determines which fonts are available on my computer?

The fonts available on your computer may be different from the fonts on other computers. The available fonts depend on your printer and the setup of your computer.

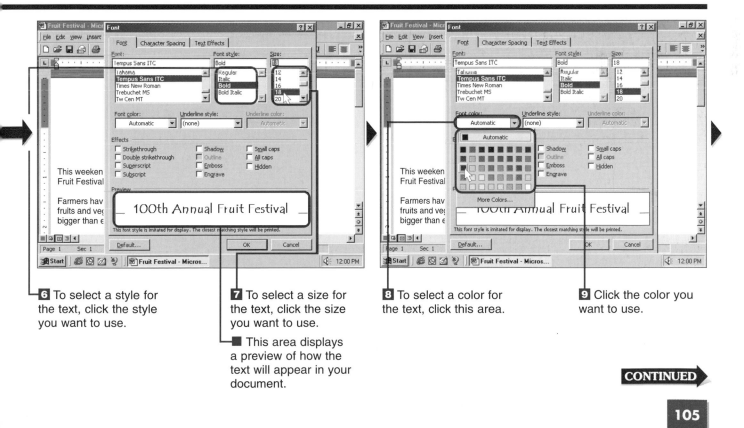

6 To select a style for the text, click the style you want to use.

7 To select a size for the text, click the size you want to use.

■ This area displays a preview of how the text will appear in your document.

8 To select a color for the text, click this area.

9 Click the color you want to use.

CONTINUED ▶

CHANGE APPEARANCE OF TEXT

Word offers many underline styles you can use to underline text in your document.

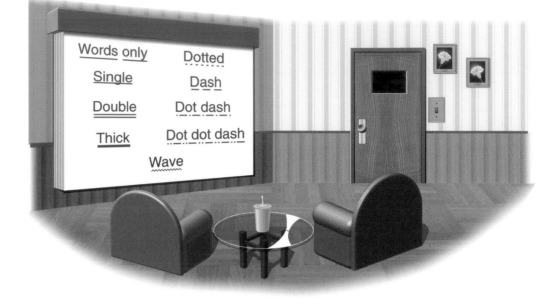

Words only   Dotted

Single   Dash

Double   Dot dash

Thick   Dot dot dash

Wave

CHANGE APPEARANCE OF TEXT (CONTINUED)

10 To select an underline style for the text, click this area.

11 Click the underline style you want to use.

12 To select a color for the underline, click this area.

*Note: You can only select an underline color if you selected an underline style in steps **10** and **11**.*

13 Click the underline color you want to use.

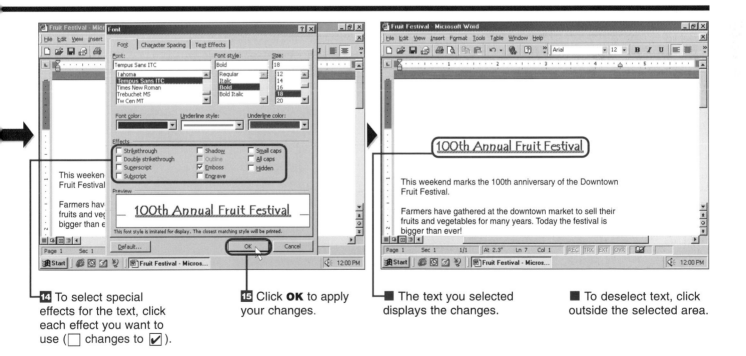

What special effects can I add to text in my document?

Word offers many special effects.

~~Strikethrough~~

~~Double strikethrough~~

TEXT ^{Superscript}

TEXT _{Subscript}

Shadow

Outline

Emboss

Engrave

SMALL CAPS

ALL CAPS

Hidden

14 To select special effects for the text, click each effect you want to use (☐ changes to ☑).

15 Click **OK** to apply your changes.

■ The text you selected displays the changes.

■ To deselect text, click outside the selected area.

CHANGE FONT FOR ALL NEW DOCUMENTS

You can change the font that Word uses for all new documents you create. This is useful when you want all future documents to appear in a specific font.

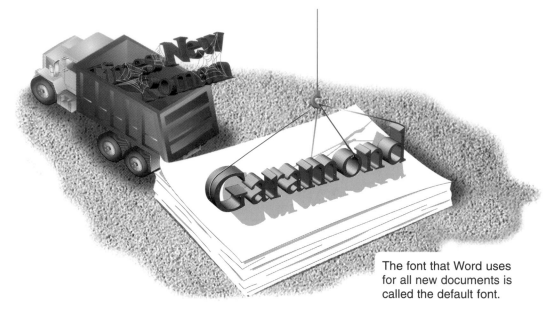

The font that Word uses for all new documents is called the default font.

CHANGE FONT FOR ALL NEW DOCUMENTS

1 Click **Format**.

2 Click **Font**.

■ The Font dialog box appears.

3 Click the **Font** tab.

4 To select a font for all new documents, click the font you want to use.

5 To select a style for the text, click the style you want to use.

6 To select a size for the text, click the size you want to use.

Will changing the font for all new documents affect the documents I have already created?

No. Word will not change the font in documents you have already created. To change the font of text in existing documents, see pages 104 to 107.

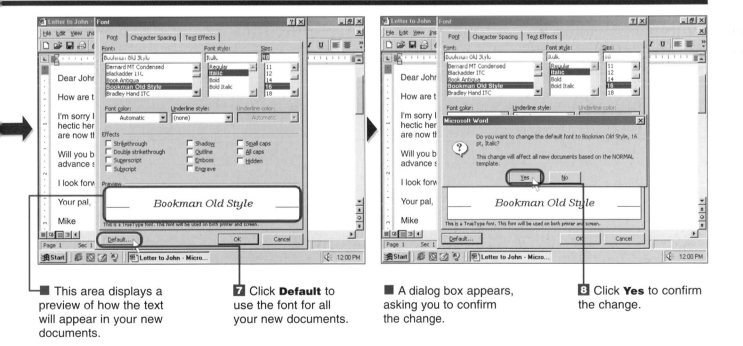

■ This area displays a preview of how the text will appear in your new documents.

7 Click **Default** to use the font for all your new documents.

■ A dialog box appears, asking you to confirm the change.

8 Click **Yes** to confirm the change.

CHANGE SPACING BETWEEN CHARACTERS

You can alter the look of text by changing the spacing between characters.

When you change the spacing between characters, the spacing between words also changes.

CHANGE SPACING BETWEEN CHARACTERS

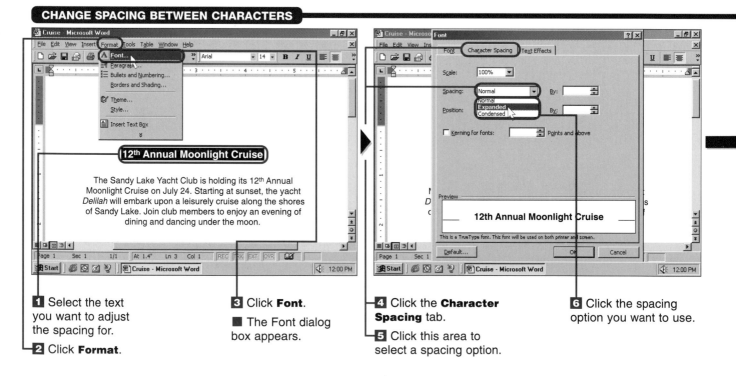

1 Select the text you want to adjust the spacing for.

2 Click **Format**.

3 Click **Font**.

■ The Font dialog box appears.

4 Click the **Character Spacing** tab.

5 Click this area to select a spacing option.

6 Click the spacing option you want to use.

Why would I change the spacing between characters?

Increasing the amount of space between characters can give headings a unique look. You can decrease the amount of space between characters to fit more text on a line in your document.

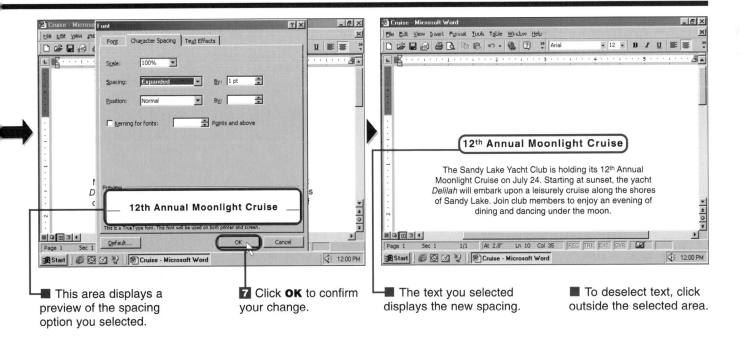

■ This area displays a preview of the spacing option you selected.

7 Click **OK** to confirm your change.

■ The text you selected displays the new spacing.

■ To deselect text, click outside the selected area.

You can animate text in your document by making the text move or flash. Animation effects are ideal for emphasizing text in a document that will be viewed on your computer screen.

1 Select the text you want to animate. To select text, see page 14.

2 Click **Format**.

3 Click **Font**.

■ The Font dialog box appears.

4 Click the **Text Effects** tab.

5 Click the animation effect you want to use.

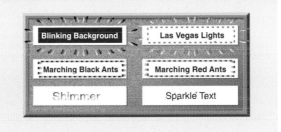

What types of animation effects does Word offer?

Word offers several animation effects that you can use to draw attention to text in your document.

Blinking Background	Las Vegas Lights
Marching Black Ants	Marching Red Ants
Shimmer	Sparkle Text

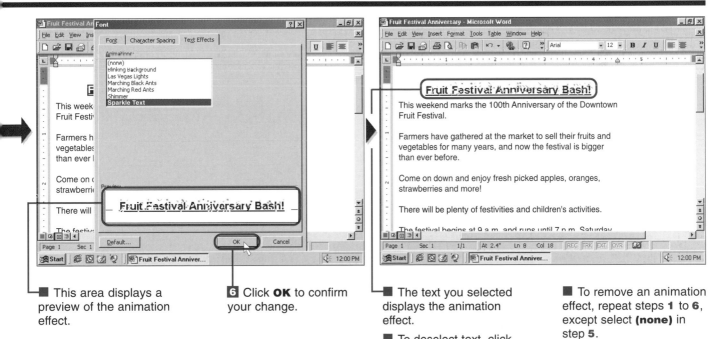

■ This area displays a preview of the animation effect.

6 Click **OK** to confirm your change.

■ The text you selected displays the animation effect.

■ To deselect text, click outside the selected area.

Note: The animation effect will not appear when you print your document. For information on printing, see page 184.

■ To remove an animation effect, repeat steps **1** to **6**, except select **(none)** in step **5**.

USING STYLES

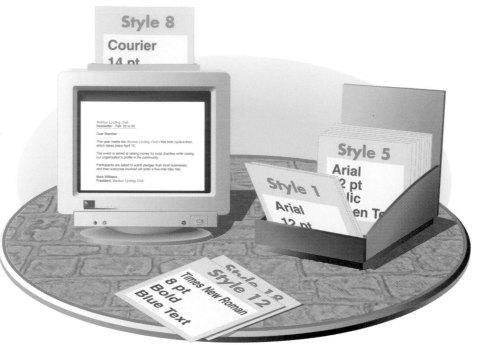

You can create a style to store formatting you like. You can then use the style to quickly apply the formatting to text in your documents.

CREATE A STYLE

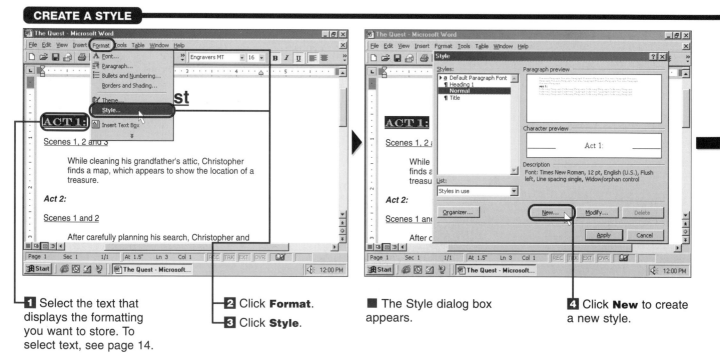

1 Select the text that displays the formatting you want to store. To select text, see page 14.

2 Click **Format**.

3 Click **Style**.

■ The Style dialog box appears.

4 Click **New** to create a new style.

What is the difference between character and paragraph styles?

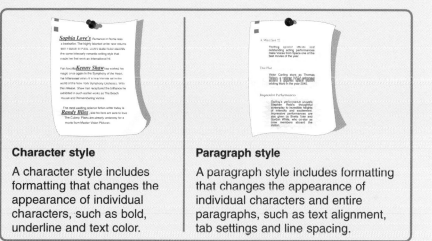

Character style

A character style includes formatting that changes the appearance of individual characters, such as bold, underline and text color.

Paragraph style

A paragraph style includes formatting that changes the appearance of individual characters and entire paragraphs, such as text alignment, tab settings and line spacing.

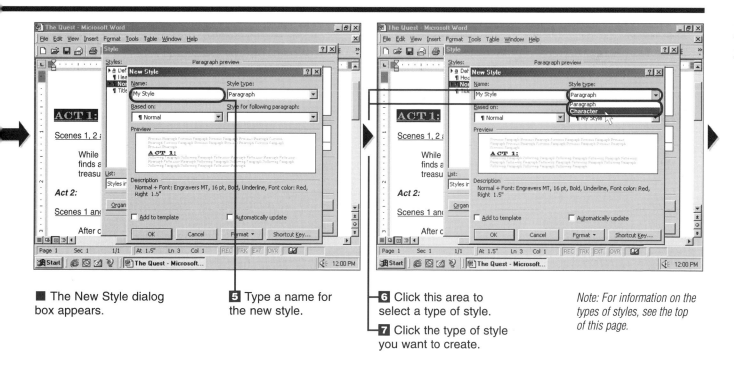

■ The New Style dialog box appears.

5 Type a name for the new style.

6 Click this area to select a type of style.

7 Click the type of style you want to create.

Note: For information on the types of styles, see the top of this page.

USING STYLES

After you create a style, you can apply the style to text in your document.

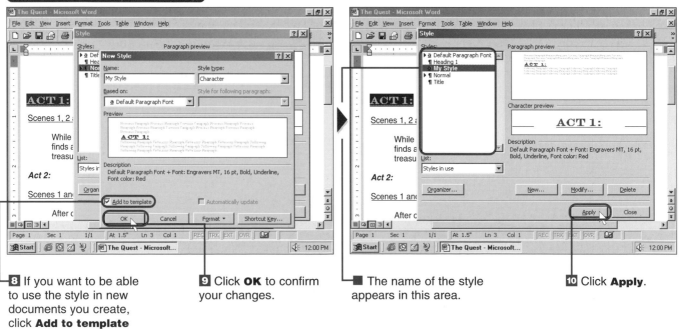

8 If you want to be able to use the style in new documents you create, click **Add to template** (☐ changes to ✔).

9 Click **OK** to confirm your changes.

■ The name of the style appears in this area.

10 Click **Apply**.

How can using styles help me?

Styles can save you time when you want to apply the same formatting to many different areas in a document. Styles also help you keep the appearance of text in a document consistent.

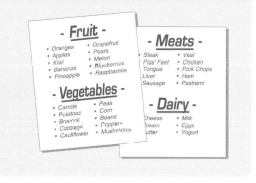

APPLY A STYLE

1 Select the text you want to apply a style to. To select text, see page 14.

2 Click ▼ in this area to display a list of styles.

Note: If the Style area is not displayed, click ≫ on the Formatting toolbar to display all the buttons.

3 Click the style you want to use.

Note: Word provides several built-in styles.

■ Word applies the style to the text you selected.

■ To deselect text, click outside the selected area.

You can change a style you created. When you change a style, Word automatically changes all the text you formatted with the style.

CHANGE A STYLE

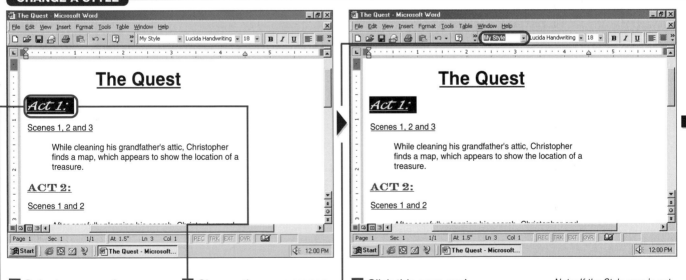

1 Select an area of text you formatted with the style you want to change. To select text, see page 14.

2 Change the appearance of the text you selected. To change the appearance of text, see pages 104 to 107.

3 Click this area and then press the **Enter** key.

Note: If the Style area is not displayed, click ☒ on the Formatting toolbar to display all the buttons.

When would I want to change a style?

You may want to change an existing style to quickly change the appearance of a document. You can try several formats until the document appears the way you want.

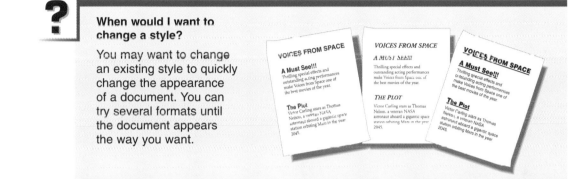

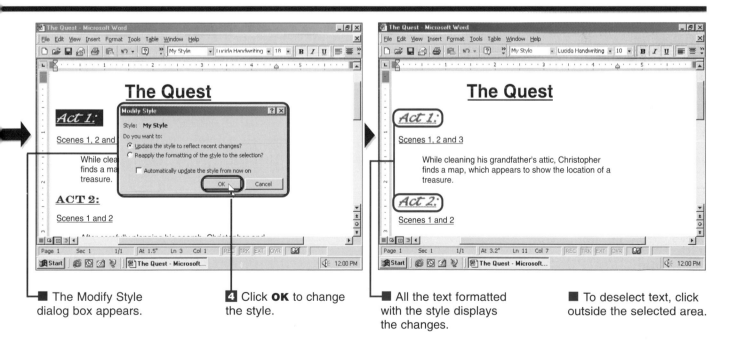

■ The Modify Style dialog box appears.

4 Click **OK** to change the style.

■ All the text formatted with the style displays the changes.

■ To deselect text, click outside the selected area.

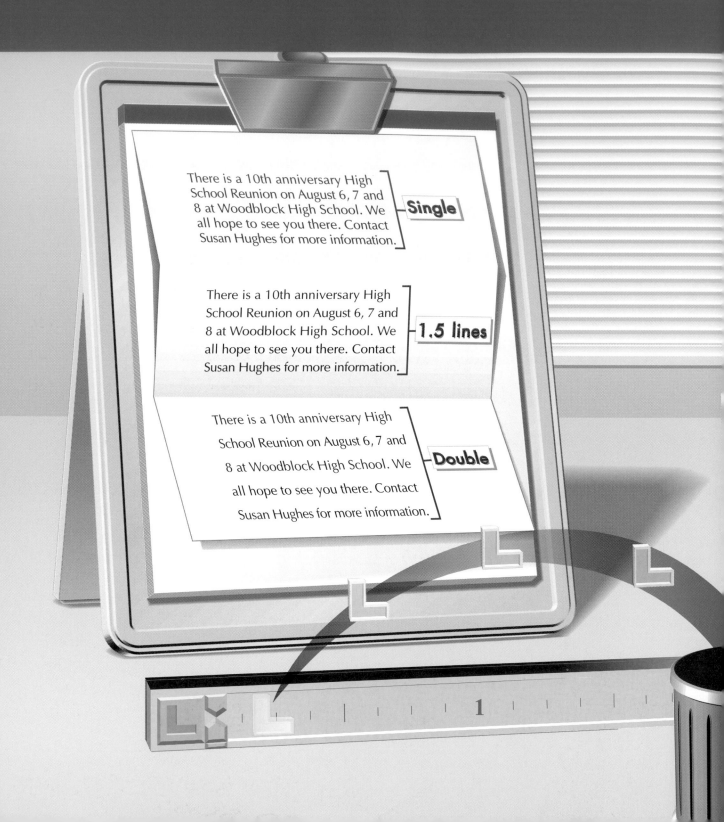

CHAPTER 6

Format Paragraphs

Do you want to change the line spacing, create a drop cap and indent paragraphs in your document? This chapter shows you how.

ADD BULLETS AND NUMBERS

You can separate items in a list by beginning each item with a bullet or number.

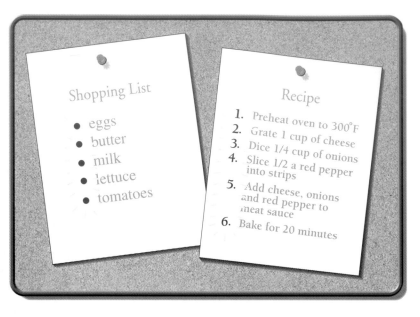

Bullets are useful for items in no particular order, such as items in a shopping list. Numbers are useful for items in a specific order, such as directions in a recipe.

ADD BULLETS AND NUMBERS

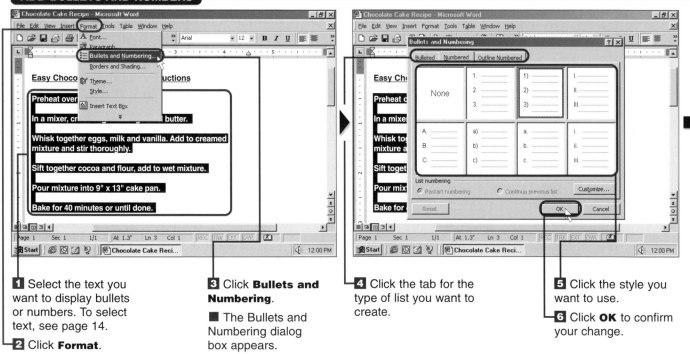

1 Select the text you want to display bullets or numbers. To select text, see page 14.

2 Click **Format**.

3 Click **Bullets and Numbering**.

■ The Bullets and Numbering dialog box appears.

4 Click the tab for the type of list you want to create.

5 Click the style you want to use.

6 Click **OK** to confirm your change.

How can I create a bulleted or numbered list as I type?

1 Type * or **1.** followed by a space. Then type the first item in the list.

2 Press the `Enter` key and Word automatically starts the next item with a bullet or number.

■ To end the bulleted or numbered list, press the `Enter` key twice.

- Monday, January 4th -
1. Dentist appointment
2. Lunch with Carrie
3. Pick up kids
4. Soccer game

SPACEBAR

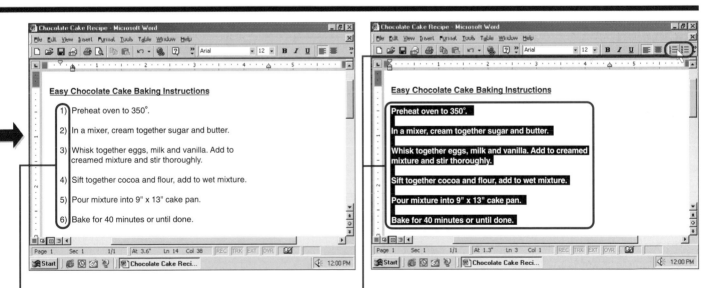

■ The bullets or numbers appear in your document.

■ To deselect text, click outside the selected area.

■ To remove bullets or numbers from your document, repeat steps **1** to **6**, except select **None** in step **5**.

QUICKLY ADD BULLETS OR NUMBERS

1 Select the text you want to display bullets or numbers. To select text, see page 14.

2 Click one of these buttons.

Add numbers

Add bullets

Note: If the button you want is not displayed, click on the Formatting toolbar to display all the buttons.

ADD BULLETS AND NUMBERS

You can enhance a list of items in your document by beginning each item with a picture bullet.

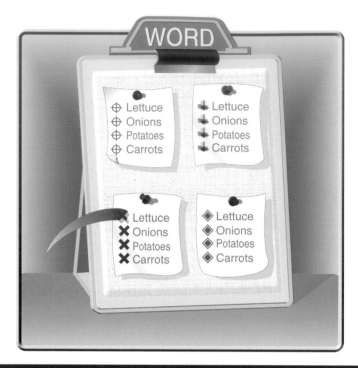

ADD PICTURE BULLETS

1 Select the text you want to display picture bullets. To select text, see page 14.

2 Click **Format**.

3 Click **Bullets and Numbering**.

■ The Bullets and Numbering dialog box appears.

4 Click the **Bulleted** tab.

5 Click **Picture**.

■ The Picture Bullet dialog box appears.

Why did the Cannot Locate Clip dialog box appear?

This dialog box appears if the picture bullet you selected is not stored on your computer. Click **Cancel** to close the dialog box. Insert the CD-ROM disc you used to install Word into your CD-ROM drive and then repeat steps **7** and **8** below to add the picture bullet to your document.

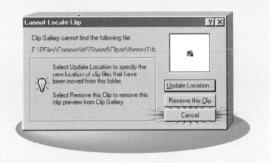

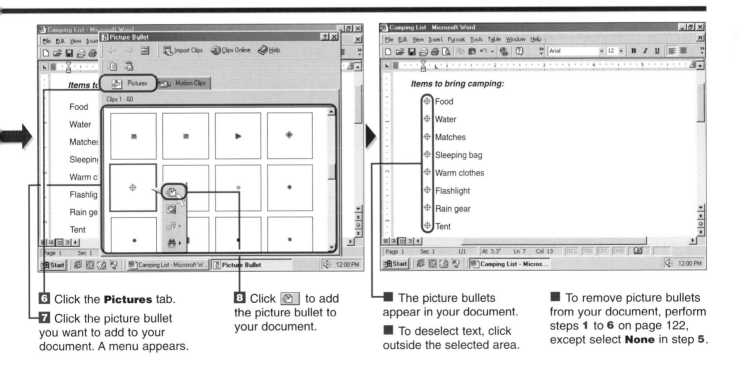

6 Click the **Pictures** tab.

7 Click the picture bullet you want to add to your document. A menu appears.

8 Click 🖼 to add the picture bullet to your document.

■ The picture bullets appear in your document.

■ To deselect text, click outside the selected area.

■ To remove picture bullets from your document, perform steps **1** to **6** on page 122, except select **None** in step **5**.

CHANGE LINE SPACING

You can change the amount
of space between the lines
of text in your document.
Changing the line spacing
can make your document
easier to review and edit.

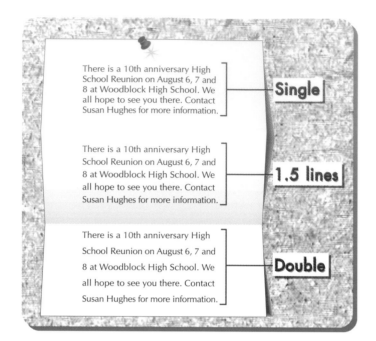

CHANGE LINE SPACING

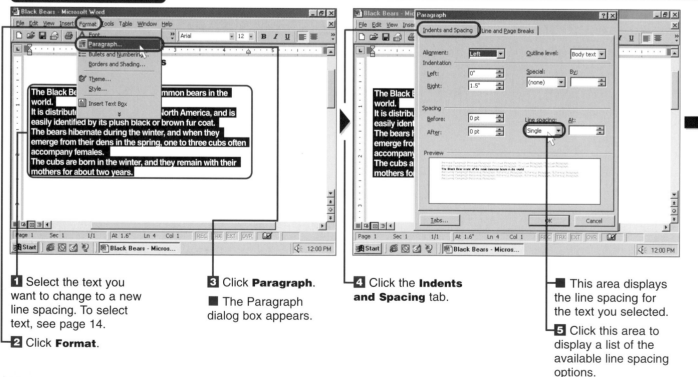

1 Select the text you
want to change to a new
line spacing. To select
text, see page 14.

2 Click **Format**.

3 Click **Paragraph**.

■ The Paragraph
dialog box appears.

4 Click the **Indents
and Spacing** tab.

■ This area displays
the line spacing for
the text you selected.

5 Click this area to
display a list of the
available line spacing
options.

Does Word ever automatically adjust the line spacing?

Word automatically increases the spacing of lines that contain large characters.

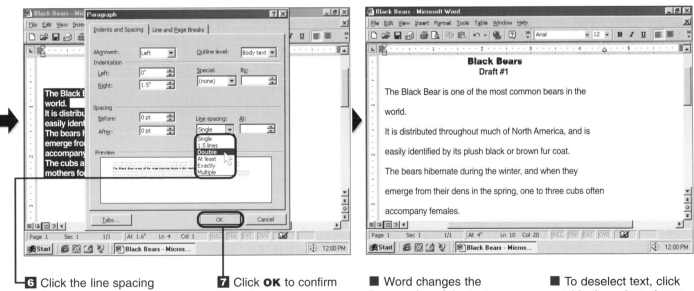

6 Click the line spacing option you want to use.

7 Click **OK** to confirm your change.

■ Word changes the line spacing of the text you selected.

■ To deselect text, click outside the selected area.

INDENT PARAGRAPHS

You can use the Indent feature to make paragraphs in your document stand out.

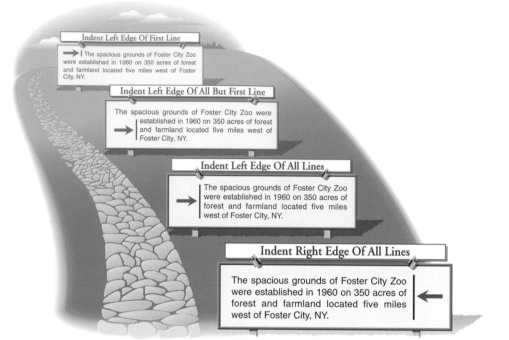

Indent Left Edge Of First Line

The spacious grounds of Foster City Zoo were established in 1960 on 350 acres of forest and farmland located five miles west of Foster City, NY.

Indent Left Edge Of All But First Line

The spacious grounds of Foster City Zoo were established in 1960 on 350 acres of forest and farmland located five miles west of Foster City, NY.

Indent Left Edge Of All Lines

The spacious grounds of Foster City Zoo were established in 1960 on 350 acres of forest and farmland located five miles west of Foster City, NY.

Indent Right Edge Of All Lines

The spacious grounds of Foster City Zoo were established in 1960 on 350 acres of forest and farmland located five miles west of Foster City, NY.

INDENT PARAGRAPHS

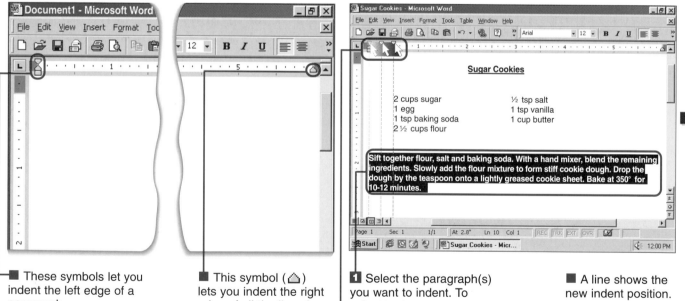

■ These symbols let you indent the left edge of a paragraph.

▽ Indent first line

△ Indent all but first line

☐ Indent all lines

■ This symbol (△) lets you indent the right edge of all the lines in a paragraph.

Note: If the symbols are not displayed, see page 46 to display the ruler.

1 Select the paragraph(s) you want to indent. To select text, see page 14.

2 Drag an indent symbol to a new position.

■ A line shows the new indent position.

What is a hanging indent?

A hanging indent moves all but the first line of a paragraph to the right. Hanging indents are useful when you are creating a résumé, glossary or bibliography.

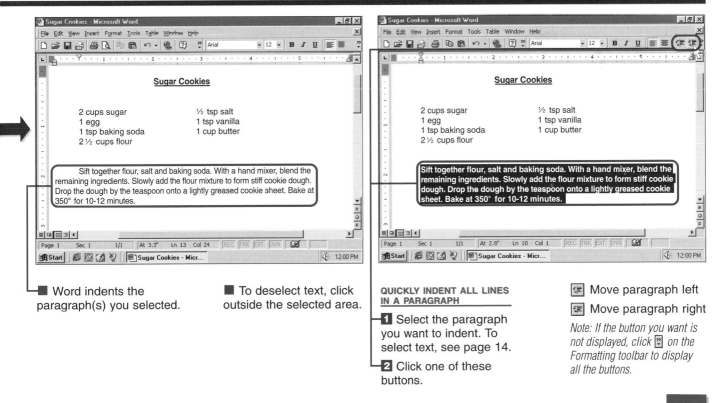

■ Word indents the paragraph(s) you selected.

■ To deselect text, click outside the selected area.

QUICKLY INDENT ALL LINES IN A PARAGRAPH

1 Select the paragraph you want to indent. To select text, see page 14.

2 Click one of these buttons.

Move paragraph left

Move paragraph right

Note: If the button you want is not displayed, click ⟩ on the Formatting toolbar to display all the buttons.

CHANGE TAB SETTINGS

You can use tabs to line up columns of information in your document. Word offers several types of tabs that you can choose from.

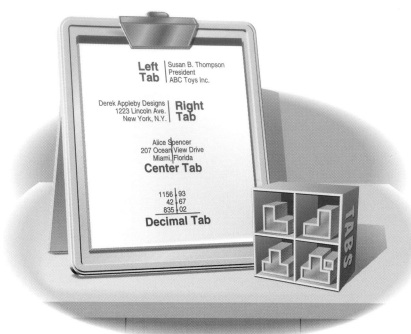

Left Tab
Susan B. Thompson
President
ABC Toys Inc.

Derek Appleby Designs
1223 Lincoln Ave.
New York, N.Y.
Right Tab

Alice Spencer
207 Ocean View Drive
Miami, Florida
Center Tab

1156 93
42 67
835 02
Decimal Tab

Word automatically places a tab every 0.5 inches across a page.

ADD A TAB

1 Select the text you want to contain the new tab. To select text, see page 14.

■ To add a tab to text you are about to type, click where you want to type the text.

2 Click this area until the type of tab you want to add appears.

Note: If the area is not displayed, see page 46 to display the ruler.

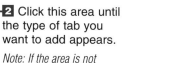

⌊	Left tab
⊥	Center tab
⌋	Right tab
⊥	Decimal tab

What happens if I use spaces instead of tabs to line up columns of text?

If you use spaces instead of tabs to line up columns of text, the information may not line up properly when you print your document.

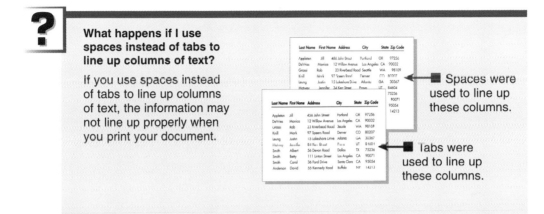

■ Spaces were used to line up these columns.

■ Tabs were used to line up these columns.

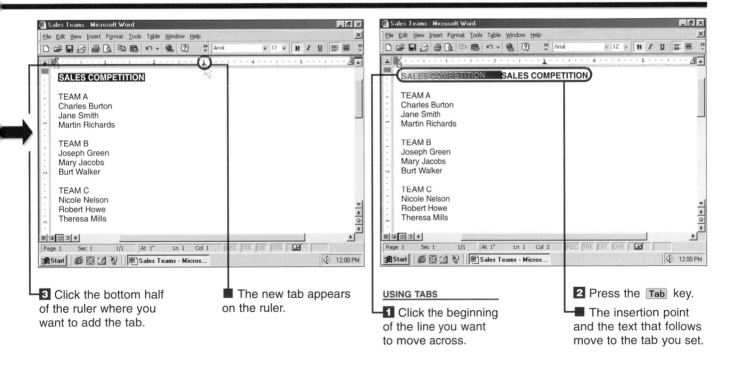

3 Click the bottom half of the ruler where you want to add the tab.

■ The new tab appears on the ruler.

USING TABS

1 Click the beginning of the line you want to move across.

2 Press the **Tab** key.

■ The insertion point and the text that follows move to the tab you set.

CHANGE TAB SETTINGS

You can move a
tab to a different
position on the
ruler.

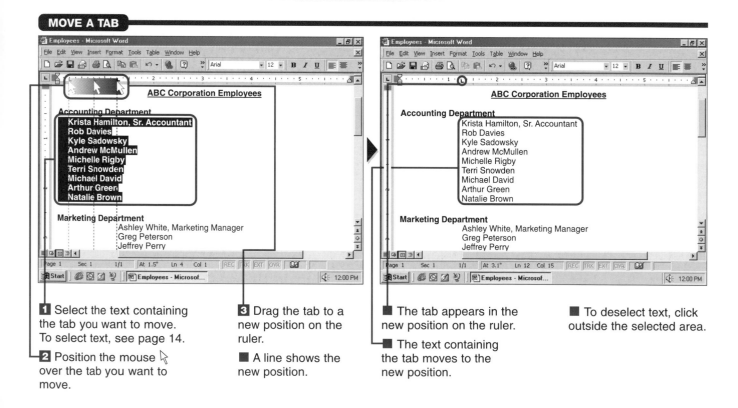

1 Select the text containing
the tab you want to move.
To select text, see page 14.

2 Position the mouse ⌖
over the tab you want to
move.

3 Drag the tab to a
new position on the
ruler.

■ A line shows the
new position.

■ The tab appears in the
new position on the ruler.

■ The text containing
the tab moves to the
new position.

■ To deselect text, click
outside the selected area.

When you no longer
need a tab, you can
remove the tab from
your document.

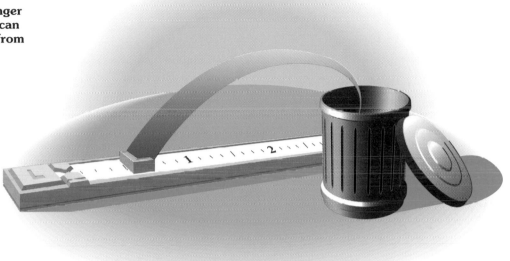

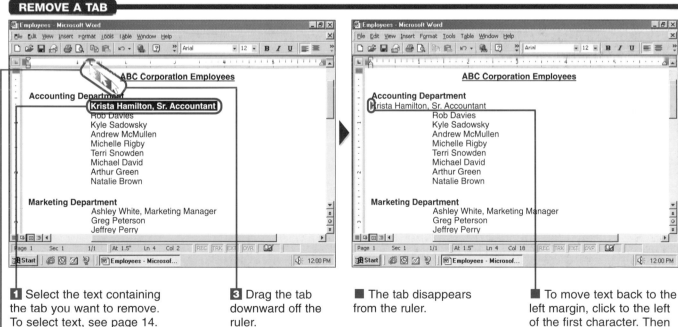

1 Select the text containing
the tab you want to remove.
To select text, see page 14.

2 Position the mouse
over the tab you want to
remove.

3 Drag the tab
downward off the
ruler.

■ The tab disappears
from the ruler.

■ To move text back to the
left margin, click to the left
of the first character. Then
press the `◆Backspace` key.

CHANGE TAB SETTINGS

You can insert a line or row of dots, called leader characters, before a tab to help lead the eye from one column of information to another.

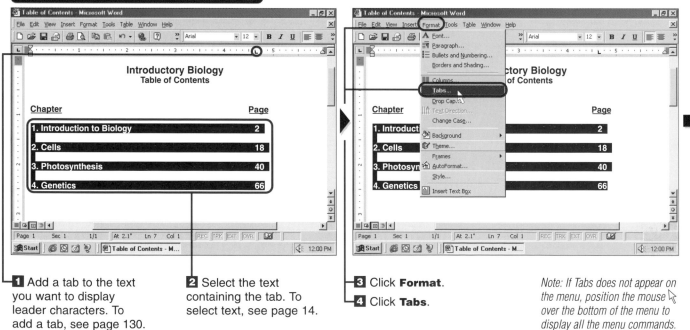

TABLE OF CONTENTS

Chapter 1......................10
Chapter 2......................32
Chapter 3......................48
Chapter 4......................72
Chapter 5......................85
Chapter 6......................96
Chapter 7......................112

TABLE OF CONTENTS

Chapter 8..............135
Chapter 9..............152
Chapter 10..............174
Chapter 11..............193
Chapter 12..............205
Chapter 13..............214
Chapter 14..............224

ADD A TAB WITH LEADER CHARACTERS

1 Add a tab to the text you want to display leader characters. To add a tab, see page 130.

2 Select the text containing the tab. To select text, see page 14.

3 Click **Format**.

4 Click **Tabs**.

Note: If Tabs does not appear on the menu, position the mouse over the bottom of the menu to display all the menu commands.

■ The Tabs dialog box appears.

Why would I use leader characters?

Carson, S...... 555-5670
Hyland, M...... 555-2346
Inglis, K......... 555-4328
Kerr, D.......... 555-7621
Moore, S....... 555-3066
Schmidt, S.... 555-8087
Smith, M....... 555-5190
Taylor, D....... 555-3487
Trott, P.......... 555-1729
Walker, B...... 555-5430

JOB APPLICATION

Please enter information
in the areas provided.

Last Name: _____
First Name: _____
Address: _____

_____

City/State: _____
Zip Code: _____
Phone No: _____

Leader characters make
information such as a
table of contents or a list
of telephone numbers
easier to read.

Leader characters
are also used in
forms to create areas
where people can
enter information.

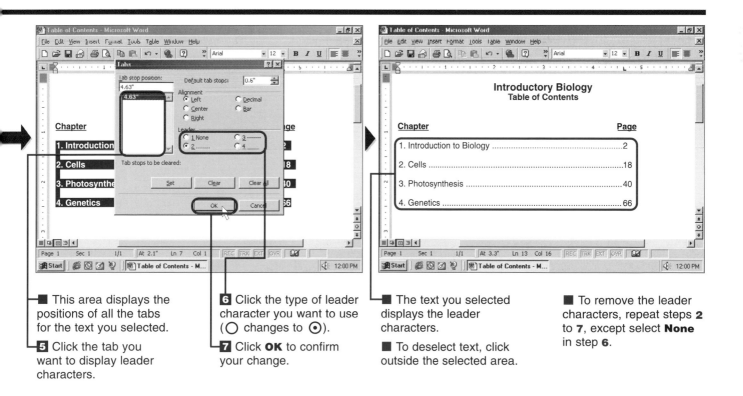

■ This area displays the
positions of all the tabs
for the text you selected.

5 Click the tab you
want to display leader
characters.

6 Click the type of leader
character you want to use
(○ changes to ⊙).

7 Click **OK** to confirm
your change.

■ The text you selected
displays the leader
characters.

■ To deselect text, click
outside the selected area.

■ To remove the leader
characters, repeat steps **2**
to **7**, except select **None**
in step **6**.

You can create a
large capital letter
at the beginning
of a paragraph
to enhance the
appearance of
the paragraph.

Word can only display a
drop cap properly in the
Print Layout and Web
Layout views. For more
information on the views,
see page 44.

CREATE A DROP CAP

1 Click the paragraph
you want to display a
drop cap.

2 Click **Format**.

3 Click **Drop Cap**.

*Note: If Drop Cap does not
appear on the menu, position
the mouse ⌖ over the bottom
of the menu to display all the
menu commands.*

■ The Drop Cap dialog
box appears.

4 Click the way you
want the drop cap to
appear in the paragraph.

■ This area displays
the font the drop cap
will display.

5 To select another font
for the drop cap, click ▼
in this area.

6 Click the font you want
the drop cap to display.

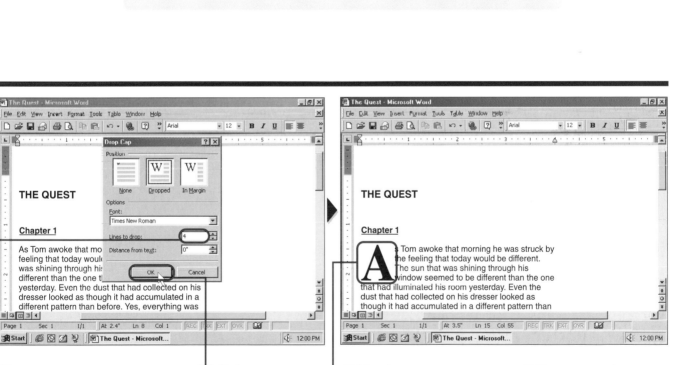

Can I create a drop cap using more than one letter?

You can create a drop cap using several letters or an entire word at the beginning of a paragraph. Select the letters or word you want to make a drop cap and then perform steps **2** to **8** below. To select text, see page 14.

■ This area displays the number of lines that will wrap around the drop cap.

7 To change the number of lines, double-click this area and then type the number of lines.

8 Click **OK** to create the drop cap.

■ The drop cap appears in your document.

■ To deselect the drop cap, click outside the drop cap.

■ To remove a drop cap, repeat steps **1** to **4**, except select **None** in step **4**. Then perform step **8**.

ADD A BORDER

You can add a border to text in your document to draw attention to important information.

ADD A BORDER

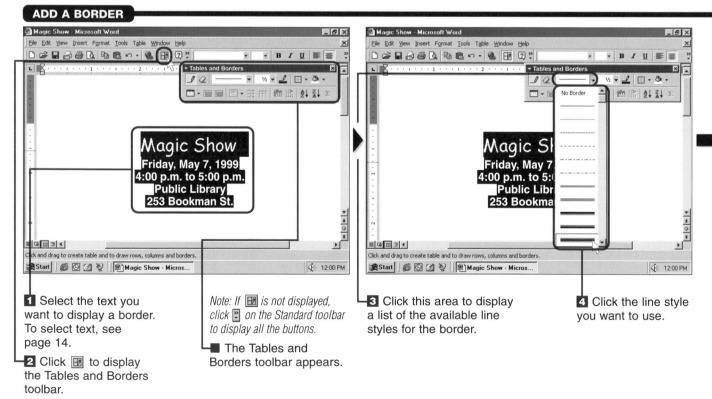

1 Select the text you want to display a border. To select text, see page 14.

2 Click 🗗 to display the Tables and Borders toolbar.

Note: If 🗗 is not displayed, click 🔊 on the Standard toolbar to display all the buttons.

■ The Tables and Borders toolbar appears.

3 Click this area to display a list of the available line styles for the border.

4 Click the line style you want to use.

138

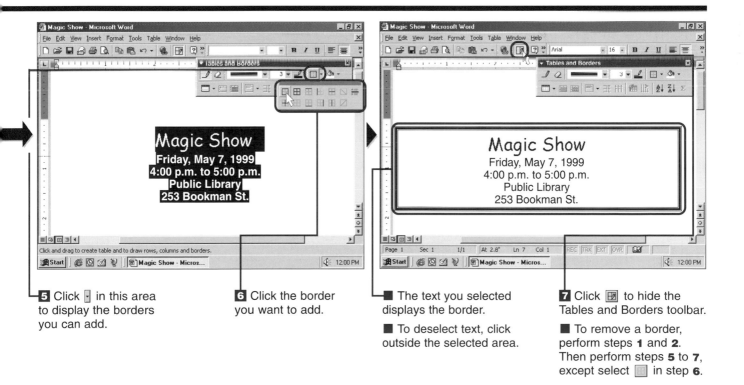

How can I quickly add a line across my page?

When you type one of the sets of characters in this chart and then press the `Enter` key, Word automatically adds a line across your page.

Type the following:		Line Style
3 hyphens	(---)	———————
3 underscore characters	(___)	———————
3 equal signs	(===)	═══════

5 Click ⦙ in this area to display the borders you can add.

6 Click the border you want to add.

■ The text you selected displays the border.

■ To deselect text, click outside the selected area.

7 Click ⊞ to hide the Tables and Borders toolbar.

■ To remove a border, perform steps **1** and **2**. Then perform steps **5** to **7**, except select ⊞ in step **6**.

You can emphasize
an area of text in
your document by
adding shading.

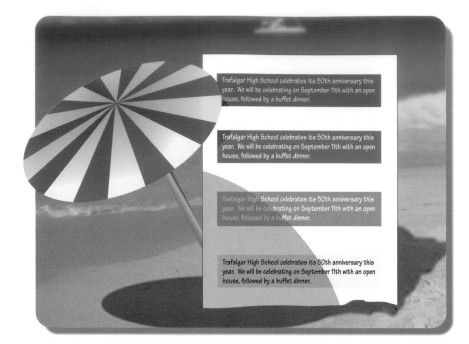

ADD SHADING

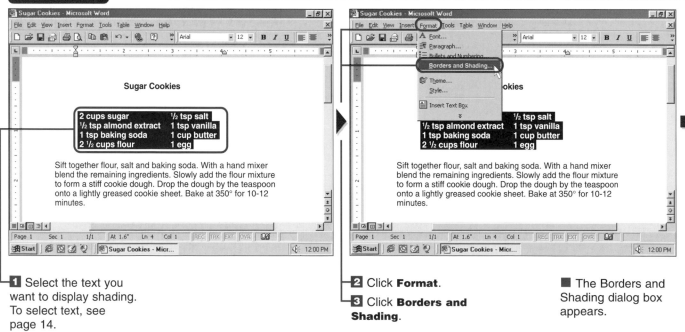

1 Select the text you
want to display shading.
To select text, see
page 14.

2 Click **Format**.

3 Click **Borders and
Shading**.

■ The Borders and
Shading dialog box
appears.

How will the shading I add to my document appear when I print the document?

When you print your document on a color printer, the shading will appear on the printed page as it appears on your screen. When you print your document on a black-and-white printer, any colored shading you added will appear as a shade of gray on the printed page.

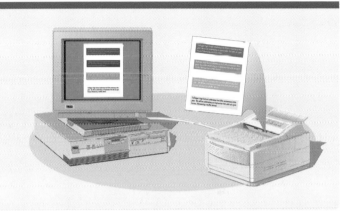

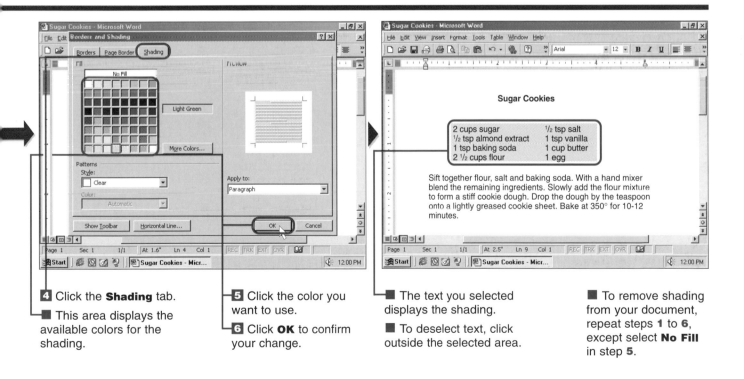

■ **4** Click the **Shading** tab.

■ This area displays the available colors for the shading.

■ **5** Click the color you want to use.

■ **6** Click **OK** to confirm your change.

■ The text you selected displays the shading.

■ To deselect text, click outside the selected area.

■ To remove shading from your document, repeat steps **1** to **6**, except select **No Fill** in step **5**.

HYPHENATE TEXT

You can have Word hyphenate the text in your document.

Hyphenating text helps eliminate gaps at the ends of the lines in a document. This may allow you to fit more text on a page.

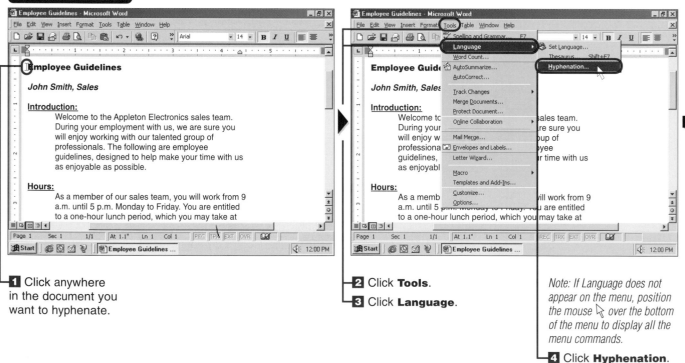

1 Click anywhere in the document you want to hyphenate.

2 Click **Tools**.

3 Click **Language**.

Note: If Language does not appear on the menu, position the mouse over the bottom of the menu to display all the menu commands.

4 Click **Hyphenation**.

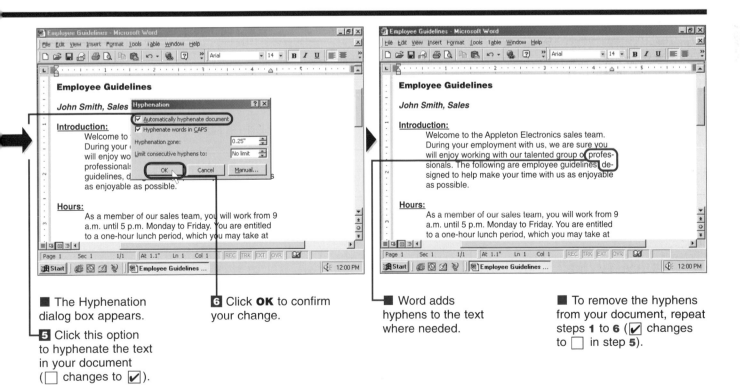

What will happen to the hyphenated text in my document if I edit the document?

When you add or delete text in your document, Word will automatically adjust the hyphenation in the document for you.

XYZ's financial ana- lysts have predicted a spectacular year for the lucrative com- pany.

XYZ Corporation's financial analysts have predicted a spectacu- lar year for the lucra- tive company.

■ The Hyphenation dialog box appears.

5 Click this option to hyphenate the text in your document (☐ changes to ☑).

6 Click **OK** to confirm your change.

■ Word adds hyphens to the text where needed.

■ To remove the hyphens from your document, repeat steps **1** to **6** (☑ changes to ☐ in step **5**).

The Olympic Flame

One constant that remains from ancient times, is the Olympic flame. It has remained since the beginning.

In ancient times the Olympic games took on a very religious significance. Olympia, the grounds on which the first games were played, was considered sacred.

The ancient Greeks believed very deeply in a relationship between life and death and the connection that existed between religion and burial traditions.

time the ancient Olympic games were held, the Olympic flame was lit to symbolize the re-birth of the spirit of their dead heroes.

Today, that tradition continues. In 1936, for the first time in modern Olympic history, the sacred Olympic flame was carried to Berlin, Germany where the 11th Olympiad took place. Since that time and to this present day, runners, through a relay, transport the flame, from Greece, every four years to the city that is to host the Olympics. The runner, carrying the torch, into the stadium at the opening Olympic ceremony and lights the Olympic torch which burns throughout the games until it is extinguished during the closing ceremony.

CHAPTER 7

Format Pages

Are you wondering how to change the appearance of pages in your document? In this chapter you will learn how to add page numbers, change margins, create newspaper columns and more.

You are invited... **TO A**

SURPRISE

BIRTHDAY Party!

INSERT A PAGE BREAK

If you want to start a new page at a specific place in your document, you can insert a page break. A page break indicates where one page ends and another begins.

INSERT A PAGE BREAK

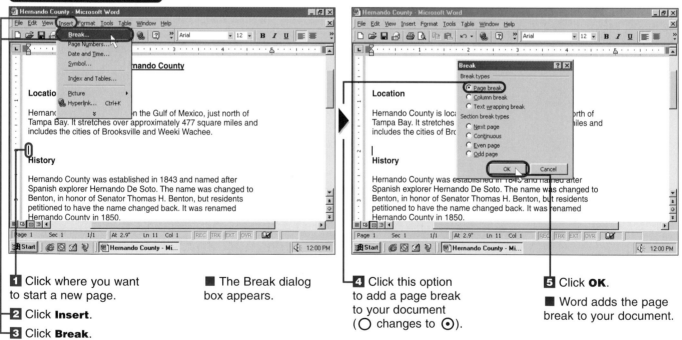

1 Click where you want to start a new page.

2 Click **Insert**.

3 Click **Break**.

■ The Break dialog box appears.

4 Click this option to add a page break to your document (○ changes to ⊙).

5 Click **OK**.

■ Word adds the page break to your document.

Will Word ever insert page breaks automatically?

When you fill a page with text, Word automatically starts a new page by inserting a page break for you.

DELETE A PAGE BREAK

1 Click ▤ to display your document in the Normal view.

■ The **Page Break** line shows where one page ends and another begins. The line will not appear when you print your document.

Note: You may need to scroll through your document to view the line.

2 Click the **Page Break** line.

3 Press the Delete key to remove the page break.

INSERT A SECTION BREAK

You can divide your document into sections so you can format each section separately.

Dividing your document into sections allows you to apply formatting to only part of your document. For example, you may want to add newspaper columns or change the margins for only part of your document.

INSERT A SECTION BREAK

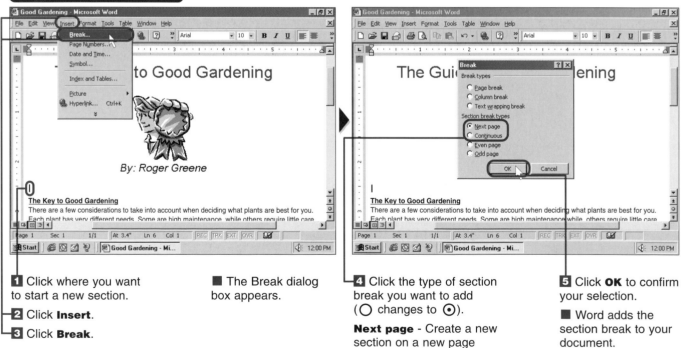

1 Click where you want to start a new section.

2 Click **Insert**.

3 Click **Break**.

■ The Break dialog box appears.

4 Click the type of section break you want to add (○ changes to ⊙).

Next page - Create a new section on a new page

Continuous - Create a new section on the current page

5 Click **OK** to confirm your selection.

■ Word adds the section break to your document.

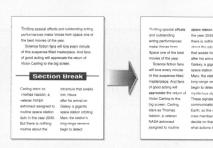

Will the appearance of my document change when I delete a section break?

When you delete a section break, the text above the break assumes the appearance of the text below the break. For example, if the text appears in columns below a section break, the text above the break will also appear in columns when you delete the break.

DELETE A SECTION BREAK

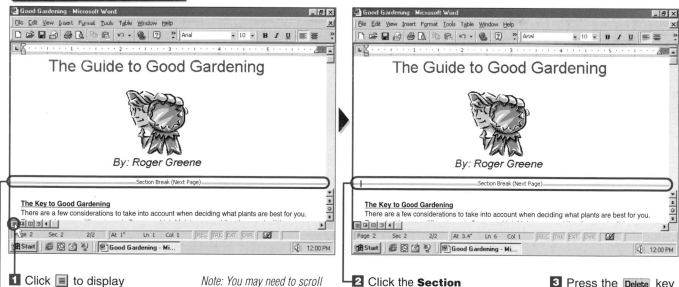

1 Click ▤ to display your document in the Normal view.

■ The **Section Break** line shows where one section ends and another begins. The line will not appear when you print your document.

Note: You may need to scroll through your document to view the line.

2 Click the **Section Break** line.

3 Press the Delete key to remove the section break.

ADD PAGE NUMBERS

You can have Word number the pages in your document.

1 Click **Insert**.

2 Click **Page Numbers**.

■ The Page Numbers dialog box appears.

3 Click this area to select a position for the page numbers.

4 Click the position where you want the page numbers to appear.

Will Word adjust the page numbers if I make changes to my document?

If you add, remove or rearrange text in your document, Word will automatically adjust the page numbers for you.

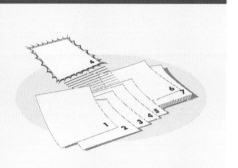

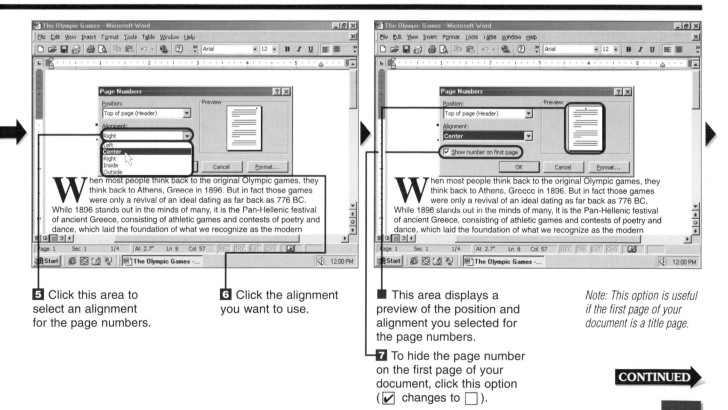

5 Click this area to select an alignment for the page numbers.

6 Click the alignment you want to use.

■ This area displays a preview of the position and alignment you selected for the page numbers.

7 To hide the page number on the first page of your document, click this option (☑ changes to ☐).

Note: This option is useful if the first page of your document is a title page.

CONTINUED ▶

ADD PAGE NUMBERS

Word offers several formats you can use for your page numbers. You can choose the format that best suits your document.

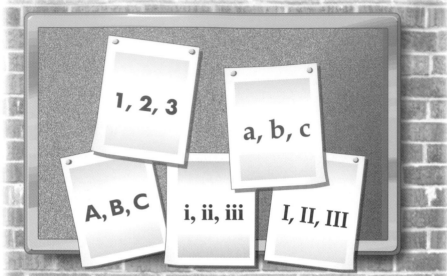

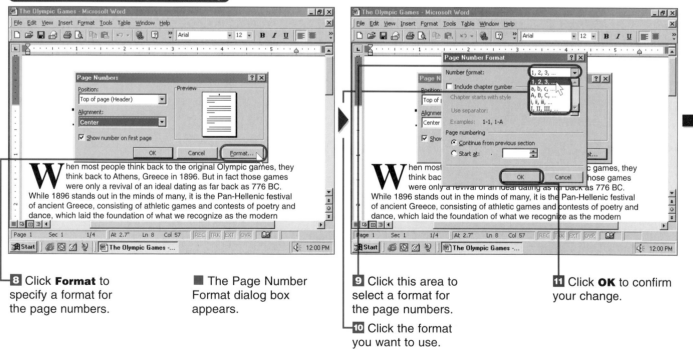

8 Click **Format** to specify a format for the page numbers.

■ The Page Number Format dialog box appears.

9 Click this area to select a format for the page numbers.

10 Click the format you want to use.

11 Click **OK** to confirm your change.

How do I remove page numbers from my document?

To remove page numbers, you must delete the page number from the document's header or footer. To delete information from a header or footer, see the top of page 155.

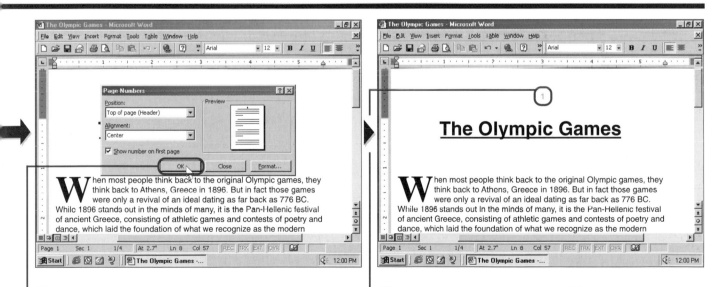

12 Click **OK** to add the page numbers to your document.

■ The document displays the page numbers.

■ Word can only display page numbers in the Print Layout view. For more information on the views, see page 44.

ADD A HEADER OR FOOTER

You can add a header and footer to every page in your document. A header or footer can display information such as the date, chapter title or your name.

■ A **header** appears at the top of each page.

■ A **footer** appears at the bottom of each page.

Word can only display headers and footers in the Print Layout view. For more information on the views, see page 44.

ADD A HEADER OR FOOTER TO EVERY PAGE

1 Click **View**.

2 Click **Header and Footer**.

■ Word displays the Header and Footer toolbar.

■ The text in the document is dimmed.

3 To create a header, type the header text. You can format the text as you would format any text in a document. To format text, see pages 94 to 107.

4 Click 🔲 to display the Footer area.

How do I delete information from a header or footer?

Perform steps **1** and **2** below to display the headers and footers in your document. Select the text you want to delete from the header or footer and then press the Delete key. To select text, see page 14.

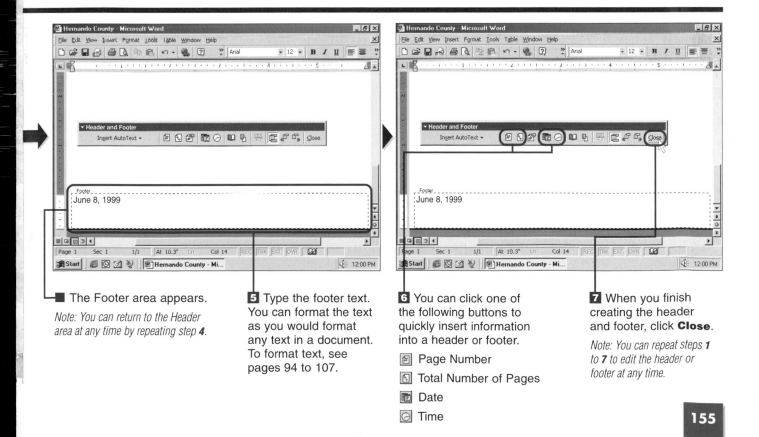

■ The Footer area appears.

Note: You can return to the Header area at any time by repeating step 4.

5 Type the footer text. You can format the text as you would format any text in a document. To format text, see pages 94 to 107.

6 You can click one of the following buttons to quickly insert information into a header or footer.

Page Number

Total Number of Pages

Date

Time

7 When you finish creating the header and footer, click **Close**.

*Note: You can repeat steps **1** to **7** to edit the header or footer at any time.*

ADD A HEADER OR FOOTER

You can have different headers and footers on different pages in your document.

VARY HEADERS OR FOOTERS WITHIN DOCUMENT

1 Click **View**.

2 Click **Header and Footer**.

■ Word displays the Header and Footer toolbar.

■ The text in the document is dimmed.

3 Click 📄 to set up different headers and footers for different pages in your document.

■ The Page Setup dialog box appears.

**What header and footer
areas does Word provide?**

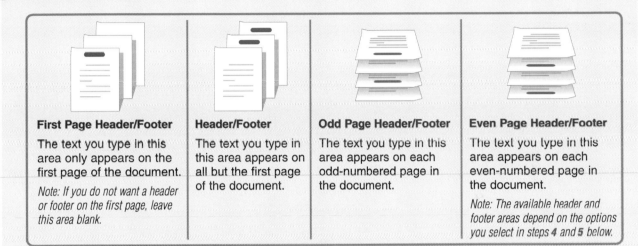

First Page Header/Footer

The text you type in this
area only appears on the
first page of the document.

*Note: If you do not want a header
or footer on the first page, leave
this area blank.*

Header/Footer

The text you type in
this area appears on
all but the first page
of the document.

Odd Page Header/Footer

The text you type in this
area appears on each
odd-numbered page in
the document.

Even Page Header/Footer

The text you type in this
area appears on each
even-numbered page in
the document.

*Note: The available header and
footer areas depend on the options
you select in steps 4 and 5 below.*

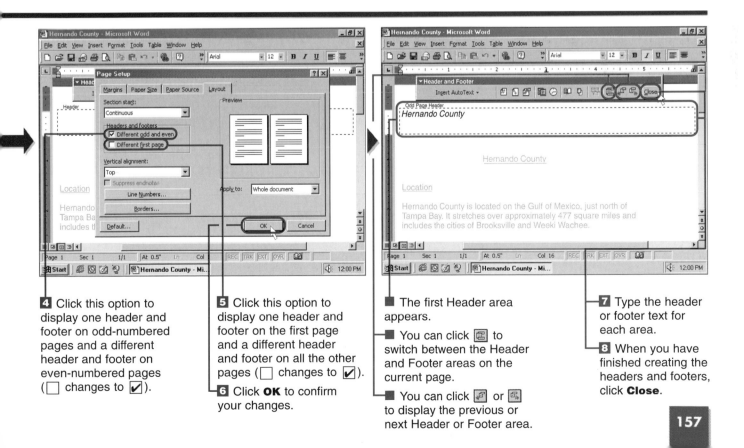

4 Click this option to
display one header and
footer on odd-numbered
pages and a different
header and footer on
even-numbered pages
(☐ changes to ✔).

5 Click this option to
display one header and
footer on the first page
and a different header
and footer on all the other
pages (☐ changes to ✔).

6 Click **OK** to confirm
your changes.

■ The first Header area
appears.

■ You can click 🗐 to
switch between the Header
and Footer areas on the
current page.

■ You can click 🗐 or 🗐
to display the previous or
next Header or Footer area.

7 Type the header
or footer text for
each area.

8 When you have
finished creating the
headers and footers,
click **Close**.

ADD FOOTNOTES OR ENDNOTES

You can add a footnote or endnote to provide additional information about text in your document. Footnotes and endnotes can provide information such as an explanation, comment or reference.

1 Senator Benton introduced a bill in the State Legislature, which was responsible for opening the land for settlement.

Word displays footnotes and endnotes as they will appear on a printed page in the Print Layout view. For more information on the views, see page 44.

ADD FOOTNOTES OR ENDNOTES

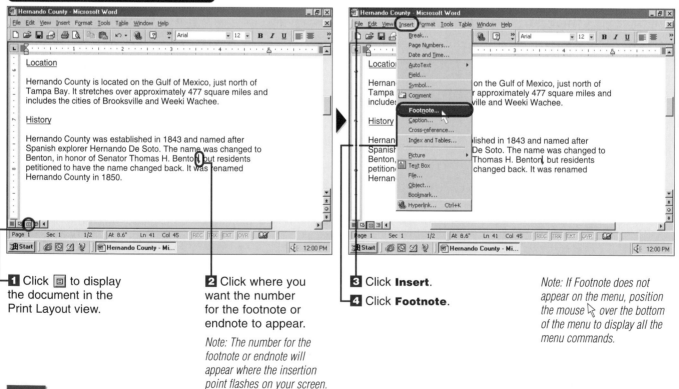

1 Click 🔳 to display the document in the Print Layout view.

2 Click where you want the number for the footnote or endnote to appear.

Note: The number for the footnote or endnote will appear where the insertion point flashes on your screen.

3 Click **Insert**.

4 Click **Footnote**.

Note: If Footnote does not appear on the menu, position the mouse ⧸ over the bottom of the menu to display all the menu commands.

What is the difference between footnotes and endnotes?

Footnotes

Footnotes appear at the bottom of a page. Word ensures that the text for a footnote always appears on the same page as the footnote number.

Endnotes

Endnotes appear at the end of a document.

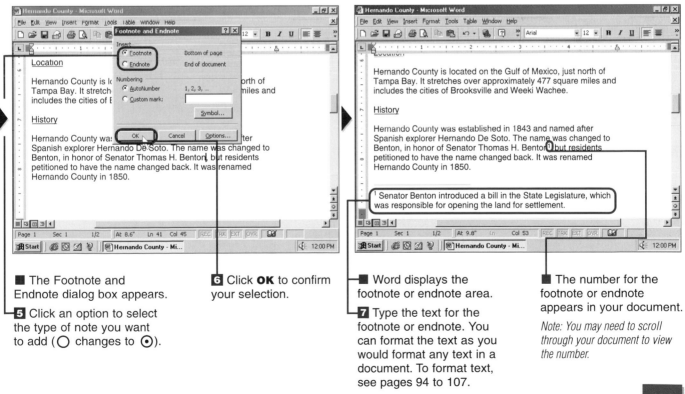

■ The Footnote and Endnote dialog box appears.

5 Click an option to select the type of note you want to add (○ changes to ⊙).

6 Click **OK** to confirm your selection.

■ Word displays the footnote or endnote area.

7 Type the text for the footnote or endnote. You can format the text as you would format any text in a document. To format text, see pages 94 to 107.

■ The number for the footnote or endnote appears in your document.

Note: You may need to scroll through your document to view the number.

ADD FOOTNOTES OR ENDNOTES

You can edit a footnote or endnote you added to a document. You can also delete a footnote or endnote you no longer need.

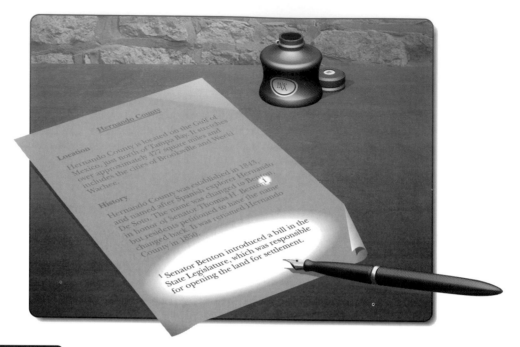

EDIT A FOOTNOTE OR ENDNOTE

1 To view the text for a footnote or endnote, position the mouse I over the footnote or endnote number in your document.

■ A yellow box appears, displaying the text for the footnote or endnote.

2 To edit the text for a footnote or endnote, click 🔲 to display the document in the Print Layout view.

3 Double-click the number for the footnote or endnote you want to edit.

How do I print endnotes on a separate page?

Word automatically prints endnotes after the last line in a document. To print endnotes on a separate page, insert a page break directly above the endnote area. To insert a page break, see page 146.

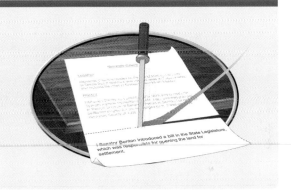

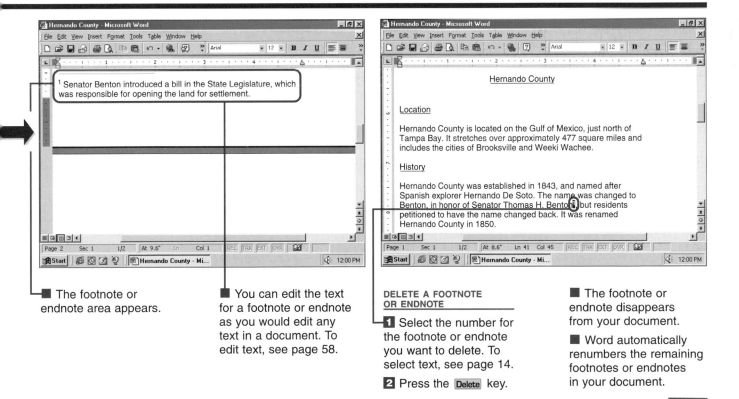

■ The footnote or endnote area appears.

■ You can edit the text for a footnote or endnote as you would edit any text in a document. To edit text, see page 58.

DELETE A FOOTNOTE OR ENDNOTE

1 Select the number for the footnote or endnote you want to delete. To select text, see page 14.

2 Press the Delete key.

■ The footnote or endnote disappears from your document.

■ Word automatically renumbers the remaining footnotes or endnotes in your document.

CENTER TEXT ON A PAGE

You can vertically center text on each page of your document. This is useful for creating title pages and short memos.

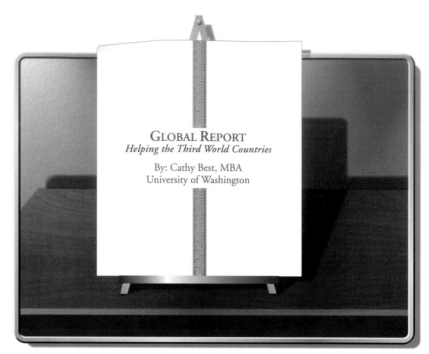

CENTER TEXT ON A PAGE

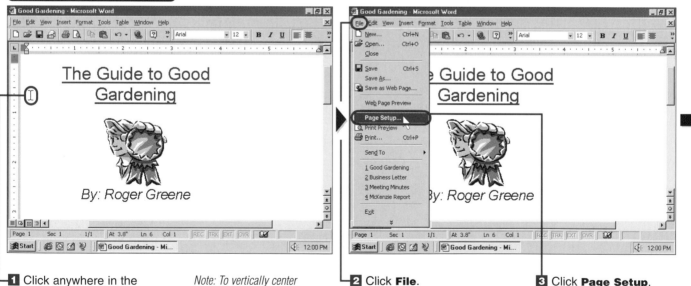

1 Click anywhere in the document or section you want to vertically center.

Note: To vertically center only some of the text in a document, you must divide the document into sections. To divide a document into sections, see page 148.

2 Click **File**.

3 Click **Page Setup**.

■ The Page Setup dialog box appears.

How can I display the entire page on my screen so I can clearly see how the centered text looks on the page?

You can use the Print Preview feature to display the entire page on your screen. This lets you see how the centered text will appear on a printed page. For information on the Print Preview feature, see page 180.

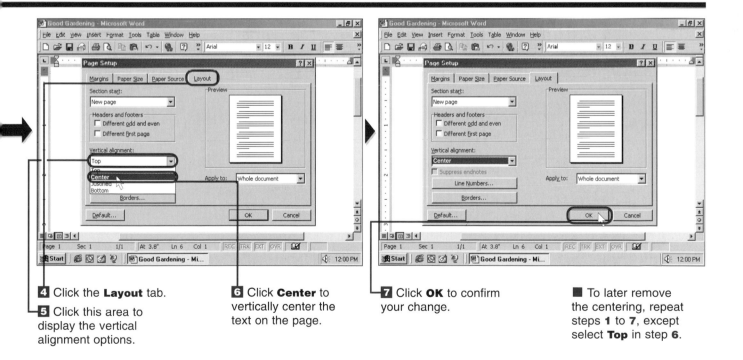

4 Click the **Layout** tab.

5 Click this area to display the vertical alignment options.

6 Click **Center** to vertically center the text on the page.

7 Click **OK** to confirm your change.

■ To later remove the centering, repeat steps **1** to **7**, except select **Top** in step **6**.

CHANGE MARGINS

A margin is the amount of space between the text in your document and the edge of your paper. You can change the margins to suit your needs.

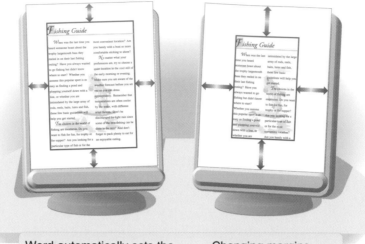

Word automatically sets the top and bottom margins at 1 inch and the left and right margins at 1.25 inches.

Changing margins lets you accommodate letterhead and other specialty paper.

CHANGE MARGINS

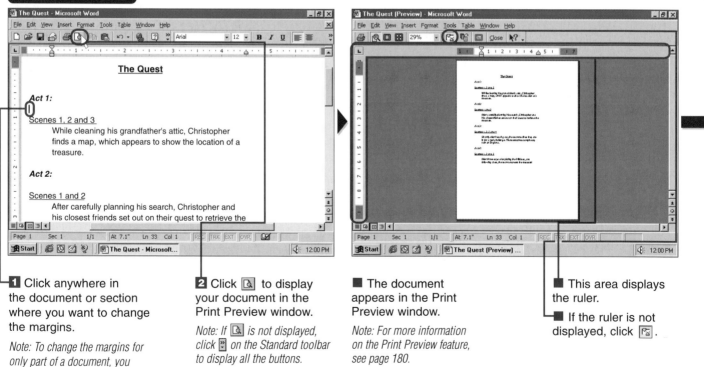

1 Click anywhere in the document or section where you want to change the margins.

Note: To change the margins for only part of a document, you must divide the document into sections. To divide a document into sections, see page 148.

2 Click 🔍 to display your document in the Print Preview window.

Note: If 🔍 is not displayed, click ❯ on the Standard toolbar to display all the buttons.

■ The document appears in the Print Preview window.

Note: For more information on the Print Preview feature, see page 180.

■ This area displays the ruler.

■ If the ruler is not displayed, click 🔳.

How can I quickly change the left and right margins for only part of my document?

You can change the Indentation of paragraphs to quickly change the left and right margins for only part of your document. To indent paragraphs, see page 128.

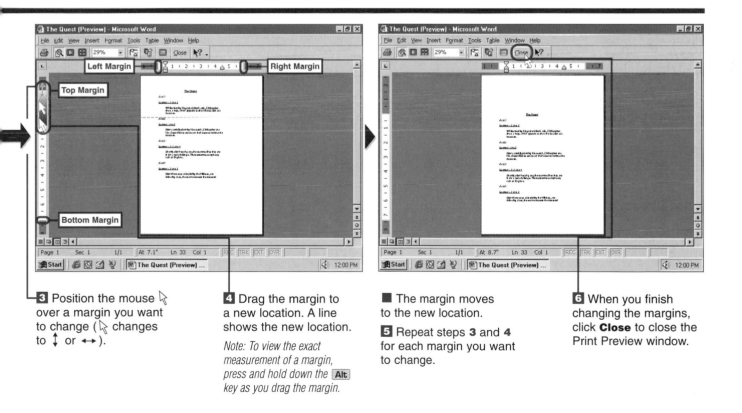

3 Position the mouse over a margin you want to change (changes to ↕ or ↔).

4 Drag the margin to a new location. A line shows the new location.

Note: To view the exact measurement of a margin, press and hold down the Alt *key as you drag the margin.*

■ The margin moves to the new location.

5 Repeat steps **3** and **4** for each margin you want to change.

6 When you finish changing the margins, click **Close** to close the Print Preview window.

CHANGE PAPER SIZE

Word sets each page in your document to print on letter-sized paper. If you want to use a different paper size, you can change this setting.

CHANGE PAPER SIZE

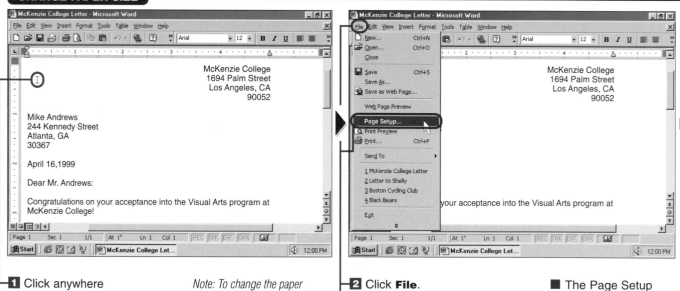

1 Click anywhere in the document or section you want to print on a different paper size.

Note: To change the paper size for only part of a document, you must divide the document into sections. To divide a document into sections, see page 148.

2 Click **File**.

3 Click **Page Setup**.

■ The Page Setup dialog box appears.

What paper sizes can I use?

The available paper sizes depend on the printer you are using. Most printers can print on letter-sized and legal-sized paper. You can consult the manual that came with your printer to determine which paper sizes the printer can use.

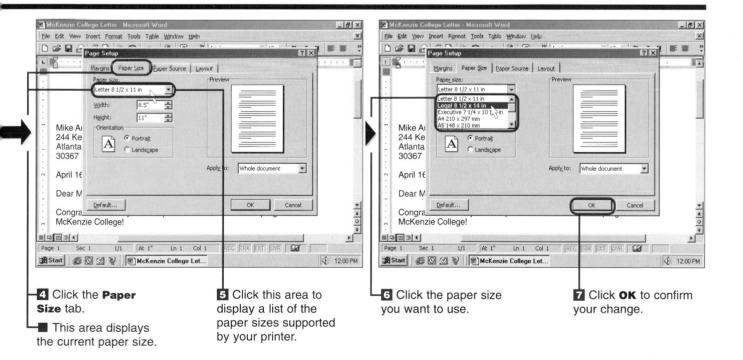

4 Click the **Paper Size** tab.

■ This area displays the current paper size.

5 Click this area to display a list of the paper sizes supported by your printer.

6 Click the paper size you want to use.

7 Click **OK** to confirm your change.

CHANGE PAGE ORIENTATION

You can change the orientation of pages in your document. The page orientation determines the direction that information prints on a page.

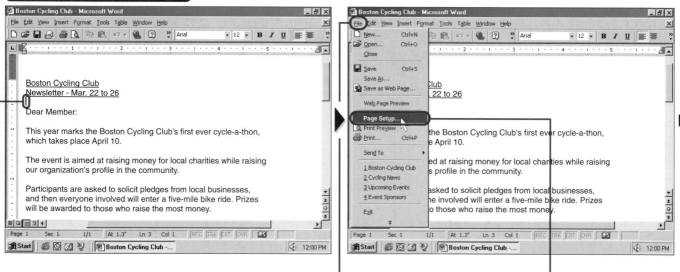

1 Click anywhere in the document or section you want to change to a different page orientation.

Note: To change the page orientation for only part of a document, you must divide the document into sections. To divide a document into sections, see page 148.

2 Click **File**.

3 Click **Page Setup**.

■ The Page Setup dialog box appears.

Which page orientation should I use?

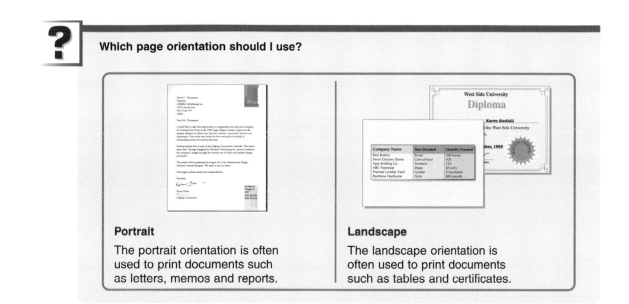

Portrait

The portrait orientation is often used to print documents such as letters, memos and reports.

Landscape

The landscape orientation is often used to print documents such as tables and certificates.

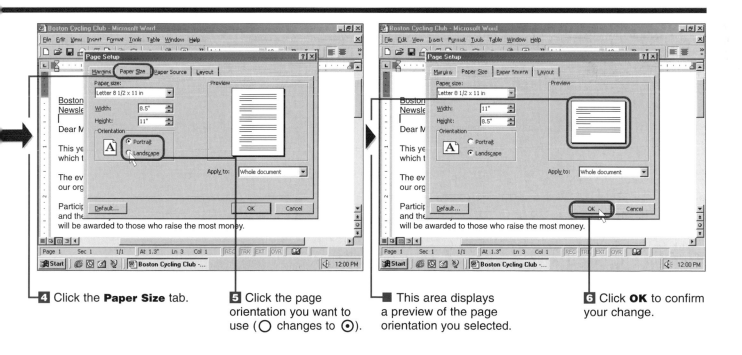

4 Click the **Paper Size** tab.

5 Click the page orientation you want to use (○ changes to ⊙).

■ This area displays a preview of the page orientation you selected.

6 Click **OK** to confirm your change.

CONTROL PAGE BREAKS

You can control the
page breaks in a long
document to tell Word
how you want text to
flow from one page
to the next.

CONTROL PAGE BREAKS

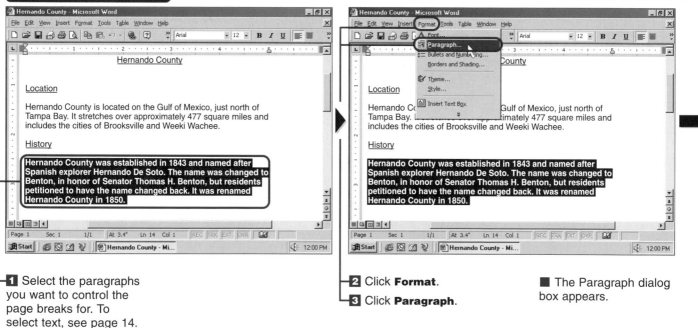

1 Select the paragraphs
you want to control the
page breaks for. To
select text, see page 14.

2 Click **Format**.

3 Click **Paragraph**.

■ The Paragraph dialog
box appears.

What page break options can I choose?

Widow/Orphan control

Prevents a single line from appearing at the top or bottom of a page.

Keep lines together

Keeps all the lines of a paragraph on the same page.

Keep with next

Keeps a paragraph on the same page as the next paragraph.

Page break before

Places a page break before a paragraph.

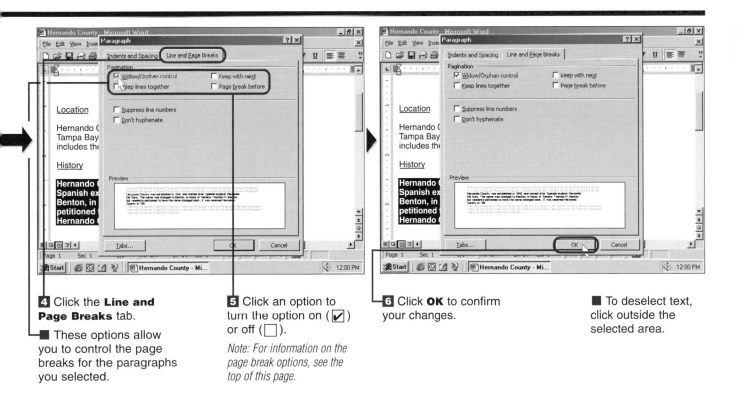

■4 Click the **Line and Page Breaks** tab.

■ These options allow you to control the page breaks for the paragraphs you selected.

■5 Click an option to turn the option on (☑) or off (☐).

Note: For information on the page break options, see the top of this page.

■6 Click **OK** to confirm your changes.

■ To deselect text, click outside the selected area.

ADD A PAGE BORDER

You can place a border around each page of your document to enhance the appearance of the document.

Word can only display page borders in the Print Layout view. For more information on the views, see page 44.

ADD A PAGE BORDER

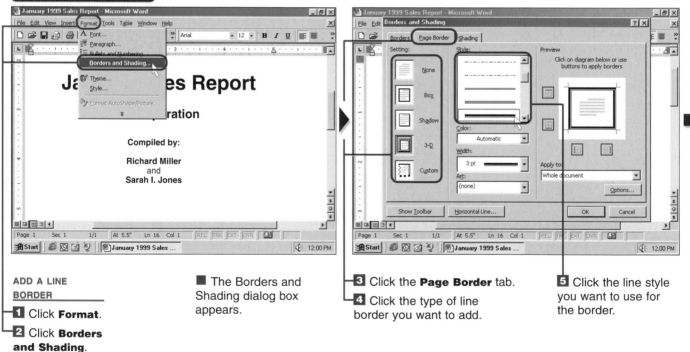

ADD A LINE BORDER

■ Click **Format**.

■ Click **Borders and Shading**.

■ The Borders and Shading dialog box appears.

3 Click the **Page Border** tab.

4 Click the type of line border you want to add.

5 Click the line style you want to use for the border.

What types of page borders can I add to my document?

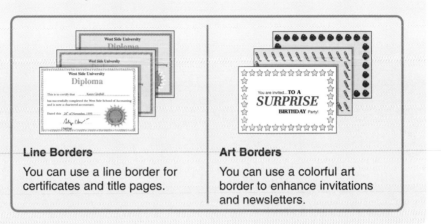

Line Borders

You can use a line border for certificates and title pages.

Art Borders

You can use a colorful art border to enhance invitations and newsletters.

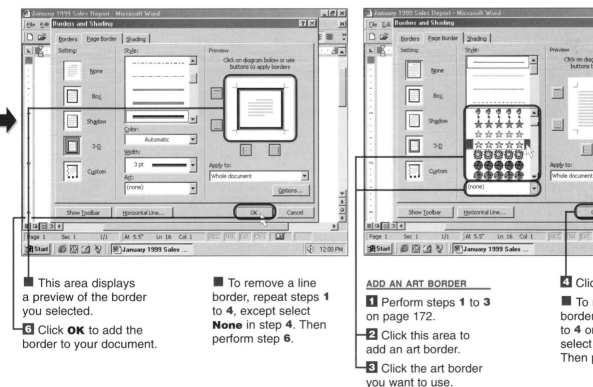

■ This area displays a preview of the border you selected.

6 Click **OK** to add the border to your document.

■ To remove a line border, repeat steps **1** to **4**, except select **None** in step **4**. Then perform step **6**.

ADD AN ART BORDER

1 Perform steps **1** to **3** on page 172.

2 Click this area to add an art border.

3 Click the art border you want to use.

4 Click **OK**.

■ To remove an art border, perform steps **1** to **4** on page 172, except select **None** in step **4**. Then perform step **6**.

APPLY A THEME

Word offers many ready-to-use designs, called themes, that you can use to give your document a new appearance.

Themes are ideal for documents that will be viewed on the Internet or on your computer screen.

Word can only display themes in the Web Layout view. For more information on the views, see page 44.

APPLY A THEME

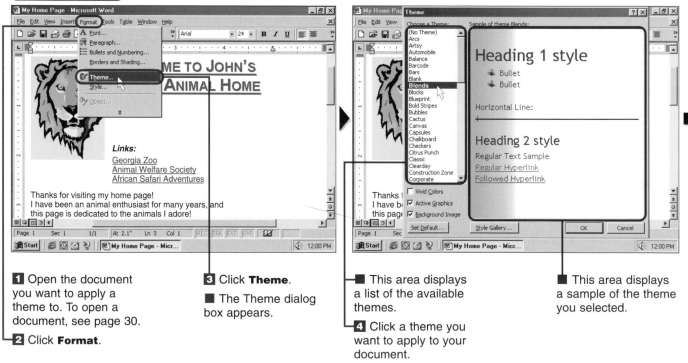

1 Open the document you want to apply a theme to. To open a document, see page 30.

2 Click **Format**.

3 Click **Theme**.

■ The Theme dialog box appears.

■ This area displays a list of the available themes.

4 Click a theme you want to apply to your document.

■ This area displays a sample of the theme you selected.

?

Why didn't a sample of the theme I selected appear?

If a sample of the theme you selected does not appear, the theme is not installed on your computer. To install the theme, insert the CD-ROM disc you used to install Word into your CD-ROM drive. Then click **Install**.

■ Repeat step **4** until the theme you want to use appears.

5 Click **OK** to apply the theme to your document.

■ Your document displays the theme you selected.

■ To remove a theme, repeat steps **1** to **5**, except select **(No Theme)** in step **4**.

CREATE NEWSPAPER COLUMNS

You can display text in columns like those found in a newspaper. This is useful for creating documents such as newsletters and brochures.

CREATE NEWSPAPER COLUMNS

1 Click anywhere in the document or section you want to display in newspaper columns.

Note: To create newspaper columns for only part of a document, you must divide the document into sections. To divide a document into sections, see page 148.

2 Click 🔲 to create newspaper columns.

Note: If 🔲 is not displayed, click 🔅 on the Standard toolbar to display all the buttons.

Why doesn't my text appear in newspaper columns?

Word can only display newspaper columns side by side in the Print Layout view. For more information on the views, see page 44.

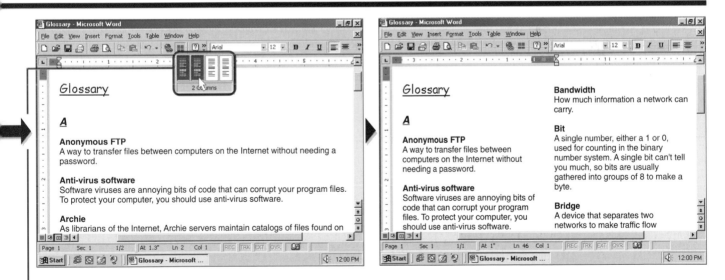

3 Drag the mouse until you highlight the number of columns you want to create.

■ The text in the document appears in newspaper columns.

■ To remove newspaper columns, repeat steps **1** to **3**, except select one column in step **3**.

CHAPTER 8

Print Documents

Would you like to produce a paper copy of a document? In this chapter you will learn how to print documents, envelopes and labels.

PREVIEW A DOCUMENT

You can use the Print Preview feature to see how your document will look when printed. This lets you confirm that the document will print the way you want.

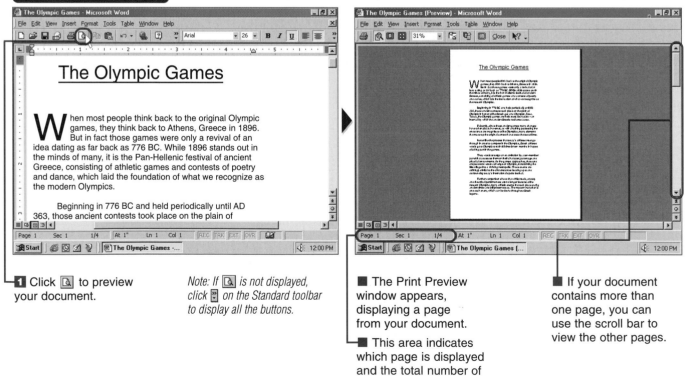

1 Click 🔍 to preview your document.

Note: If 🔍 is not displayed, click 》 on the Standard toolbar to display all the buttons.

■ The Print Preview window appears, displaying a page from your document.

■ This area indicates which page is displayed and the total number of pages in your document.

■ If your document contains more than one page, you can use the scroll bar to view the other pages.

When can I edit my document in the Print Preview window?

To change the shape of the mouse, perform step **2** below.

If the mouse looks like I when over your document, you can edit the document.

If the mouse looks like ⊕ or ⊖ when over your document, you can enlarge or reduce the size of the page displayed on your screen.

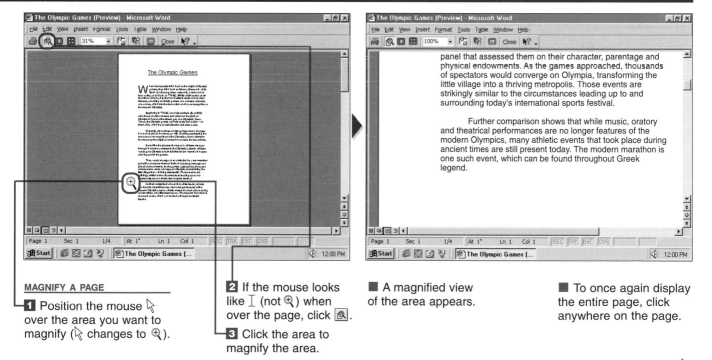

MAGNIFY A PAGE

1 Position the mouse over the area you want to magnify (⇖ changes to ⊕).

2 If the mouse looks like I (not ⊕) when over the page, click 🔍.

3 Click the area to magnify the area.

■ A magnified view of the area appears.

■ To once again display the entire page, click anywhere on the page.

CONTINUED

PREVIEW A DOCUMENT

Word can display
several pages in
the Print Preview
window at once.
This lets you view
the overall style of
a long document.

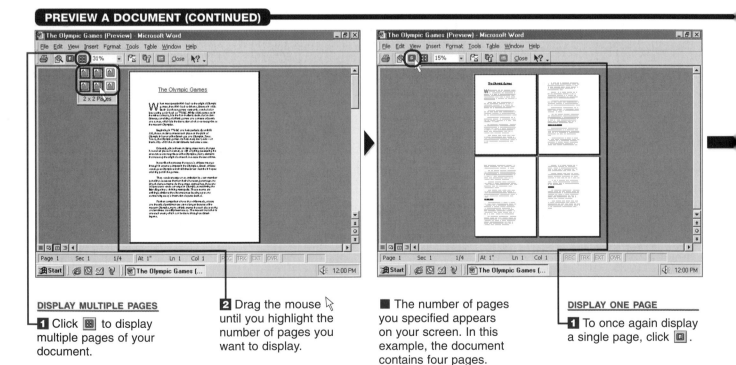

DISPLAY MULTIPLE PAGES

1 Click 🔲 to display
multiple pages of your
document.

2 Drag the mouse
until you highlight the
number of pages you
want to display.

■ The number of pages
you specified appears
on your screen. In this
example, the document
contains four pages.

DISPLAY ONE PAGE

1 To once again display
a single page, click 🔲.

182

Can I shrink the text in my document to fit on fewer pages?

If the last page in your document contains only a few lines of text, you can click 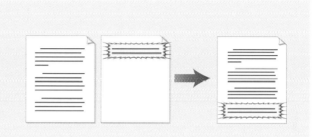 in the Print Preview window to have Word shrink the text to fit on one less page.

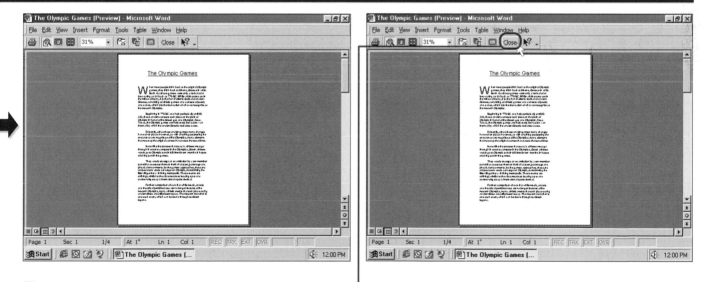

■ An entire page appears on your screen.

CLOSE PRINT PREVIEW

1 When you finish previewing your document, click **Close** to close the Print Preview window.

PRINT A DOCUMENT

You can produce a paper copy of the document displayed on your screen.

Before printing your document, make sure the printer is turned on and contains an adequate supply of paper.

PRINT A DOCUMENT

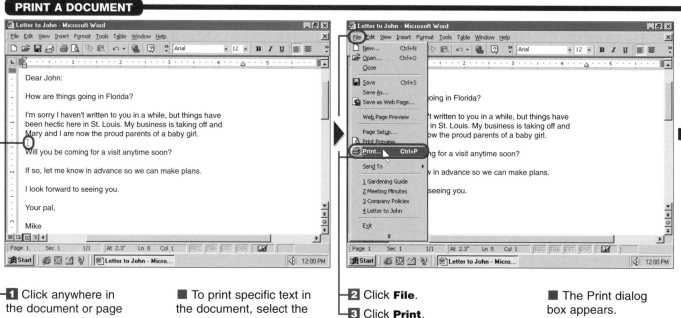

1 Click anywhere in the document or page you want to print.

■ To print specific text in the document, select the text you want to print. To select text, see page 14.

2 Click **File**.

3 Click **Print**.

■ The Print dialog box appears.

184

Which print option should I use?

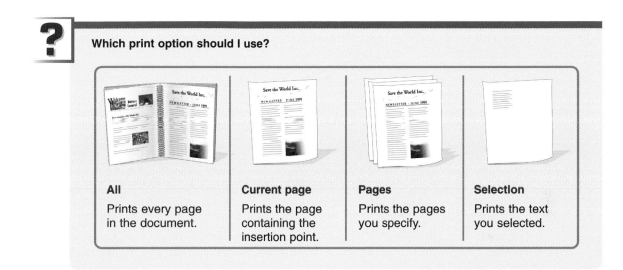

All

Prints every page in the document.

Current page

Prints the page containing the insertion point.

Pages

Prints the pages you specify.

Selection

Prints the text you selected.

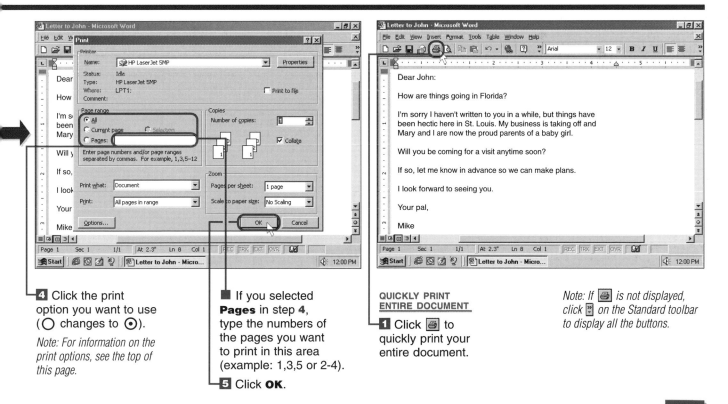

4 Click the print option you want to use (○ changes to ◉).

Note: For information on the print options, see the top of this page.

■ If you selected **Pages** in step **4**, type the numbers of the pages you want to print in this area (example: 1,3,5 or 2-4).

5 Click **OK**.

QUICKLY PRINT ENTIRE DOCUMENT

1 Click 🖨 to quickly print your entire document.

Note: If 🖨 is not displayed, click ⚌ on the Standard toolbar to display all the buttons.

You can print
an address on
an envelope.

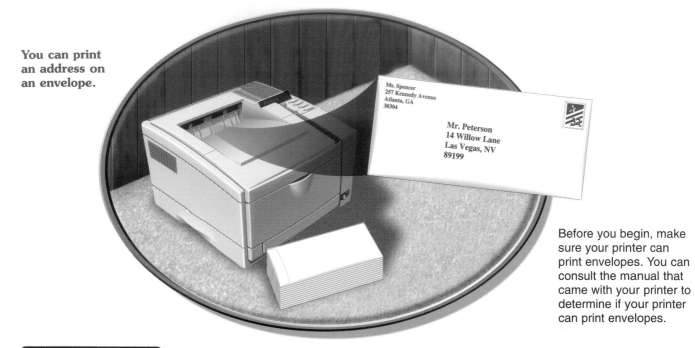

Before you begin, make
sure your printer can
print envelopes. You can
consult the manual that
came with your printer to
determine if your printer
can print envelopes.

PRINT AN ENVELOPE

1 Click **Tools**.

2 Click **Envelopes and Labels**.

■ The Envelopes
and Labels dialog
box appears.

3 Click the **Envelopes** tab.

■ This area displays the
delivery address. If Word
finds an address in your
document, Word will enter
the address for you.

4 To enter a delivery
address, click this area.
Then type the delivery
address.

*Note: To remove any existing
text before typing an address,
drag the mouse ⊺ over the text
until you highlight the text.
Then press the* Delete *key.*

Can I make an envelope part of my document?

Yes. To make an envelope part of your document, perform steps **1** to **7** below, except select **Add to Document** in step **6**. The envelope appears before the first page in your document. You can edit, format, save and print the envelope as part of your document.

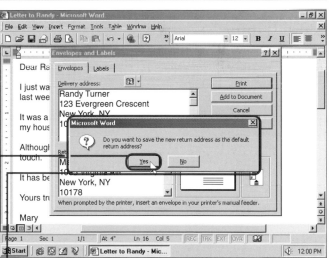

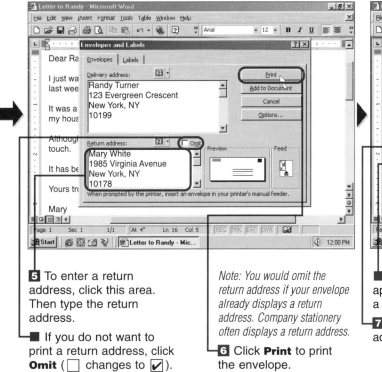

5 To enter a return address, click this area. Then type the return address.

■ If you do not want to print a return address, click **Omit** (☐ changes to ☑).

Note: You would omit the return address if your envelope already displays a return address. Company stationery often displays a return address.

6 Click **Print** to print the envelope.

■ This dialog box appears if you entered a return address.

7 To save the return address, click **Yes**.

■ If you save the return address, the address will appear as the return address every time you print an envelope. This saves you from constantly having to retype the address.

PRINT LABELS

You can use Word to print labels. Labels are useful for addressing envelopes, creating name tags and labeling file folders.

PRINT LABELS

1 Click ☐ to create a new document.

Note: If ☐ is not displayed, click ❯ on the Standard toolbar to display all the buttons.

2 Click **Tools**.

3 Click **Envelopes and Labels**.

■ The Envelopes and Labels dialog box appears.

4 Click the **Labels** tab.

5 Click **Options** to select the type of label you will use.

■ The Label Options dialog box appears.

Which label product and type should I choose?

You can check your label packaging to determine which label product and type you should choose.

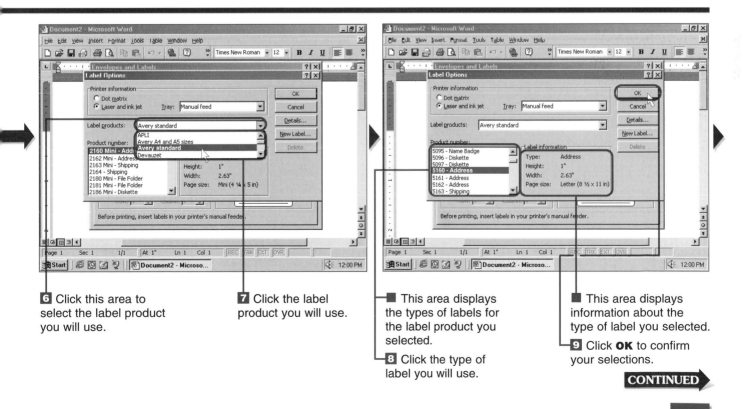

6 Click this area to select the label product you will use.

7 Click the label product you will use.

■ This area displays the types of labels for the label product you selected.

8 Click the type of label you will use.

■ This area displays information about the type of label you selected.

9 Click **OK** to confirm your selections.

CONTINUED

After you create the labels, you can enter the information you want to appear on each label.

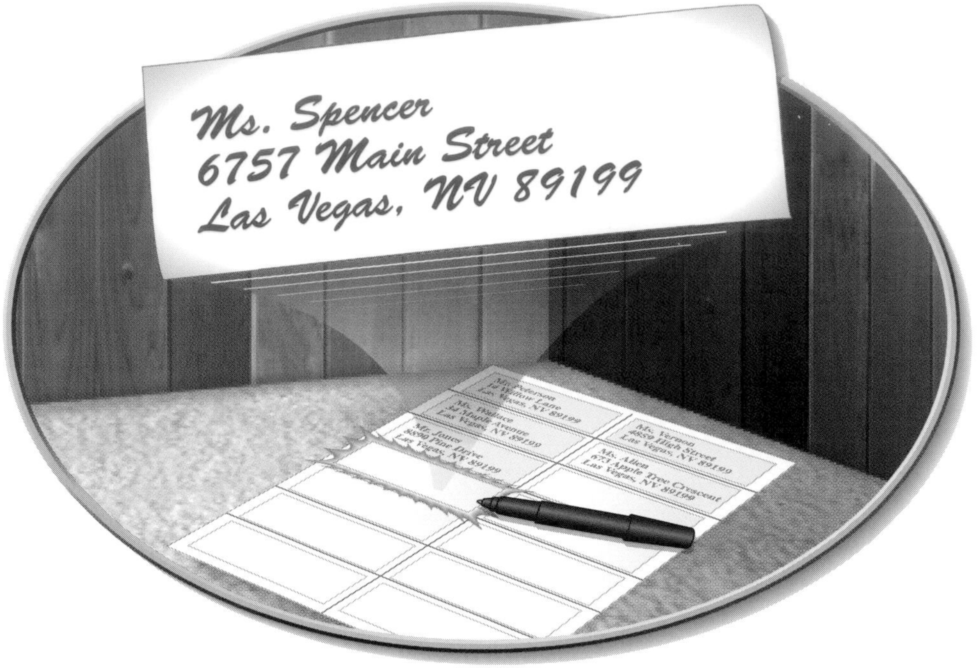

PRINT LABELS (CONTINUED)

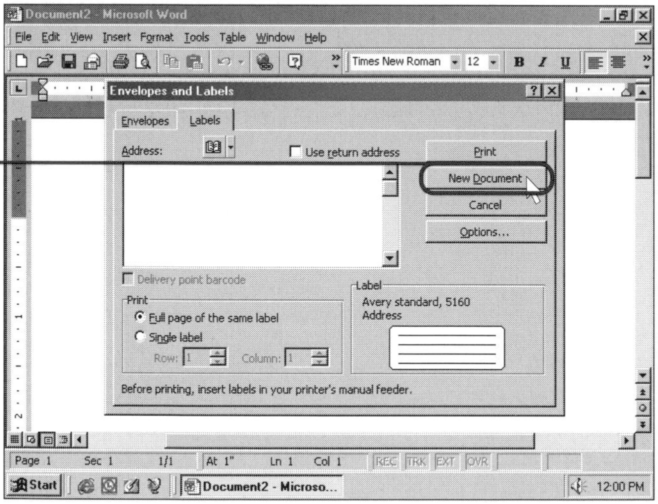

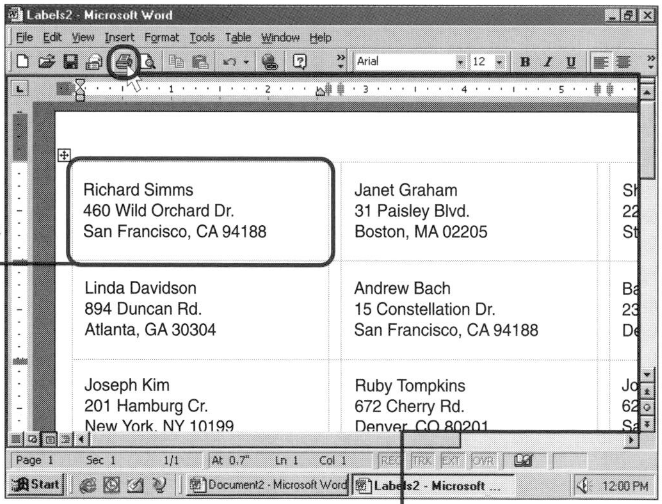

10 Click **New Document** to add the labels to a new document.

■ The labels appear in a new document.

11 Click a label where you want to enter text and then type the text. Repeat this step for each label.

Note: You can format the text on the labels as you would format any text in a document. To format text, see pages 94 to 107.

12 Click to print the labels.

Note: If is not displayed, click on the Standard toolbar to display all the buttons.

Can I quickly create a label for each person on my mailing list?

You can use the Mail Merge feature included with Word to quickly create a label for each person on your mailing list. For information on using the Mail Merge feature to create labels, see page 278.

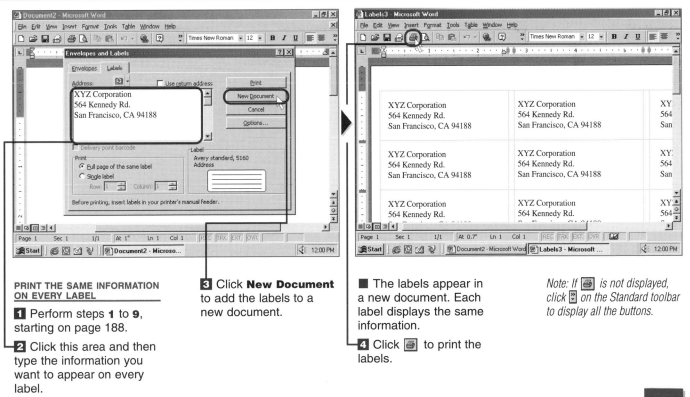

PRINT THE SAME INFORMATION ON EVERY LABEL

1 Perform steps **1** to **9**, starting on page 188.

2 Click this area and then type the information you want to appear on every label.

3 Click **New Document** to add the labels to a new document.

■ The labels appear in a new document. Each label displays the same information.

4 Click 🖨 to print the labels.

Note: If 🖨 is not displayed, click ⏵ on the Standard toolbar to display all the buttons.

CHANGE PAPER SOURCE

You can change
the location where
Word will look for
the paper to print
your document.

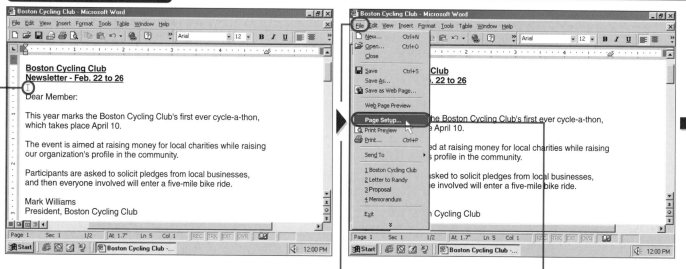

1 Click anywhere
in the document or
section you want to
print on different paper.

*Note: To change the paper
source for only part of your
document, you must divide
the document into sections.
To divide a document into
sections, see page 148.*

2 Click **File**.

3 Click **Page Setup**.

■ The Page Setup
dialog box appears.

Why would I change the paper source?

Changing the paper source is useful if your printer stores letterhead in one location and plain paper in another location. You can print the first page of your document on letterhead and print the rest of the document on plain paper.

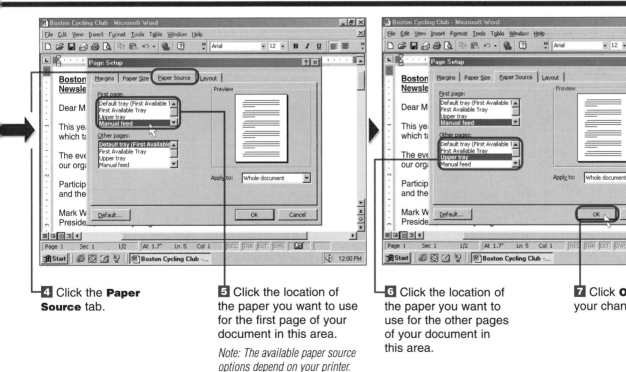

4 Click the **Paper Source** tab.

5 Click the location of the paper you want to use for the first page of your document in this area.

Note: The available paper source options depend on your printer.

6 Click the location of the paper you want to use for the other pages of your document in this area.

7 Click **OK** to confirm your changes.

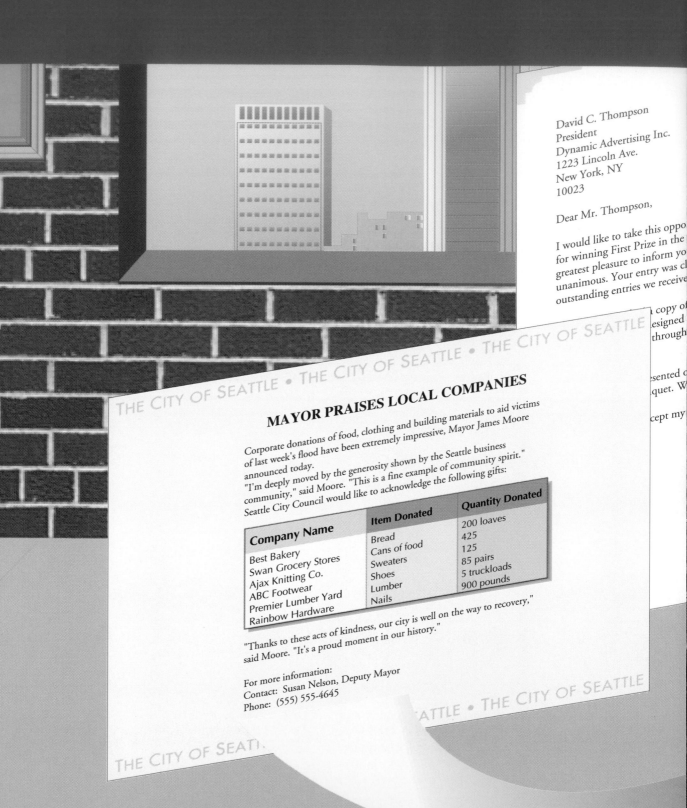

David C. Thompson
President
Dynamic Advertising Inc.
1223 Lincoln Ave.
New York, NY
10023

Dear Mr. Thompson,

I would like to take this oppo...
for winning First Prize in the...
greatest pleasure to inform yo...
unanimous. Your entry was cl...
outstanding entries we receive...

...copy of...
...esigned...
...through...

...esented...
...quet. W...

...cept my...

THE CITY OF SEATTLE • THE CITY OF SEATTLE • THE CITY OF SEATTLE

MAYOR PRAISES LOCAL COMPANIES

Corporate donations of food, clothing and building materials to aid victims of last week's flood have been extremely impressive, Mayor James Moore announced today.

"I'm deeply moved by the generosity shown by the Seattle business community," said Moore. "This is a fine example of community spirit."

Seattle City Council would like to acknowledge the following gifts:

Company Name	Item Donated	Quantity Donated
Best Bakery	Bread	200 loaves
Swan Grocery Stores	Cans of food	425
Ajax Knitting Co.	Sweaters	125
ABC Footwear	Shoes	85 pairs
Premier Lumber Yard	Lumber	5 truckloads
Rainbow Hardware	Nails	900 pounds

"Thanks to these acts of kindness, our city is well on the way to recovery," said Moore. "It's a proud moment in our history."

For more information:
Contact: Susan Nelson, Deputy Mayor
Phone: (555) 555-4645

ATTLE • THE CITY OF SEATTLE

THE CITY OF SEATTL...

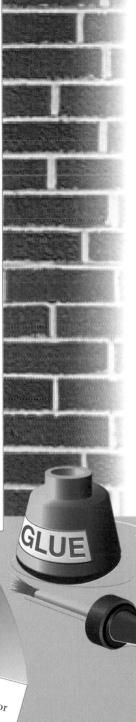

congratulate you and your company
o Design Contest. It gives me the
Judging Committee's decision was
best among the hundreds of
r.

ing Committee's remarks. This report
nic Advertising Inc. serves to enhance
ive use of colors and modern design

20 at the International Design
see you there.

lations,

264 Main St.
Seattle, WA
98104

(555) 555-1241
55) 555-1219

GLUE

For more information:
Contact: Susan Nelson, Deputy Mayor
Phone: (555) 555-4645

CHAPTER 9

Work With Multiple Documents

Are you interested in working with more than one document at a time? In this chapter you will learn how to switch between documents, move or copy text between documents and more.

CREATE A NEW DOCUMENT

You can create a
new document to
start writing a letter,
memo or report.

Think of each document
as a separate piece of
paper. Creating a new
document is like placing
a new piece of paper on
your screen.

CREATE A NEW DOCUMENT

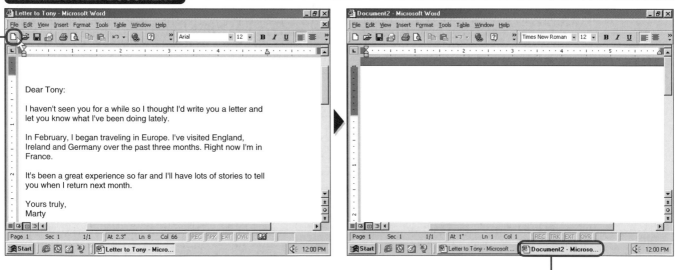

1 Click 🗋 to create
a new document.

*Note: If 🗋 is not displayed,
click ⁂ on the Standard toolbar
to display all the buttons.*

■ A new document
appears. The previous
document is now hidden
behind the new document.

■ A button for the new
document appears on
the taskbar.

SWITCH BETWEEN DOCUMENTS

Word lets you have many documents open at once. You can easily switch from one open document to another.

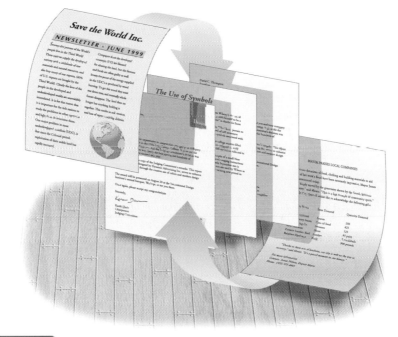

SWITCH BETWEEN DOCUMENTS

1 Click **Window** to display a list of all the documents you have open.

2 Click the name of the document you want to switch to.

■ The document appears.

■ Word displays the name of the current document at the top of your screen.

■ The taskbar displays a button for each open document. You can also switch to a document by clicking its button on the taskbar.

ARRANGE OPEN DOCUMENTS

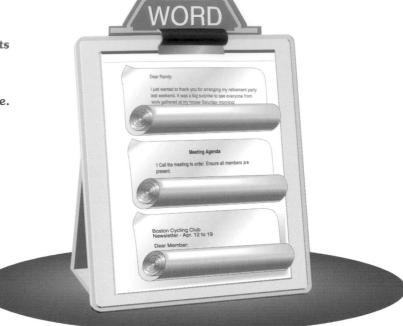

If you have several documents open, some of them may be hidden from view. You can display the contents of all your open documents at once.

ARRANGE OPEN DOCUMENTS

1 Click **Window**.

2 Click **Arrange All**.

Note: If Arrange All does not appear on the menu, position the mouse ⓀⒹ over the bottom of the menu to display all the menu commands.

■ You can now view the contents of all your open documents.

■ You can work with only one document at a time. The current document displays a blue title bar.

Note: To make another document current, click anywhere in the document.

?

How can I display more of the arranged documents on my screen?

You can remove items, such as the ruler or a toolbar, from a document to display more of the document on your screen. To hide the ruler or a toolbar, see pages 46 and 47.

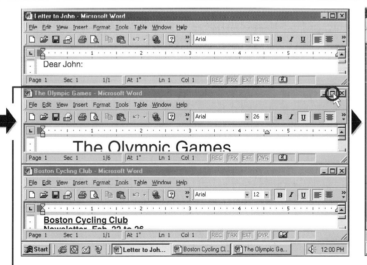

3 To once again maximize a document to fill your screen, click ▢ in the document you want to maximize.

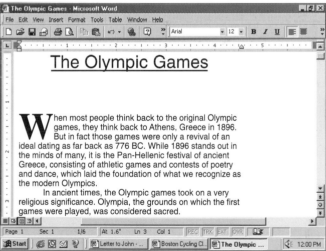

■ The document fills your screen. The other documents are hidden behind the maximized document.

MOVE OR COPY TEXT BETWEEN DOCUMENTS

You can move or copy text from one document to another. This will save you time when you want to use text from another document.

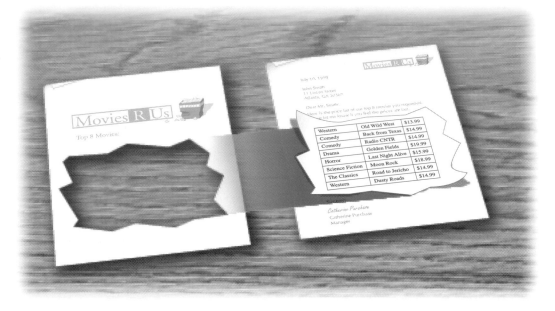

MOVE OR COPY TEXT BETWEEN DOCUMENTS

1 Select the text you want to move or copy to another document. To select text, see page 14.

2 Click one of the following buttons.

✂ Move text

📋 Copy text

Note: If the button you want is not displayed, click » *on the Standard toolbar to display all the buttons.*

Note: The Clipboard toolbar may appear when you move or copy text. To use the Clipboard toolbar, see page 65.

What is the difference between moving and copying text?

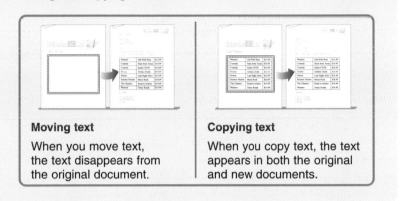

Moving text

When you move text, the text disappears from the original document.

Copying text

When you copy text, the text appears in both the original and new documents.

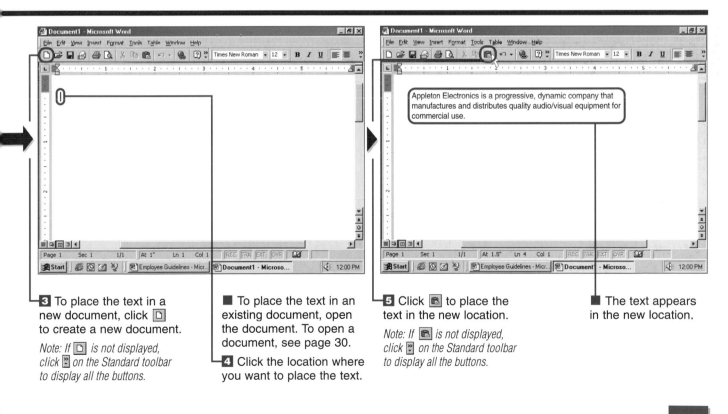

3 To place the text in a new document, click 🗋 to create a new document.

Note: If 🗋 is not displayed, click ⏷ on the Standard toolbar to display all the buttons.

■ To place the text in an existing document, open the document. To open a document, see page 30.

4 Click the location where you want to place the text.

5 Click 🛍 to place the text in the new location.

Note: If 🛍 is not displayed, click ⏷ on the Standard toolbar to display all the buttons.

■ The text appears in the new location.

CHAPTER 10

Work With Tables

Do you want to learn how to display information in a table? This chapter teaches you how to create and work with tables in your document.

CREATE A TABLE

You can create
a table to neatly
display columns
of information in
your document.

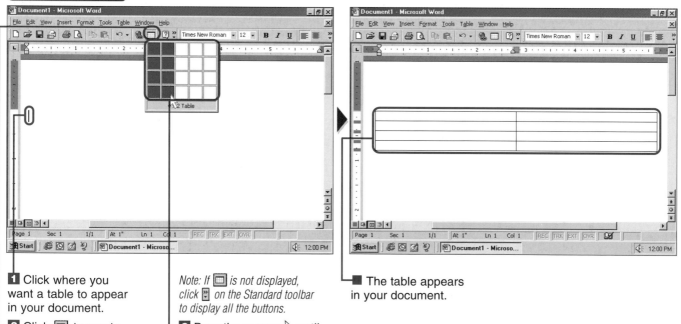

1 Click where you
want a table to appear
in your document.

2 Click ▣ to create
a table.

*Note: If ▣ is not displayed,
click ⟩⟩ on the Standard toolbar
to display all the buttons.*

3 Drag the mouse ⟨ until
you highlight the number
of columns and rows you
want the table to contain.

■ The table appears
in your document.

What are the parts of a table?

A table consists of columns, rows and cells.

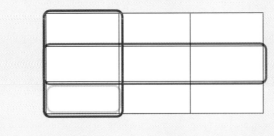

■ A column is a vertical line of boxes.

■ A row is a horizontal line of boxes.

A cell is one box.

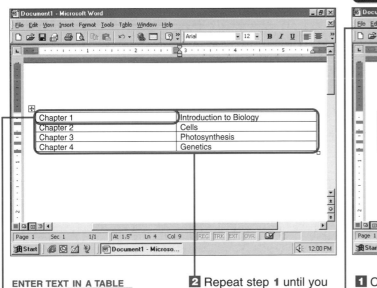

ENTER TEXT IN A TABLE

1 Click the cell where you want to enter text. Then type the text.

2 Repeat step **1** until you finish entering all the text.

■ You can format text in a table as you would format any text in a document. To format text, see pages 94 to 107.

DELETE A TABLE

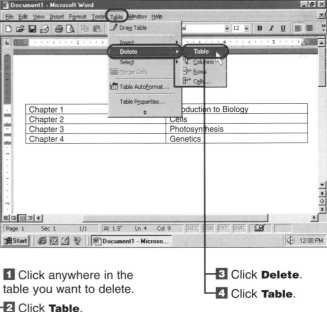

1 Click anywhere in the table you want to delete.

2 Click **Table**.

3 Click **Delete**.

4 Click **Table**.

ADD A ROW OR COLUMN

You can add a row or column to your table when you want to insert additional information.

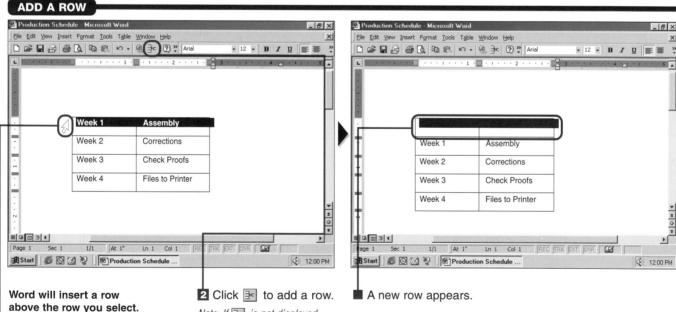

ADD A ROW

Word will insert a row above the row you select.

1 To select a row, position the mouse I to the left of the row (I changes to ↗). Then click to select the row.

2 Click ▐ to add a row.

Note: If ▐ is not displayed, click ░ on the Standard toolbar to display all the buttons.

■ A new row appears.

Can I add a row to the bottom of a table?

Yes. To add a row to the bottom of a table, click the bottom right cell in the table and then press the `Tab` key.

ADD A COLUMN

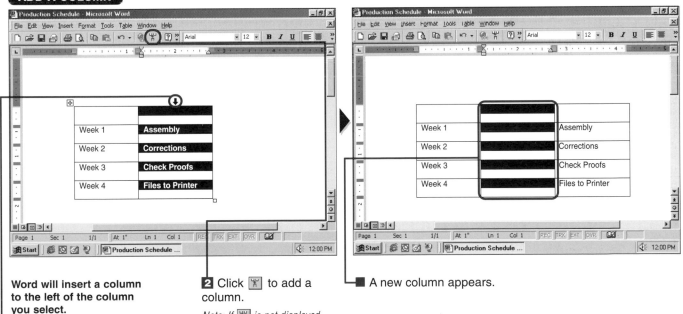

Word will insert a column to the left of the column you select.

1 To select a column, position the mouse I over the top of the column (I changes to ⬇). Then click to select the column.

2 Click 🏿 to add a column.

Note: If 🏿 is not displayed, click ▣ on the Standard toolbar to display all the buttons.

■ A new column appears.

DELETE A ROW OR COLUMN

You can delete a row or column that you no longer need from your table.

When deleting a row or column, the Clipboard toolbar may appear. To hide the Clipboard toolbar, see page 47.

When deleting a row or column, the Clipboard toolbar may appear. To hide the Clipboard toolbar, see page 47.

DELETE A ROW

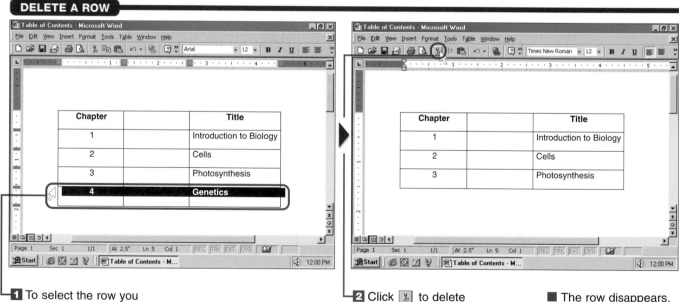

1 To select the row you want to delete, position the mouse I to the left of the row (I changes to ⇗). Then click to select the row.

2 Click ✂ to delete the row.

Note: If ✂ is not displayed, click ⁑ on the Standard toolbar to display all the buttons.

■ The row disappears.

208

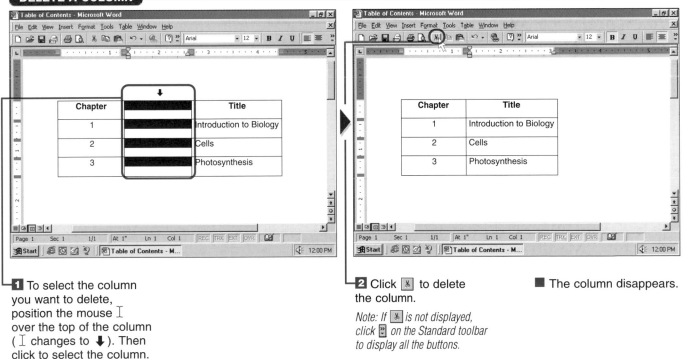

? Can I delete the information in a row or column without removing the row or column from my table?

Yes. To select the cells displaying the information you want to delete, drag the mouse I over the cells. Then press the Delete key to delete the information.

DELETE A COLUMN

1 To select the column you want to delete, position the mouse I over the top of the column (I changes to ↓). Then click to select the column.

2 Click ✂ to delete the column.

Note: If ✂ is not displayed, click ⮞ on the Standard toolbar to display all the buttons.

■ The column disappears.

CHANGE COLUMN WIDTH
OR ROW HEIGHT

After you create
a table, you can
change the width
of columns and
the height of rows.

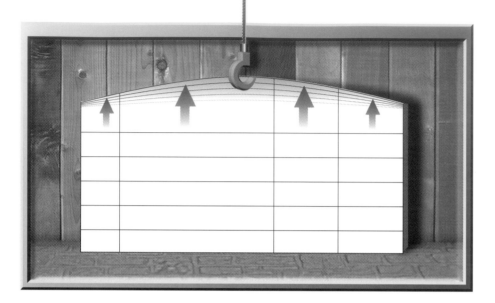

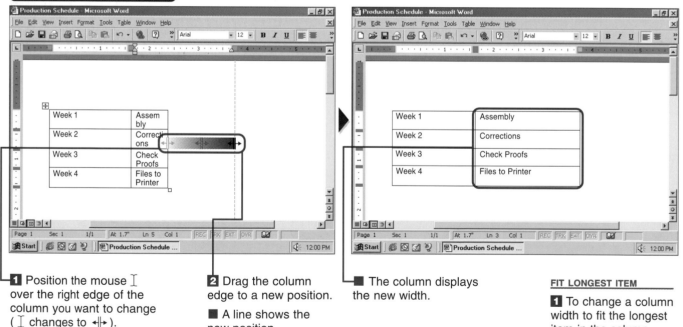

1 Position the mouse I
over the right edge of the
column you want to change
(I changes to +‖+).

2 Drag the column
edge to a new position.

■ A line shows the
new position.

■ The column displays
the new width.

FIT LONGEST ITEM

1 To change a column
width to fit the longest
item in the column,
double-click the right
edge of the column.

210

Does Word ever automatically adjust the column width or row height?

When you enter text in a table, Word may automatically increase the width of a column or the height of a row to accommodate the text you type.

CHANGE ROW HEIGHT

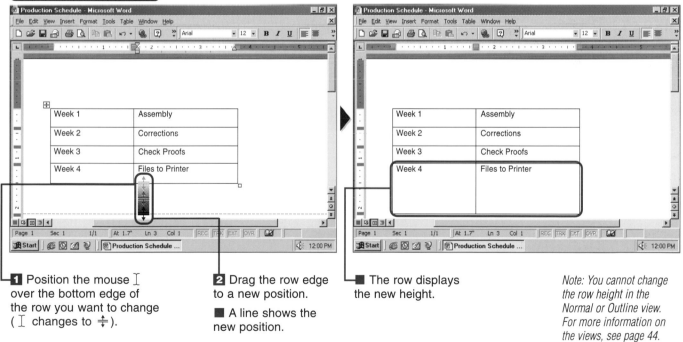

1 Position the mouse I over the bottom edge of the row you want to change (I changes to ÷).

2 Drag the row edge to a new position.

■ A line shows the new position.

■ The row displays the new height.

Note: You cannot change the row height in the Normal or Outline view. For more information on the views, see page 44.

MERGE CELLS

You can combine two or more cells in your table to create one large cell. This is useful when you want to display a title in a cell at the top of your table.

MERGE CELLS

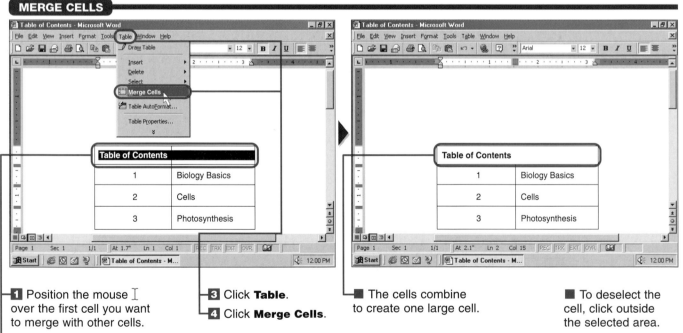

1 Position the mouse I over the first cell you want to merge with other cells.

2 Drag the mouse I until you highlight all the cells you want to merge.

3 Click **Table**.

4 Click **Merge Cells**.

■ The cells combine to create one large cell.

■ To deselect the cell, click outside the selected area.

SPLIT CELLS

You can split one
cell in your table into
several smaller cells.

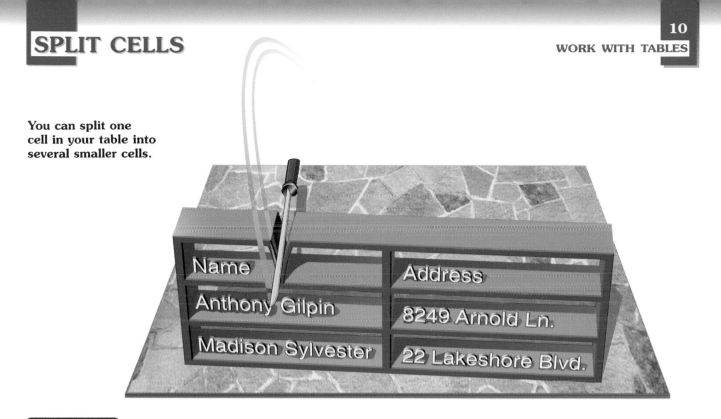

SPLIT CELLS

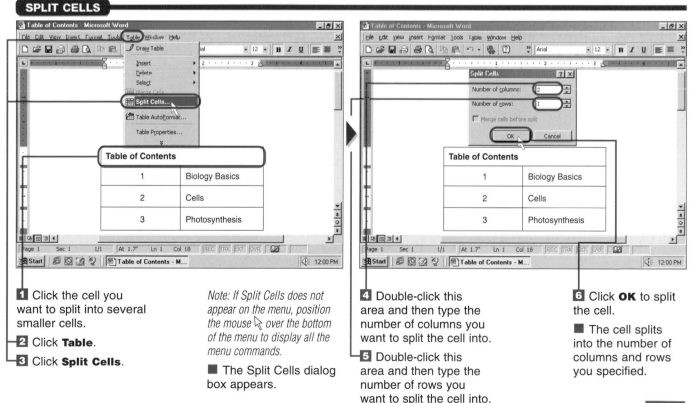

1 Click the cell you
want to split into several
smaller cells.

2 Click **Table**.

3 Click **Split Cells**.

*Note: If Split Cells does not
appear on the menu, position
the mouse ⟍ over the bottom
of the menu to display all the
menu commands.*

■ The Split Cells dialog
box appears.

4 Double-click this
area and then type the
number of columns you
want to split the cell into.

5 Double-click this
area and then type the
number of rows you
want to split the cell into.

6 Click **OK** to split
the cell.

■ The cell splits
into the number of
columns and rows
you specified.

ALIGN TEXT IN CELLS

You can enhance the appearance of your table by changing the position of text in cells.

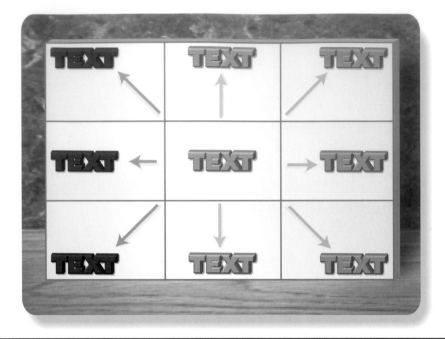

ALIGN TEXT IN CELLS

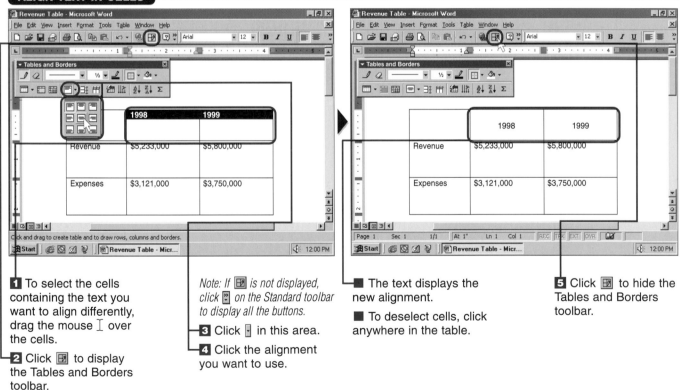

1 To select the cells containing the text you want to align differently, drag the mouse I over the cells.

2 Click ⊞ to display the Tables and Borders toolbar.

Note: If ⊞ is not displayed, click ⟫ on the Standard toolbar to display all the buttons.

3 Click ⋅ in this area.

4 Click the alignment you want to use.

■ The text displays the new alignment.

■ To deselect cells, click anywhere in the table.

5 Click ⊞ to hide the Tables and Borders toolbar.

You can change the direction of text in cells. This can help emphasize row and column headings in your table.

Word can only display the new text direction in the Print Layout and Web Layout views. For more information on the views, see page 44.

CHANGE TEXT DIRECTION

1 To select the cells containing the text you want to change to a new direction, drag the mouse I over the cells.

2 Click 📰 to display the Tables and Borders toolbar.

Note: If 📰 is not displayed, click 💥 on the Standard toolbar to display all the buttons.

3 Click 📖 to change the direction of the text. Repeat this step until the text appears the way you want.

■ The text appears in the new direction.

■ To deselect cells, click anywhere in the table.

4 Click 📰 to hide the Tables and Borders toolbar.

CHANGE TABLE BORDERS

You can enhance the appearance of your table by changing the borders.

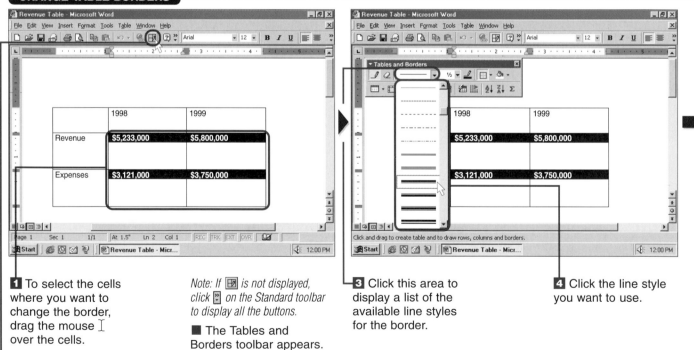

1 To select the cells where you want to change the border, drag the mouse ⊺ over the cells.

2 Click 🖽 to display the Tables and Borders toolbar.

Note: If 🖽 is not displayed, click 🔀 on the Standard toolbar to display all the buttons.

■ The Tables and Borders toolbar appears.

3 Click this area to display a list of the available line styles for the border.

4 Click the line style you want to use.

? Why would I change the border for only some of the cells in my table?

Changing the border for specific cells in your table can help you emphasize important information in the table.

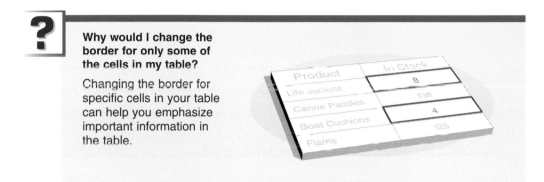

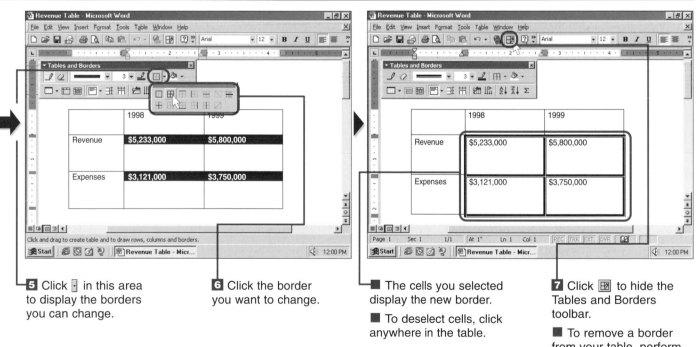

5 Click ⊟ in this area to display the borders you can change.

6 Click the border you want to change.

■ The cells you selected display the new border.

■ To deselect cells, click anywhere in the table.

7 Click ▦ to hide the Tables and Borders toolbar.

■ To remove a border from your table, perform steps **1** and **2**. Then perform steps **5** to **7**, except select ▦ in step **6**.

ADD SHADING TO CELLS

You can draw
attention to an
area of your table
by adding shading
to the cells.

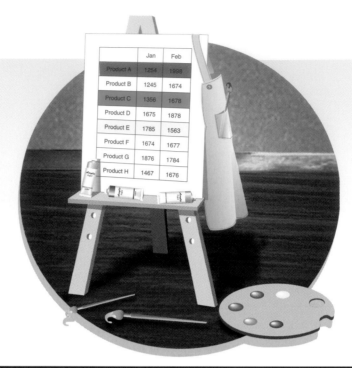

	Jan	Feb
Product A	1254	1998
Product B	1245	1674
Product C	1356	1678
Product D	1675	1878
Product E	1785	1563
Product F	1674	1677
Product G	1876	1784
Product H	1467	1676

ADD SHADING TO CELLS

1 To select the cells you
want to display shading,
drag the mouse I over
the cells.

2 Click 📠 to display
the Tables and Borders
toolbar.

*Note: If 📠 is not displayed,
click ⏩ on the Standard toolbar
to display all the buttons.*

■ The Tables and
Borders toolbar appears.

?

Why would I use shading in my table?

If you use a table to create a form that people fill out, you may want to use dark shading to indicate areas where you do not want people to enter information. You can also use shading to emphasize titles and headings.

Applicant Information	Spouse	Dependant
First Name		
Last Name		
Occupation		
Office Use Only		

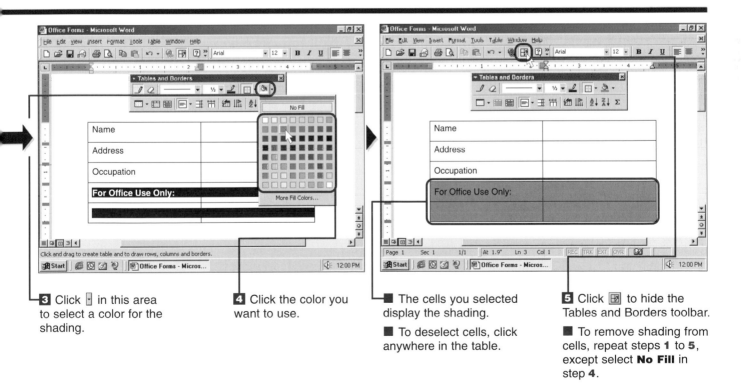

3 Click ⬝ in this area to select a color for the shading.

4 Click the color you want to use.

■ The cells you selected display the shading.

■ To deselect cells, click anywhere in the table.

5 Click 🔲 to hide the Tables and Borders toolbar.

■ To remove shading from cells, repeat steps **1** to **5**, except select **No Fill** in step **4**.

FORMAT A TABLE

Word offers many ready-to-use designs that you can choose from to give your table a new appearance.

FORMAT A TABLE

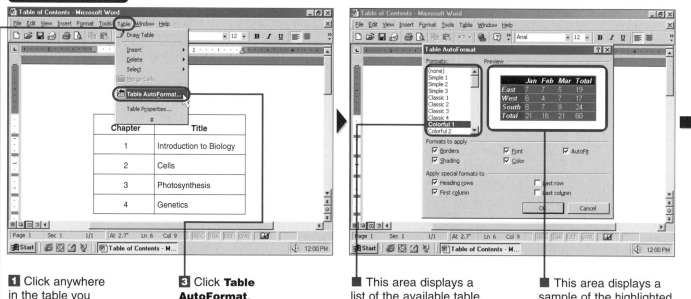

1 Click anywhere in the table you want to change.

2 Click **Table**.

3 Click **Table AutoFormat**.

■ The Table AutoFormat dialog box appears.

■ This area displays a list of the available table designs.

■ This area displays a sample of the highlighted table design.

4 Press the ↓ or ↑ key until the table design you want to use appears.

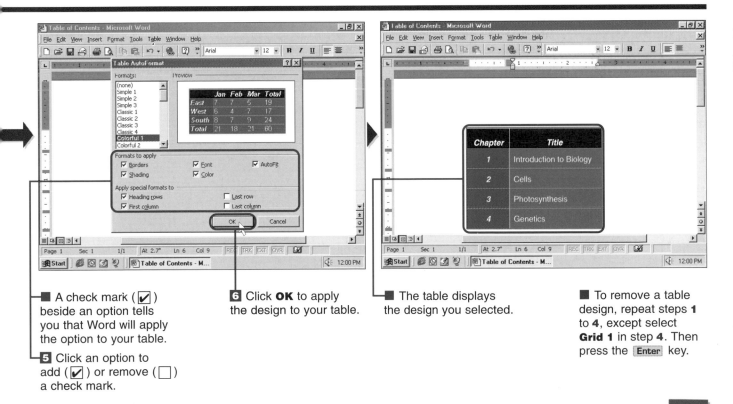

? What is the AutoFit option used for?

The AutoFit option changes the size of your table based on the amount of text in the table. If you do not want Word to change the size of your table, you can turn off the AutoFit option in step **5** below (☑ changes to ☐).

■ A check mark (☑) beside an option tells you that Word will apply the option to your table.

5 Click an option to add (☑) or remove (☐) a check mark.

6 Click **OK** to apply the design to your table.

■ The table displays the design you selected.

■ To remove a table design, repeat steps **1** to **4**, except select **Grid 1** in step **4**. Then press the **Enter** key.

You can move
a table from
one location in
your document
to another.

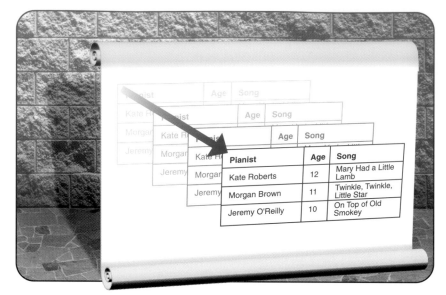

You can move a table
in the Print Layout or
Web Layout views. For
more information on
the views, see page 44.

MOVE A TABLE

1 Position the mouse ⌶
over the table you want
to move. A handle (⊞)
appears.

*Note: You may have to scroll
to the left to view the handle.*

2 Position the mouse ⌶
over the handle
(⌶ changes to ✛).

3 Drag the table to a
new location.

■ A dashed outline
indicates the new location.

■ The table appears
in the new location.

You can change
the size of a table
to improve the
layout of the table.

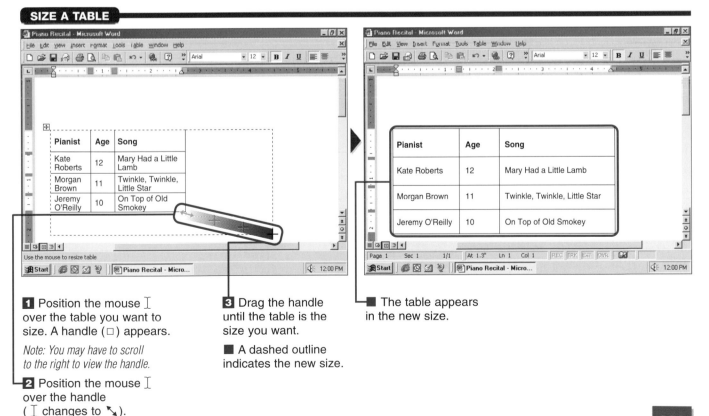

You can size a table in
the Print Layout or Web
Layout views. For more
information on the
views, see page 44.

SIZE A TABLE

1 Position the mouse I
over the table you want to
size. A handle (□) appears.

*Note: You may have to scroll
to the right to view the handle.*

2 Position the mouse I
over the handle
(I changes to ↘).

3 Drag the handle
until the table is the
size you want.

■ A dashed outline
indicates the new size.

■ The table appears
in the new size.

CHAPTER 11

Work With Graphics

Are you interested in using graphics to enhance the appearance of your document? This chapter shows you how.

ADD AN AUTOSHAPE

Word provides many
ready-made shapes,
called AutoShapes,
that you can add to
your document.

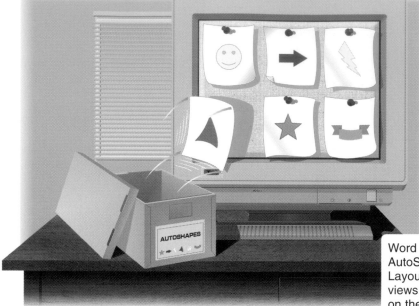

Word can only display
AutoShapes in the Print
Layout and Web Layout
views. For more information
on the views, see page 44.

ADD AN AUTOSHAPE

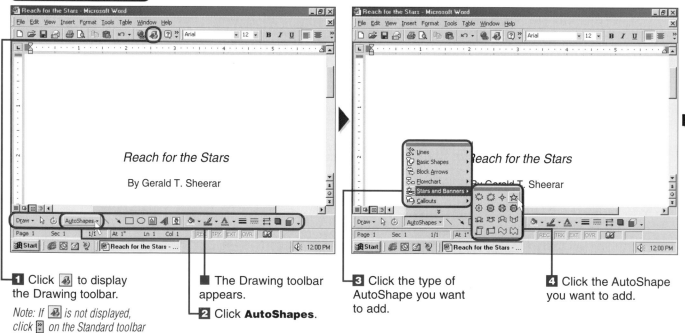

■1 Click ⊿ to display
the Drawing toolbar.

*Note: If ⊿ is not displayed,
click ⁇ on the Standard toolbar
to display all the buttons.*

■ The Drawing toolbar
appears.

■2 Click **AutoShapes**.

■3 Click the type of
AutoShape you want
to add.

■4 Click the AutoShape
you want to add.

How can I add text to an AutoShape?

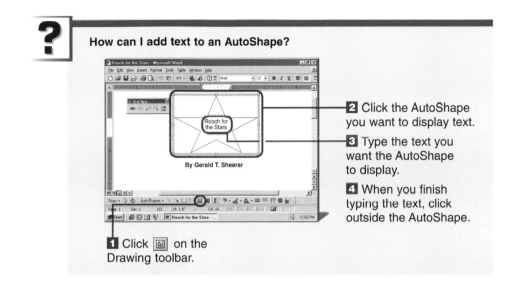

1 Click 🖺 on the Drawing toolbar.

2 Click the AutoShape you want to display text.

3 Type the text you want the AutoShape to display.

4 When you finish typing the text, click outside the AutoShape.

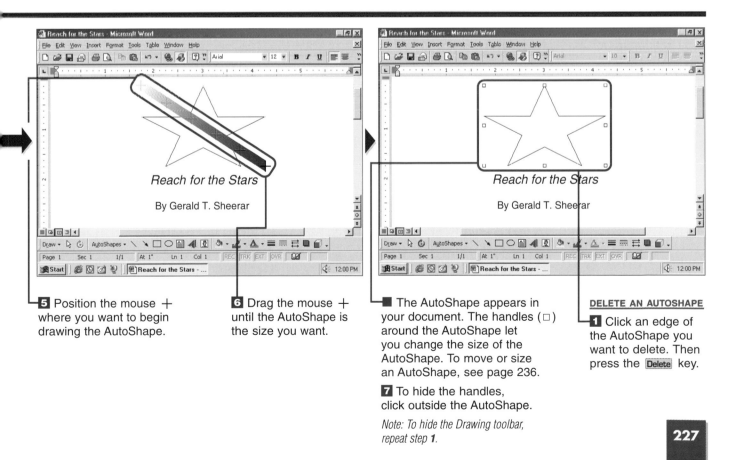

5 Position the mouse + where you want to begin drawing the AutoShape.

6 Drag the mouse + until the AutoShape is the size you want.

■ The AutoShape appears in your document. The handles (□) around the AutoShape let you change the size of the AutoShape. To move or size an AutoShape, see page 236.

7 To hide the handles, click outside the AutoShape.

Note: To hide the Drawing toolbar, repeat step 1.

DELETE AN AUTOSHAPE

1 Click an edge of the AutoShape you want to delete. Then press the Delete key.

ADD A TEXT EFFECT

You can use the WordArt feature to add a text effect to your document. Text effects can enhance the appearance of a title or draw attention to important information.

Word can only display text effects in the Print Layout and Web Layout views. For more information on the views, see page 44.

ADD A TEXT EFFECT

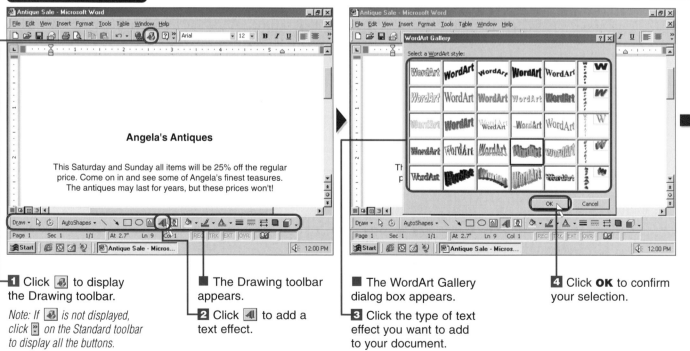

1 Click 🔲 to display the Drawing toolbar.

Note: If 🔲 is not displayed, click 🔲 on the Standard toolbar to display all the buttons.

■ The Drawing toolbar appears.

2 Click 🔲 to add a text effect.

■ The WordArt Gallery dialog box appears.

3 Click the type of text effect you want to add to your document.

4 Click **OK** to confirm your selection.

How do I edit a text effect?

Double-click the text effect to display the Edit WordArt Text dialog box. Then edit the text in the dialog box. When you finish editing the text effect, click **OK** to display the changes in your document.

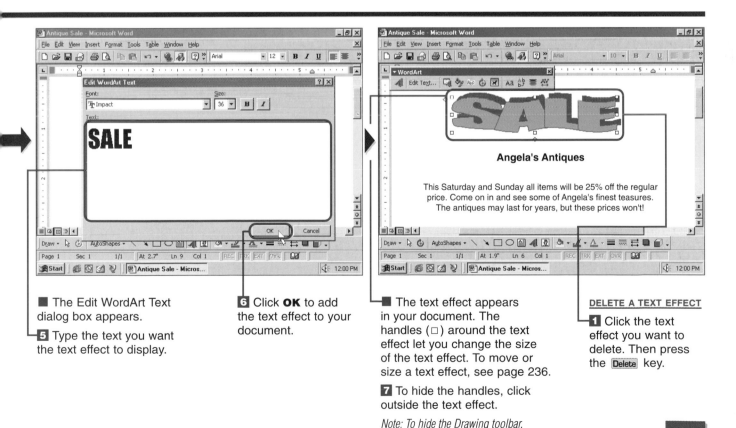

■ The Edit WordArt Text dialog box appears.

5 Type the text you want the text effect to display.

6 Click **OK** to add the text effect to your document.

■ The text effect appears in your document. The handles (□) around the text effect let you change the size of the text effect. To move or size a text effect, see page 236.

7 To hide the handles, click outside the text effect.

Note: To hide the Drawing toolbar, repeat step 1.

DELETE A TEXT EFFECT

1 Click the text effect you want to delete. Then press the [Delete] key.

Word includes professionally designed clip art images that you can add to your document. Clip art images can help illustrate concepts and make your document more interesting.

Word provides thousands of clip art images that you can choose from.

ADD CLIP ART

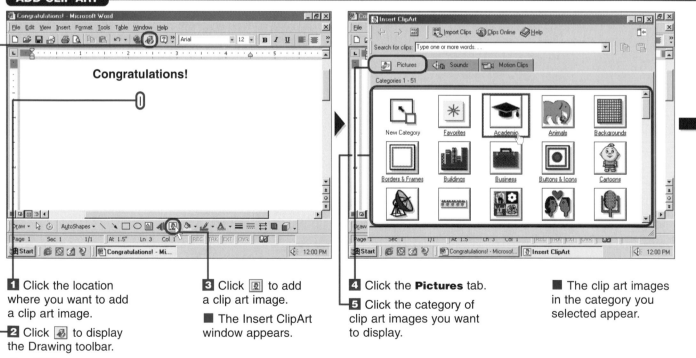

1 Click the location where you want to add a clip art image.

2 Click 🖉 to display the Drawing toolbar.

Note: If 🖉 is not displayed, click 🔽 on the Standard toolbar to display all the buttons.

3 Click 🖾 to add a clip art image.

■ The Insert ClipArt window appears.

4 Click the **Pictures** tab.

5 Click the category of clip art images you want to display.

■ The clip art images in the category you selected appear.

?

Where can I find more clip art images?

If you are connected to the Internet, you can visit Microsoft's Clip Gallery Live Web site to find additional clip art images. In the Insert ClipArt window, click **Clips Online**. In the dialog box that appears, click **OK** to connect to the Web site.

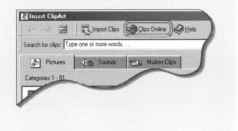

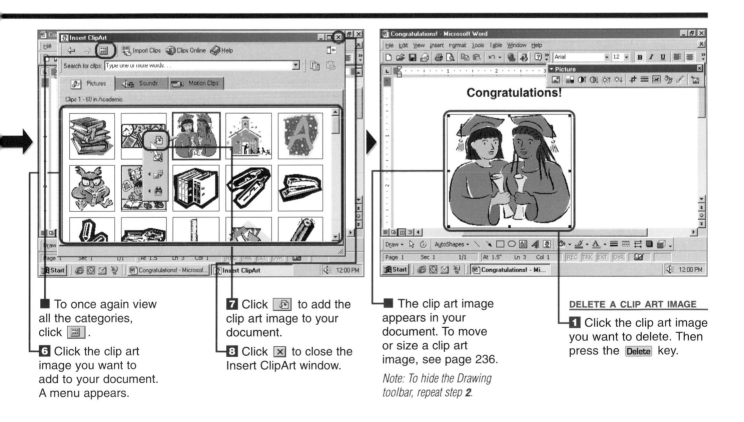

■ To once again view all the categories, click 🖳.

6 Click the clip art image you want to add to your document. A menu appears.

7 Click 🗿 to add the clip art image to your document.

8 Click ✕ to close the Insert ClipArt window.

■ The clip art image appears in your document. To move or size a clip art image, see page 236.

Note: To hide the Drawing toolbar, repeat step 2.

DELETE A CLIP ART IMAGE

1 Click the clip art image you want to delete. Then press the Delete key.

ADD A PICTURE

You can add a picture stored on your computer to your document.

Adding a picture is useful if you want to display your company logo or a picture of your family in your document.

ADD A PICTURE

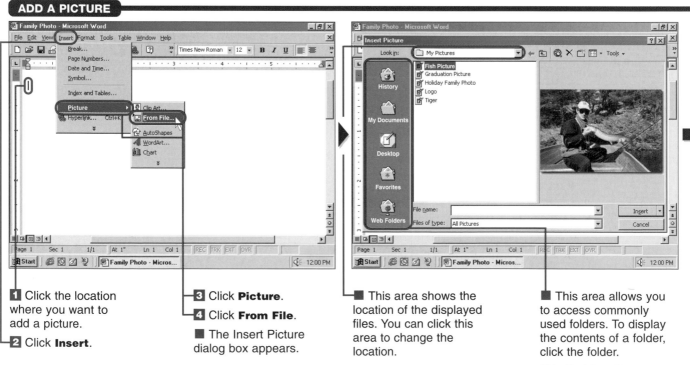

1 Click the location where you want to add a picture.

2 Click **Insert**.

3 Click **Picture**.

4 Click **From File**.

■ The Insert Picture dialog box appears.

■ This area shows the location of the displayed files. You can click this area to change the location.

■ This area allows you to access commonly used folders. To display the contents of a folder, click the folder.

Note: For information on the commonly used folders, see the top of page 25.

Where can I get pictures that I can use in my documents?

You can use a drawing program to create your own pictures or use a scanner to scan pictures into your computer. You can also find collections of pictures at most computer stores and on the Internet.

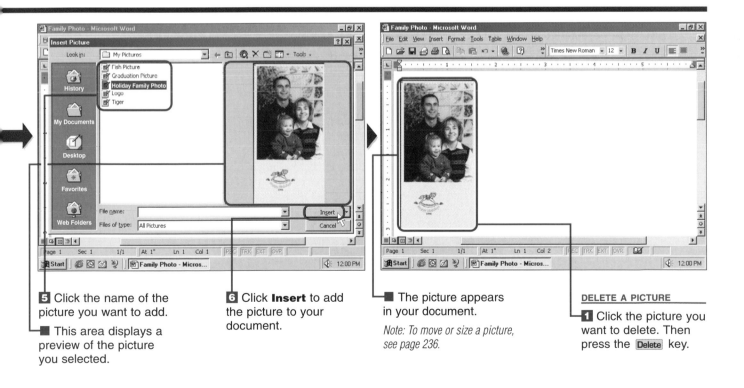

5 Click the name of the picture you want to add.

■ This area displays a preview of the picture you selected.

6 Click **Insert** to add the picture to your document.

■ The picture appears in your document.

Note: To move or size a picture, see page 236.

DELETE A PICTURE

1 Click the picture you want to delete. Then press the Delete key.

ADD A TEXT BOX

You can add a text box to your document. Text boxes are useful for displaying additional information in your document.

Word can only display text boxes in the Print Layout and Web Layout views. For more information on the views, see page 44.

ADD A TEXT BOX

1 Click 🖉 to display the Drawing toolbar.

Note: If 🖉 is not displayed, click 🔹 on the Standard toolbar to display all the buttons.

■ The Drawing toolbar appears.

2 Click 🔲 to add a text box.

3 Position the mouse + where you want to begin drawing the text box.

4 Drag the mouse + until the text box is the size you want.

How do I edit the text in a text box?

Click the text box and then edit the text as you would edit any text in a document. When you finish editing the text, click outside the text box.

■ The text box appears in your document.

5 Type the text you want the text box to display.

■ The handles (□) around the text box let you change the size of the text box. To move or size a text box, see page 236.

6 To hide the handles, click outside the text box.

Note: To hide the Drawing toolbar, repeat step 1.

DELETE A TEXT BOX

1 Click an edge of the text box you want to delete. Then press the Delete key.

MOVE OR SIZE A GRAPHIC

You can change the
location or size of
a graphic in your
document.

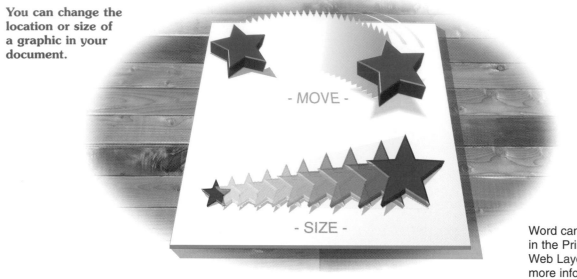

- MOVE -

- SIZE -

Word can display graphics
in the Print Layout and
Web Layout views. For
more information on the
views, see page 44.

MOVE A GRAPHIC

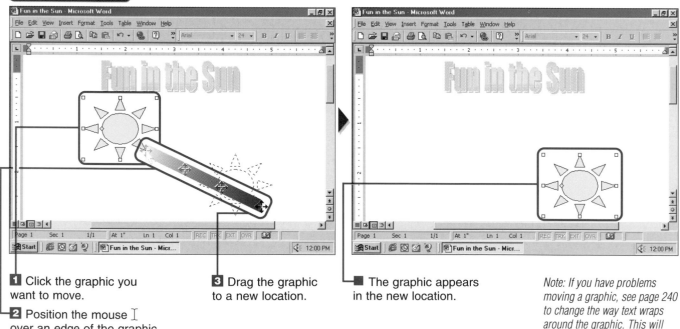

1 Click the graphic you
want to move.

2 Position the mouse I
over an edge of the graphic
(I changes to ✛ or ↖).

3 Drag the graphic
to a new location.

■ The graphic appears
in the new location.

*Note: If you have problems
moving a graphic, see page 240
to change the way text wraps
around the graphic. This will
give you more control over
the placement of the graphic.*

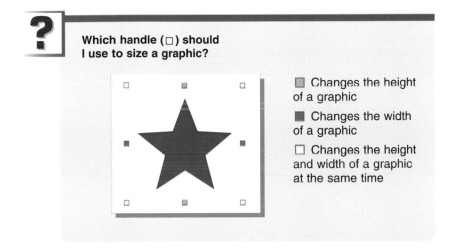

? **Which handle (□) should I use to size a graphic?**

■ Changes the height of a graphic

■ Changes the width of a graphic

□ Changes the height and width of a graphic at the same time

SIZE A GRAPHIC

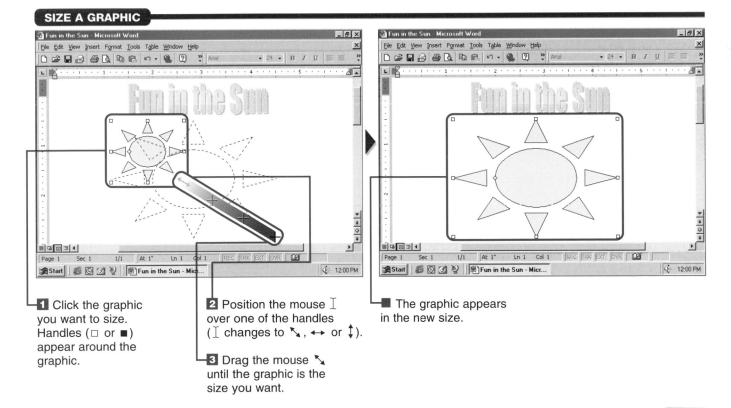

1 Click the graphic you want to size. Handles (□ or ■) appear around the graphic.

2 Position the mouse I over one of the handles (I changes to ↖, ↔ or ↕).

3 Drag the mouse ↖ until the graphic is the size you want.

■ The graphic appears in the new size.

CHANGE COLOR OF GRAPHIC

You can change
the color of a
graphic in your
document.

Word can display graphics
in the Print Layout and
Web Layout views. For
more information on the
views, see page 44.

CHANGE COLOR OF GRAPHIC

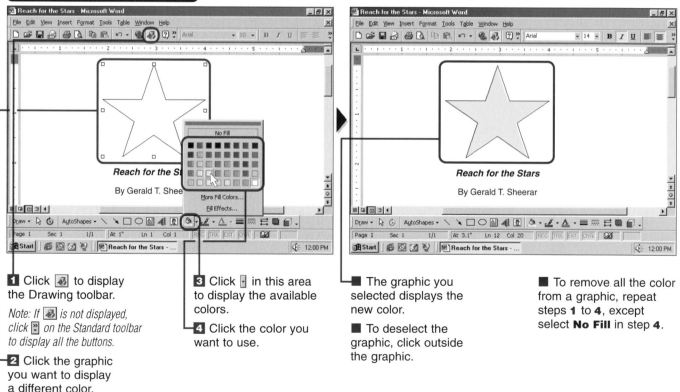

1 Click 🖌 to display
the Drawing toolbar.

*Note: If 🖌 is not displayed,
click 🔲 on the Standard toolbar
to display all the buttons.*

2 Click the graphic
you want to display
a different color.

3 Click 🔹 in this area
to display the available
colors.

4 Click the color you
want to use.

■ The graphic you
selected displays the
new color.

■ To deselect the
graphic, click outside
the graphic.

■ To remove all the color
from a graphic, repeat
steps **1** to **4**, except
select **No Fill** in step **4**.

238

You can make a graphic appear three-dimensional.

Word can display graphics in the Print Layout and Web Layout views. For more information on the views, see page 44.

MAKE A GRAPHIC 3-D

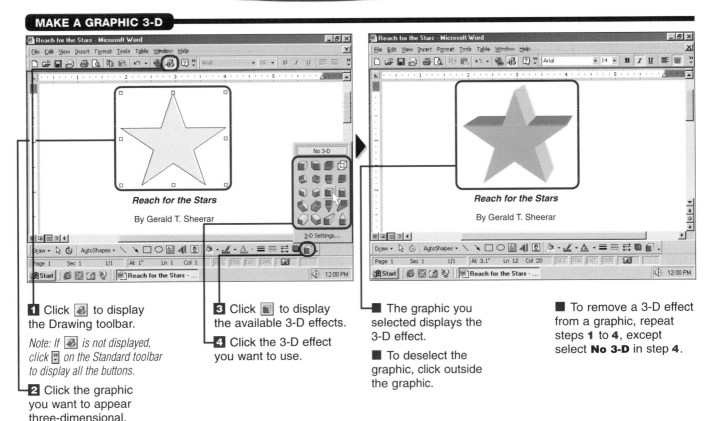

Reach for the Stars

By Gerald T. Sheerar

1 Click 🔲 to display the Drawing toolbar.

Note: If 🔲 is not displayed, click 🔲 on the Standard toolbar to display all the buttons.

2 Click the graphic you want to appear three-dimensional.

3 Click 🔲 to display the available 3-D effects.

4 Click the 3-D effect you want to use.

■ The graphic you selected displays the 3-D effect.

■ To deselect the graphic, click outside the graphic.

■ To remove a 3-D effect from a graphic, repeat steps **1** to **4**, except select **No 3-D** in step **4**.

WRAP TEXT AROUND A GRAPHIC

After you add a graphic to your document, you can choose how you want to wrap text around the graphic.

Siberian tigers grow up to 9 feet in length, with males larger than females.

Males weigh up to 650 pounds, while females may reach 365 pounds. Their fur is long and thick, with dark stripes. This provides tigers with the ability to hide from their prey.

Siberian tigers grow up to 9 feet in length, with males larger than females. Male tigers weigh up to 650 pounds. Females weigh up to 365 pounds. Their fur is long and thick, with dark stripes. This provides tigers with the ability to hide from their prey.

Word can display graphics in the Print Layout and Web Layout views. For more information on the views, see page 44.

WRAP TEXT AROUND A GRAPHIC

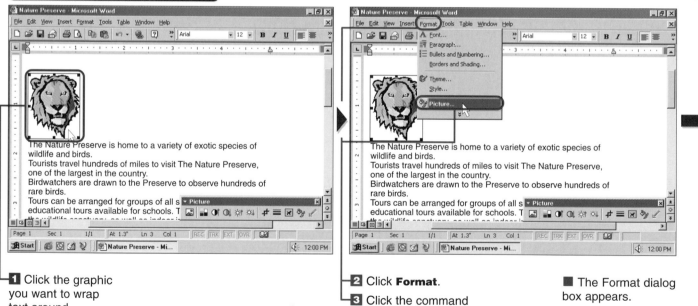

1 Click the graphic you want to wrap text around.

2 Click **Format**.

3 Click the command for the type of graphic you selected, such as **AutoShape**, **Picture** or **WordArt**.

■ The Format dialog box appears.

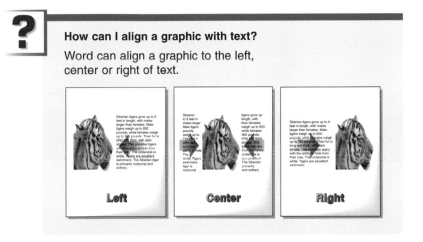

How can I align a graphic with text?

Word can align a graphic to the left, center or right of text.

Left   Center   Right

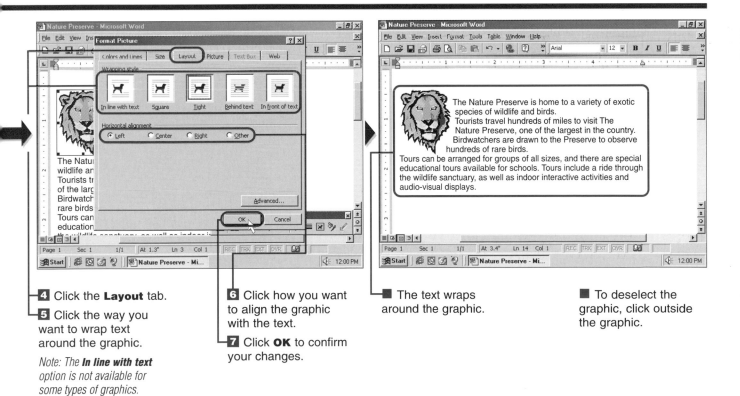

■ **4** Click the **Layout** tab.

■ **5** Click the way you want to wrap text around the graphic.

*Note: The **In line with text** option is not available for some types of graphics.*

■ **6** Click how you want to align the graphic with the text.

■ **7** Click **OK** to confirm your changes.

■ The text wraps around the graphic.

■ To deselect the graphic, click outside the graphic.

Template 1

14 pt, Arial, Italic, Blue

Dear Member:
There will be a general meeting on Saturday, June 19 at the Lincoln Memorial High School Auditorium. We look forward to seeing you there. The upcoming canned food

10 pt, Times New Roman, Black

CHAPTER 12

Time-Saving Features

Would you like to spend less time creating your documents? In this chapter you will learn how to work with the time-saving tools Word provides, such as templates, wizards and macros.

USING TEMPLATES AND WIZARDS

You can use templates and wizards to save time when creating common types of documents, such as letters, memos and reports.

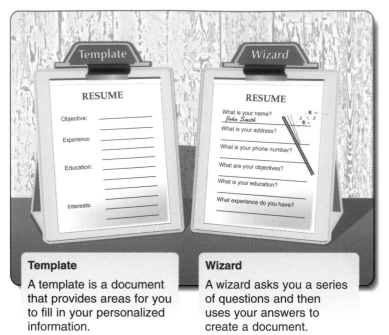

Template

A template is a document that provides areas for you to fill in your personalized information.

Wizard

A wizard asks you a series of questions and then uses your answers to create a document.

USING TEMPLATES AND WIZARDS

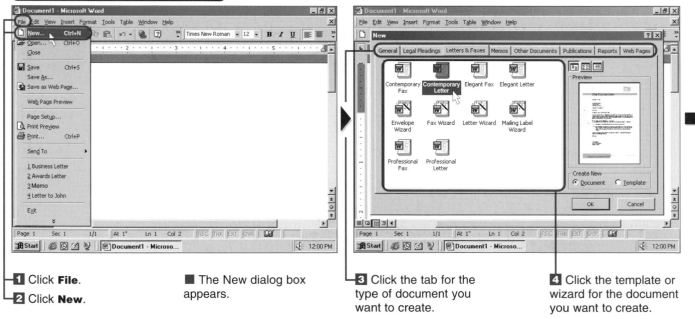

1 Click **File**.

2 Click **New**.

■ The New dialog box appears.

3 Click the tab for the type of document you want to create.

4 Click the template or wizard for the document you want to create.

*Note: A wizard has **Wizard** in its name.*

244

Why does a dialog box appear when I select a template or wizard?

A dialog box appears if the template or wizard you selected is not stored on your computer. Insert the CD-ROM disc you used to install Word into your CD-ROM drive. Then click **OK** to install the template or wizard.

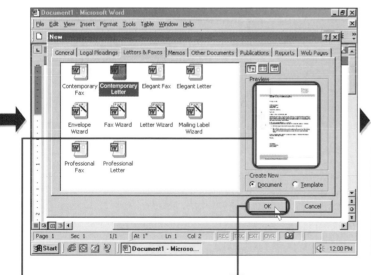

■ If a preview of the document you selected is available, the preview appears in this area.

5 Click **OK** to create the document.

■ The document appears on your screen.

Note: If you selected a wizard in step 4, Word will ask you a series of questions before creating the document.

6 Type your personalized information in the appropriate areas to complete the document.

CREATE A TEMPLATE

You can create a template from any document. Using a template you have created helps you quickly create other documents that use the same formatting, page settings and text.

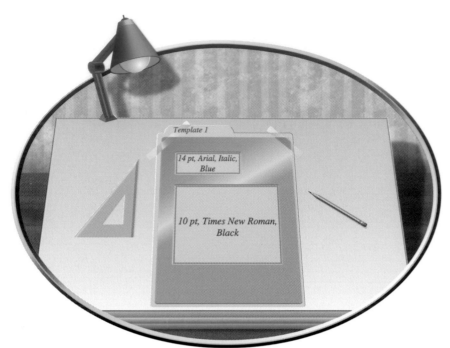

CREATE A TEMPLATE

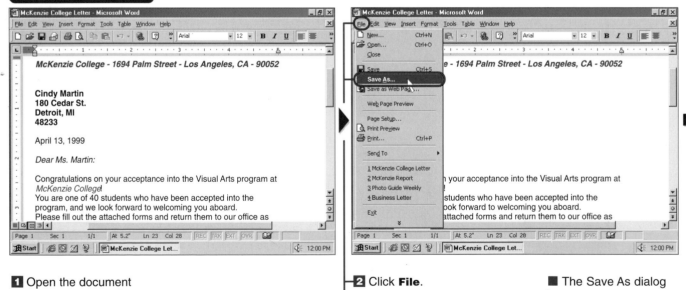

1 Open the document you want to use as the basis for the template. To open a document, see page 30.

2 Click **File**.

3 Click **Save As**.

■ The Save As dialog box appears.

How do I use a template I created?

Word stores templates you create in the Templates folder. To open a template stored in the Templates folder, perform steps **1** to **6** starting on page 244, except select the **General** tab in step **3**.

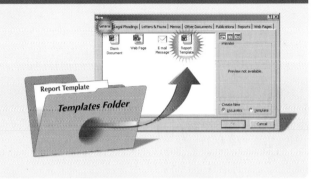

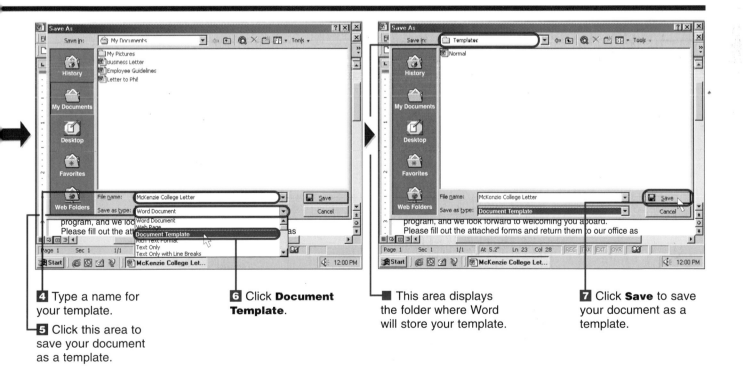

4 Type a name for your template.

5 Click this area to save your document as a template.

6 Click **Document Template**.

■ This area displays the folder where Word will store your template.

7 Click **Save** to save your document as a template.

RECORD A MACRO

A macro saves you time by combining a series of commands into a single command.

RECORD A MACRO

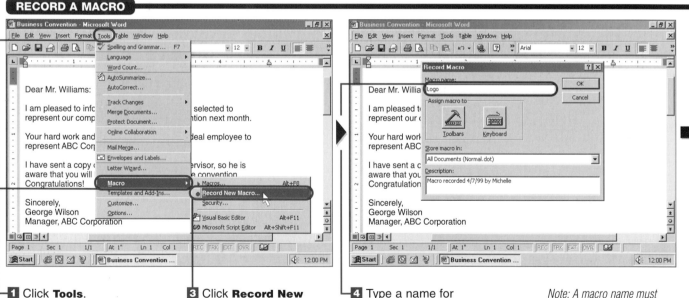

1 Click **Tools**.

2 Click **Macro**.

Note: If Macro does not appear on the menu, position the mouse ⟀ over the bottom of the menu to display all the menu commands.

3 Click **Record New Macro**.

■ The Record Macro dialog box appears.

4 Type a name for the macro.

Note: A macro name must begin with a letter and cannot contain spaces.

Should I practice before I record a macro?

Before recording a macro, you should plan and practice all the actions you want the macro to include. Word will record any mistakes or corrections you make while recording the macro.

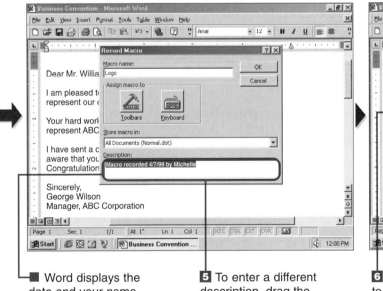

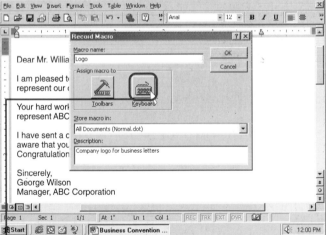

■ Word displays the date and your name as a description for the macro.

5 To enter a different description, drag the mouse I over the text in this area to select the text. Then type a new description.

6 Click **Keyboard** to assign a keyboard shortcut to the macro.

■ The Customize Keyboard dialog box appears.

CONTINUED

RECORD A MACRO

Macros are ideal for tasks you frequently perform in your documents.

Alt + F3...
Inserting logo

Macros can help speed up many repetitive formatting and editing tasks, such as removing extra spaces from text. Macros are also useful for inserting items such as your company logo or symbols into your documents.

RECORD A MACRO (CONTINUED)

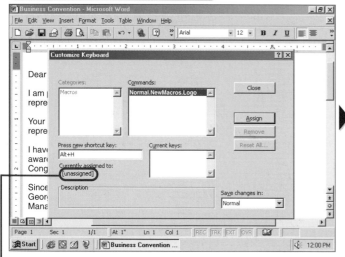

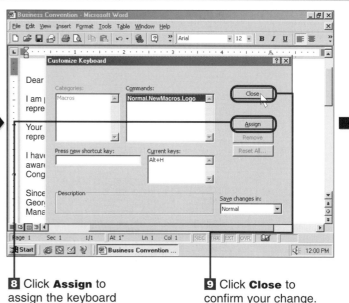

7 To specify a keyboard shortcut for the macro, press and hold down the **Alt** key as you press a letter or number key.

■ This area displays the word **[unassigned]**.

*Note: If the word **[unassigned]** is not displayed, the keyboard shortcut you specified is already assigned to another command. Press the* **Backspace** *key to delete the shortcut and then repeat step **7**, using a different letter or number.*

8 Click **Assign** to assign the keyboard shortcut to your macro.

9 Click **Close** to confirm your change.

?

Can I use the mouse while recording a macro?

While recording a macro, you can only use the mouse to select toolbar buttons or menu commands. You cannot use the mouse to move the insertion point or select text.

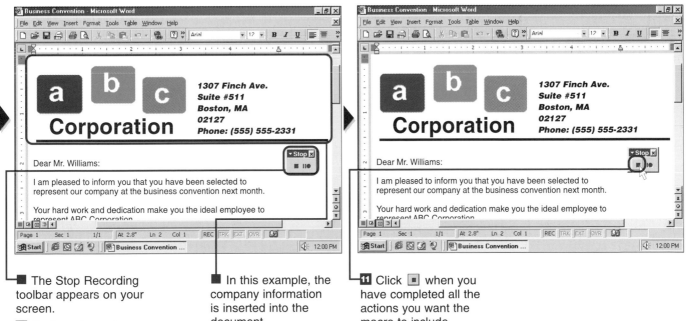

■ The Stop Recording toolbar appears on your screen.

🔟 Perform the actions you want the macro to include.

■ In this example, the company information is inserted into the document.

🔢 Click ■ when you have completed all the actions you want the macro to include.

RUN A MACRO

When you run a macro, Word automatically performs the actions you recorded.

RUN A MACRO

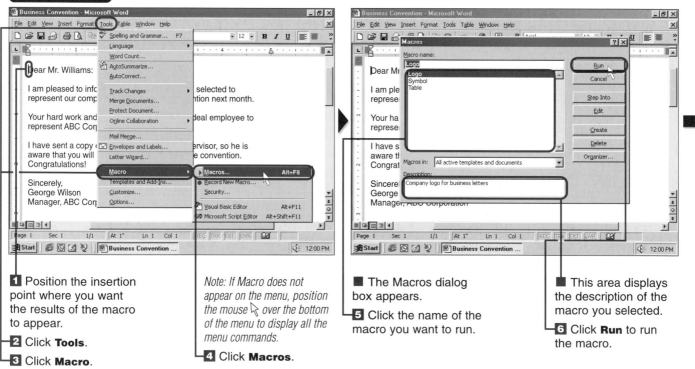

1 Position the insertion point where you want the results of the macro to appear.

2 Click **Tools**.

3 Click **Macro**.

Note: If Macro does not appear on the menu, position the mouse over the bottom of the menu to display all the menu commands.

4 Click **Macros**.

■ The Macros dialog box appears.

5 Click the name of the macro you want to run.

■ This area displays the description of the macro you selected.

6 Click **Run** to run the macro.

252

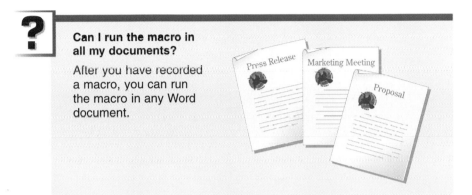

Can I run the macro in all my documents?

After you have recorded a macro, you can run the macro in any Word document.

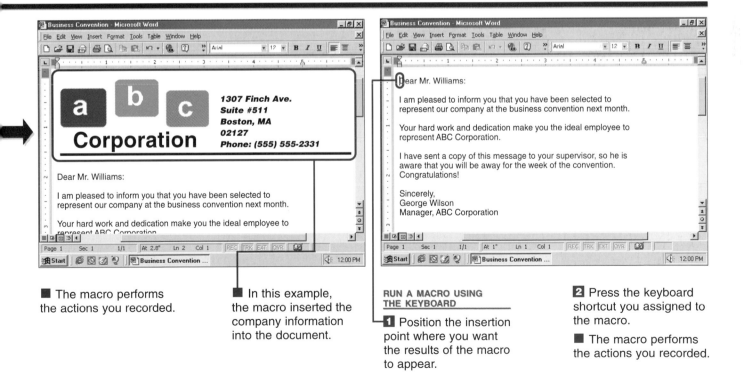

■ The macro performs the actions you recorded.

■ In this example, the macro inserted the company information into the document.

RUN A MACRO USING THE KEYBOARD

1 Position the insertion point where you want the results of the macro to appear.

2 Press the keyboard shortcut you assigned to the macro.

■ The macro performs the actions you recorded.

CREATE A NEW TOOLBAR

You can create a new
toolbar containing
buttons and commands
you frequently use.

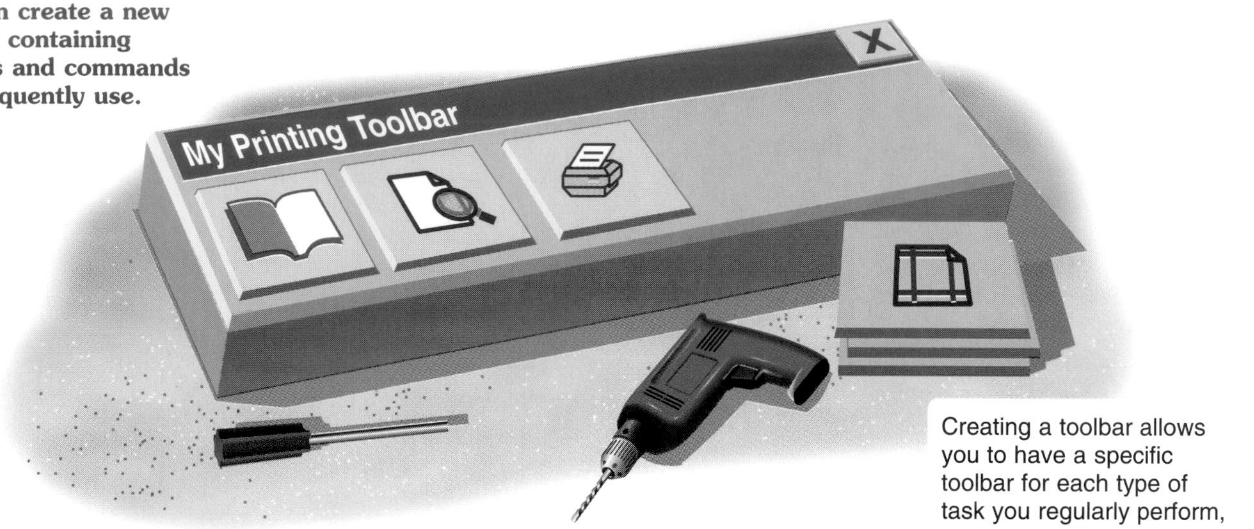

My Printing Toolbar

Creating a toolbar allows
you to have a specific
toolbar for each type of
task you regularly perform,
such as printing documents
or adding AutoShapes.

CREATE A NEW TOOLBAR

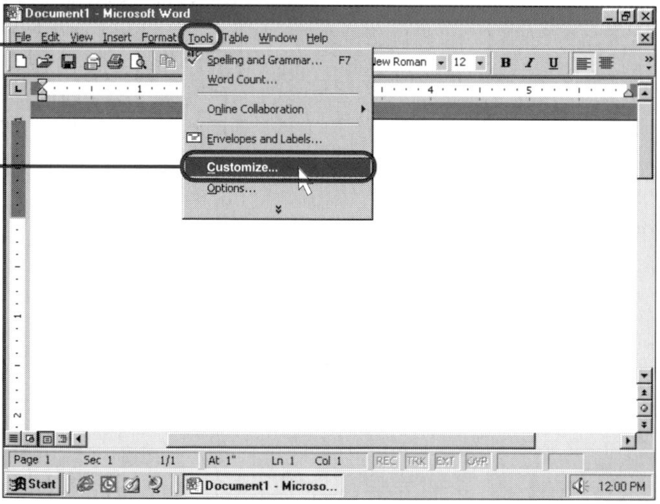

-1 Click **Tools**.

-2 Click **Customize**.

■ The Customize dialog
box appears.

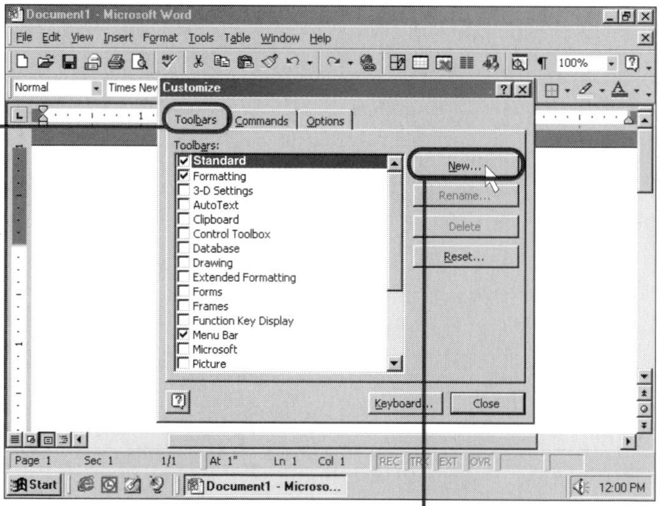

-3 Click the **Toolbars** tab.

-4 Click **New** to create
a new toolbar.

■ The New Toolbar
dialog box appears.

How can I move a toolbar I created?

After you create a new toolbar, you can move the toolbar to a new location on your screen. To move a toolbar, position the mouse ⬚ over the title bar and then drag the toolbar to a new location. For more information on working with toolbars, see pages 47 to 49.

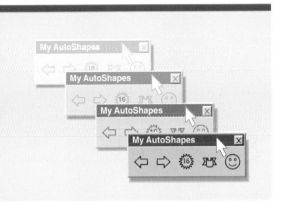

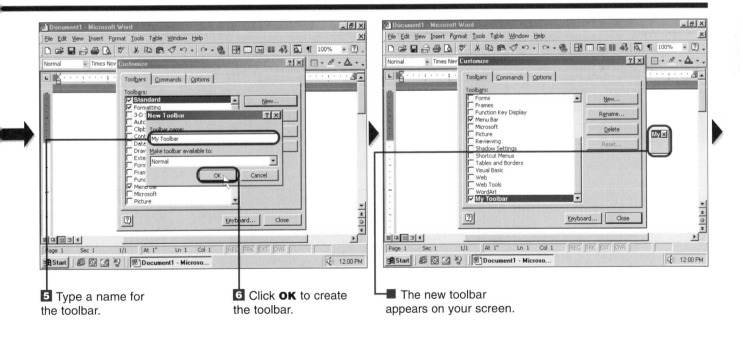

5 Type a name for the toolbar.

6 Click **OK** to create the toolbar.

■ The new toolbar appears on your screen.

CONTINUED

CREATE A NEW TOOLBAR

You can add buttons to
a toolbar you created.
Each button allows
you to perform a
different task.

Word offers hundreds
of buttons for you to
choose from.

CREATE A NEW TOOLBAR (CONTINUED)

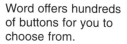

7 Click the **Commands** tab.

8 Click the category that contains the button you want to add to the toolbar.

*Note: If you do not know which category contains the button you want to add, click **All Commands** to display all the buttons.*

■ This area displays the buttons in the category you selected.

9 Position the mouse ⌖ over the button you want to add to the toolbar.

10 Drag the button to the toolbar. A line ([ ) indicates where the button will appear.

Can I add a button to a toolbar included with Word?

Yes. Display the Customize dialog box by performing steps **1** and **2** on page 254. Then perform steps **7** to **12** below to add a button to the toolbar.

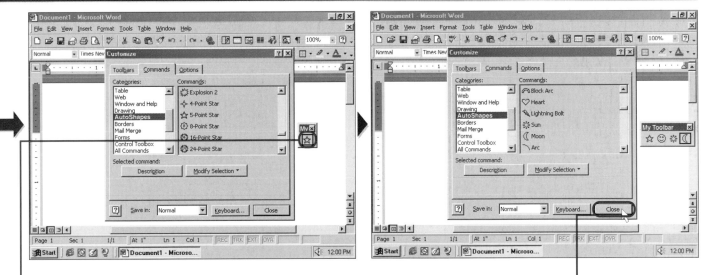

■ The button appears on the toolbar.

11 Repeat steps **8** to **10** for each button you want to add to the toolbar.

12 When you finish adding buttons to the toolbar, click **Close** to close the Customize dialog box.

CREATE A NEW TOOLBAR

You can remove
buttons you no
longer use from
your toolbar.

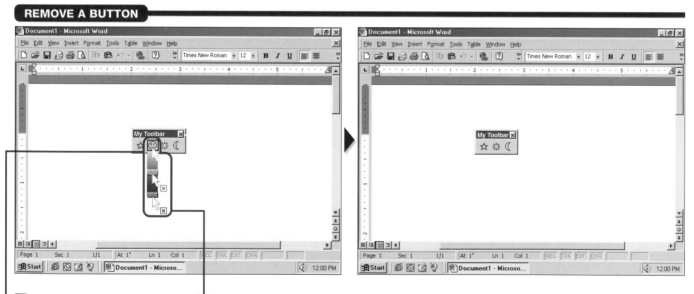

1 Display the toolbar you
want to change. To display
a toolbar, see page 47.

2 Position the mouse ⌖
over the button you want
to remove.

3 Press and hold down
the **Alt** key as you drag
the button downward off
the toolbar.

■ The button disappears
from the toolbar.

You can move buttons
on your toolbar to
place buttons for
related tasks together.
This can make it
easier to find the
buttons you need.

MOVE A BUTTON

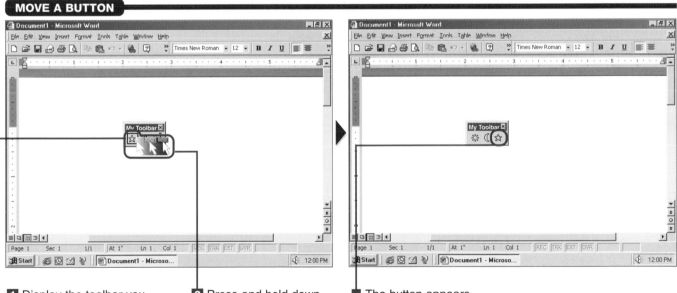

1 Display the toolbar you
want to change. To display
a toolbar, see page 47.

2 Position the mouse
over the button you want
to move.

3 Press and hold down
the Alt key as you drag
the button to a new
location.

■ A line ([ ) indicates
where the button will
appear.

■ The button appears
in the new location on
the toolbar.

Mr. John Smith
11 South Street
Los Angeles, CA 90013

Mr. Jim Hunter
14 Willow Avenue
Los Angeles, CA 90028

CHAPTER 13

Mail Merge

Would you like to quickly produce a personalized letter for each person on a mailing list? This chapter teaches you how.

MAIL
MAIL
MAIL
MAIL
MAIL
Record 25
John Smith
11 South Street
Los Angeles, CA
90013
Mr. Smith
Record 26
Jim Hunter
14 Willow Avenue
Los Angeles, CA
90028
Mr. Hunter

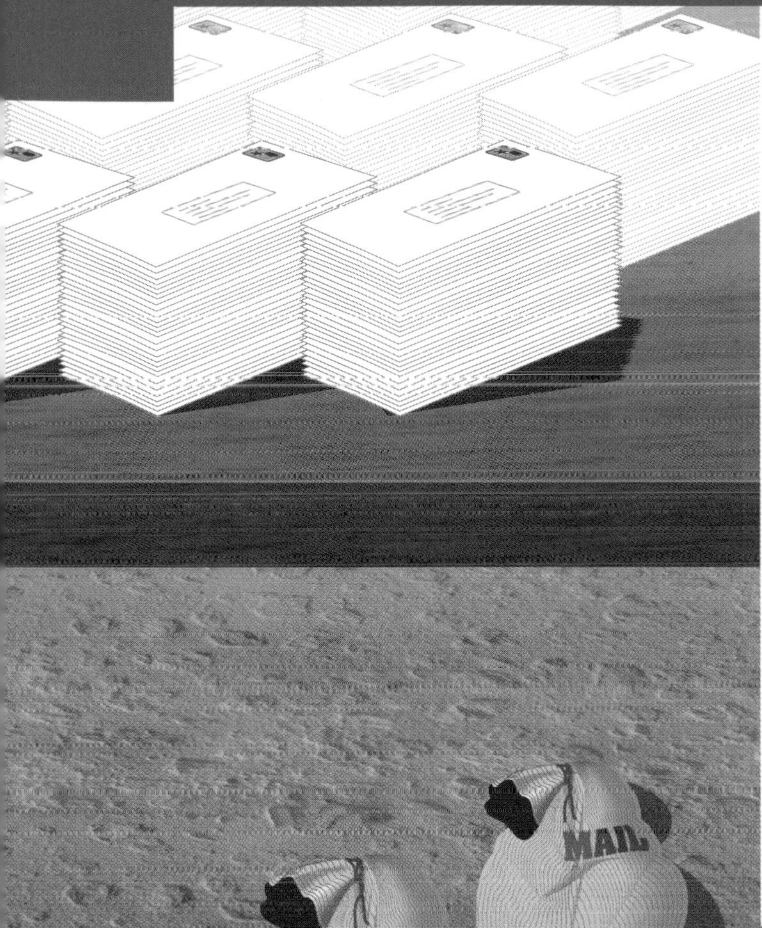

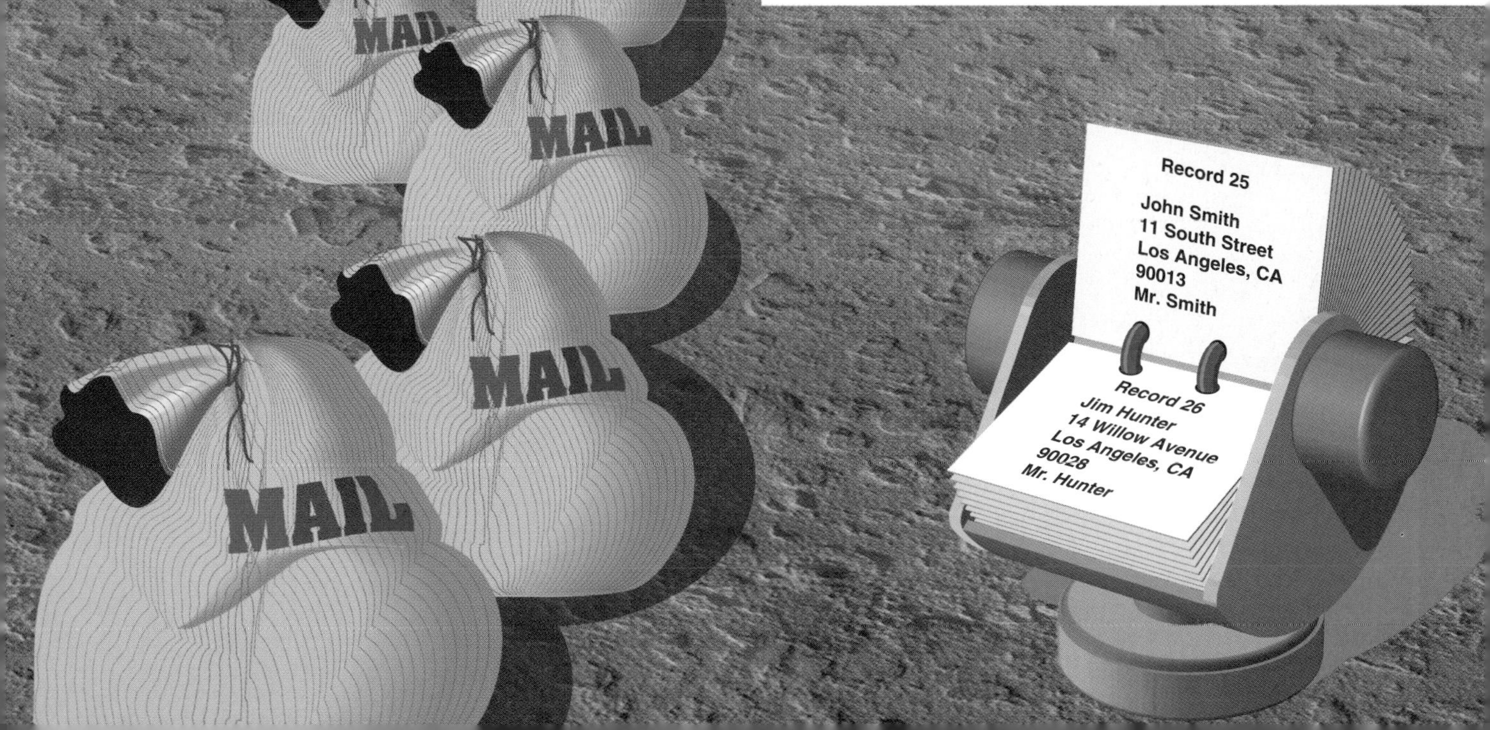

You can use the Mail Merge feature to produce a personalized letter for each person on your mailing list.

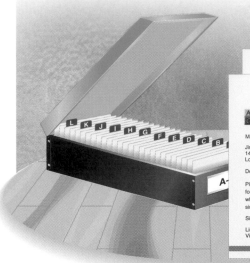

Performing a mail merge is useful if you often send the same document, such as an announcement or advertisement, to many people.

STEP 1

Create a Main Document

A main document is a letter you want to send to each person on your mailing list.

STEP 2

Create a Data Source

A data source contains the information that changes in each letter, such as the name and address of each person on your mailing list. You only need to create a data source once. After you create a data source, you can use the data source in future mailings. A data source consists of fields and records.

FirstName	LastName	Address1	City	State	PostalCode
Ted	Duxan	14 Pine Street	Los Angeles	CA	90023
John	Smith	11 South Street	Los Angeles	CA	90013
Heather	Brown	56 Maple Street	San Diego	CA	92128
Jim	Hunter	14 Willow Avenue	Los Angeles	CA	90028
Linda	Wilson	989 Main Street	Burbank	CA	91505
Ted	Green	66 River Road	Burbank	CA	91501

Field

A field is a specific category of information. Each field has a name, such as LastName or City.

Record

A record is all the information for one person on your mailing list.

What types of documents can I create using the Mail Merge feature?

Form Letters

Mailing Labels

Envelopes

Catalogs

STEP 3

Complete the Main Document

To complete the main document, you must insert special instructions into the main document. These instructions tell Word where to place the personalized information from the data source.

«FirstName» «LastName»
«Address1»
«City», «State» «PostalCode»

«Greeting»

STEP 4

Merge the Main Document and Data Source

You combine, or merge, the main document and the data source to create a personalized letter for each person on your mailing list. Word replaces the special instructions in the main document with the personalized information from the data source.

CREATE A MAIN DOCUMENT

The main document contains the text that remains the same in each letter.

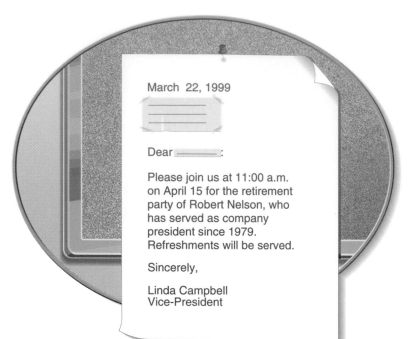

March 22, 1999

Dear _____:

Please join us at 11:00 a.m. on April 15 for the retirement party of Robert Nelson, who has served as company president since 1979. Refreshments will be served.

Sincerely,

Linda Campbell
Vice-President

CREATE A MAIN DOCUMENT

1 Click □ to create a new document.

Note: If □ is not displayed, click ≫ on the Standard toolbar to display all the buttons.

2 Type the letter you want to send to each person on your mailing list. Include the information for one person.

3 Save the document. To save a document, see page 24.

4 Click **Tools**.

5 Click **Mail Merge**.

Note: If Mail Merge does not appear on the menu, position the mouse ⊳ over the bottom of the menu to display all the menu commands.

■ The Mail Merge Helper dialog box appears.

Can I use a document I previously created as my main document?

Yes. Open the document you want to use as your main document. Then perform steps **4** to **8** below. To open a document, see page 30.

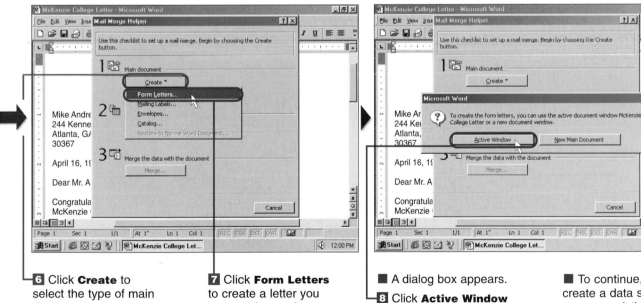

6 Click **Create** to select the type of main document you want to create.

7 Click **Form Letters** to create a letter you can send to each person on your mailing list.

■ A dialog box appears.

8 Click **Active Window** to make the document displayed on your screen the main document.

■ To continue, you must create a data source or open an existing data source. To create a data source, see page 266. To open an existing data source, see page 272.

CREATE A DATA SOURCE

The data source contains the personalized information that changes in each letter, such as the name and address of each person on your mailing list.

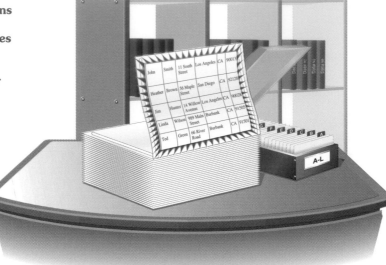

You only need to create a data source once. To open an existing data source, see page 272.

CREATE A DATA SOURCE

■ Before creating a data source, you must create a main document. To create a main document, see page 264.

1 Click **Get Data**.

2 Click **Create Data Source**.

■ The Create Data Source dialog box appears.

■ Word provides a list of commonly used field names.

3 To remove a field name you do not need, click the field name.

4 Click **Remove Field Name**.

■ The field name disappears from the list.

What is a field name?

A field name is a name given to a category of information, such as LastName or City. When you create a data source, Word provides a list of field names you can choose from. You can remove and add field names until you have all the field names you need.

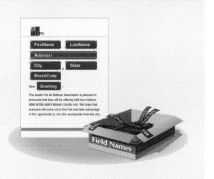

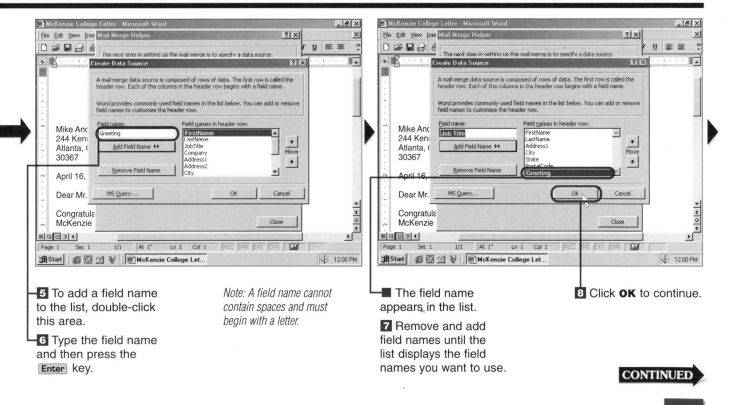

5 To add a field name to the list, double-click this area.

6 Type the field name and then press the Enter key.

Note: A field name cannot contain spaces and must begin with a letter.

■ The field name appears in the list.

7 Remove and add field names until the list displays the field names you want to use.

8 Click **OK** to continue.

CONTINUED

CREATE A DATA SOURCE

After you save the
data source, you can
enter the information
for each person on
your mailing list.

■ The Save As dialog
box appears.

9 Type a name for
the data source.

■ This area shows the
location where Word will
save the data source.
You can click this area
to change the location.

10 Click **Save** to save
the data source.

■ A dialog box appears,
stating that the data source
contains no records.

11 Click **Edit Data Source**
to enter the information
for each person on your
mailing list.

How do I browse through the information I entered?

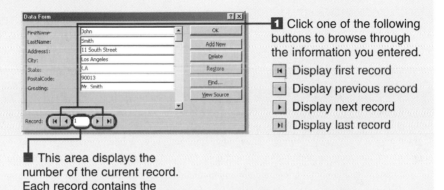

1 Click one of the following buttons to browse through the information you entered.

[◄] Display first record

[◄] Display previous record

[►] Display next record

[►] Display last record

■ This area displays the number of the current record. Each record contains the information for one person.

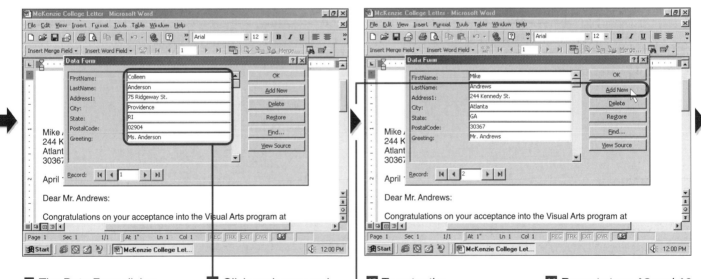

■ The Data Form dialog box appears, displaying areas where you can enter the information for a person on your mailing list.

12 Click each area and type the appropriate information for a person.

13 To enter the information for another person, click **Add New**.

14 Repeat steps **12** and **13** for each person on your mailing list.

CONTINUED

CREATE A DATA SOURCE

When you finish entering
information in the data
source, you can display
a table showing all the
information you entered.

FirstName	LastName	Address1	City	State	PostalCode
John	Smith	11 South Street	Los Angeles	CA	90013
Heather	Brown	56 Maple Street	San Diego	CA	92128
Jim	Hunter	14 Willow Avenue	Los Angeles	CA	90028
Linda	Wilson	989 Main Street	Burbank	CA	91505
Ted	Green	66 River Road	Burbank	CA	91501

CREATE A DATA SOURCE (CONTINUED)

McKenzie College Letter - Microsoft Word

Data Form

FirstName:	Rita
LastName:	Wilson
Address1:	365 Anno Rd.
City:	Salem
State:	MA
PostalCode:	01970
Greeting:	Ms. Wilson

OK
Add New
Delete
Restore
Find...
View Source

Record: 16

Mike
244 K
Atlant
30367

April

Dear Mr. Andrews:

Congratulations on your acceptance into the Visual Arts program at

McKenzie College Students - Microsoft Word

FirstName	LastName	Address1	City	State	PostalCode	Greeting
Colleen	Anderson	75 Ridgeway St.	Providence	RI	02904	Ms. Anderson
Mike	Andrews	244 Kennedy St.	Atlanta	GA	30367	Mr. Andrews
Louise	Fallahar	54 Surfside Dr.	San Jose	CA	95101	Ms. Fallahar
Geoffery	Lee	88 Malcolm Ave.	Jacksonville	FL	32203	Mr. Lee
Cindy	Martin	180 Cedar St.	Detroit	MI	48223	Ms. Martin
Patricia	Moorley	5692	Beverly	CA	90210	Ms.

15 When you finish
entering the information
for all the people on
your mailing list, click
View Source.

■ The information you
entered appears in a table.

■ The first row in the table
displays the field names
you specified. Each of the
following rows displays the
information for one person.

*Note: Text that does not fit
on one line in the table will
appear on one line when
you print the letters.*

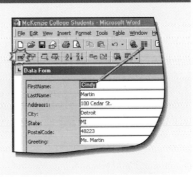

How do I change information in my data source?

When viewing the data source, you can click 🖉 to redisplay the Data Form dialog box. You can then add or change information for people on your mailing list. You can also edit the text directly in the table as you would edit any text in a document.

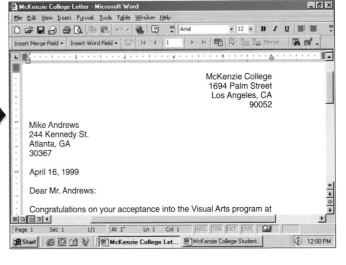

16 Click 🖫 to save the information you entered.

Note: If 🖫 is not displayed, click ∗ on the Standard toolbar to display all the buttons.

17 Click 🖻 to return to the main document.

■ The main document appears on your screen.

■ To continue, you must complete the main document. To complete the main document, see page 274.

OPEN AN EXISTING DATA SOURCE

You can use a
data source you
previously created
to perform a mail
merge.

A data source contains
the information that
changes in each letter,
such as the name and
address of each person
on your mailing list.

OPEN AN EXISTING DATA SOURCE

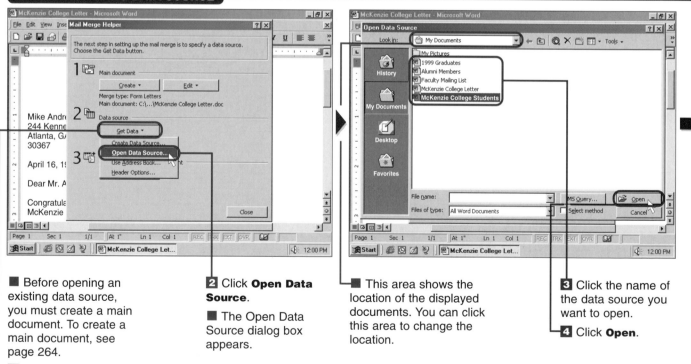

■ Before opening an
existing data source,
you must create a main
document. To create a
main document, see
page 264.

1 Click **Get Data**.

2 Click **Open Data
Source**.

■ The Open Data
Source dialog box
appears.

■ This area shows the
location of the displayed
documents. You can click
this area to change the
location.

3 Click the name of
the data source you
want to open.

4 Click **Open**.

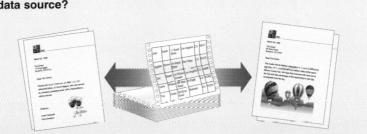

When should I use an existing data source?

Once you create a data source, you can use the data source for all your mailings. For example, you can use the same data source for each newsletter and sales brochure you send to your customers.

Before using an existing data source, you should review the data source to make sure the information is up-to-date. You can open a data source as you would open any document. To open a document, see page 30.

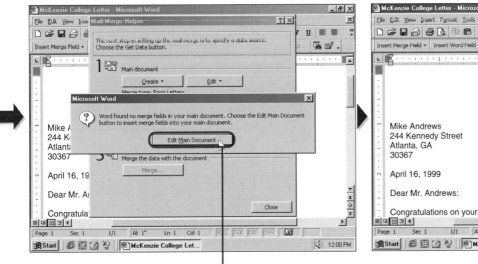

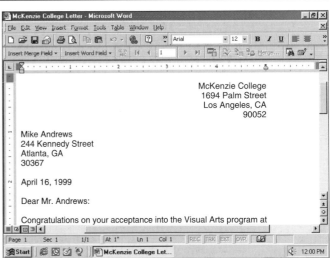

■ A dialog box appears.

5 Click **Edit Main Document** to return to the main document.

■ The main document appears on your screen.

■ To continue, you must complete the main document. To complete the main document, see page 274.

COMPLETE THE MAIN DOCUMENT

You must insert special instructions, called merge fields, to complete the main document. These instructions tell Word where to place the personalized information from the data source.

A
C
I inc.

FirstName	LastName

Address1

City	,	State

PostalCode

_____

Dear   :

Greeting

The Austin Hot Air Balloon Association is pleased to announce that they will be offering half-hour balloon rides at this year's Mower County Fair. We hope that everyone will come out to the Fair and take advantage of this opportunity to view the countryside from the sky.

COMPLETE THE MAIN DOCUMENT

McKenzie College Letter - Microsoft Word

File Edit View Insert Format Tools Table Window Help

Insert Merge Field ▾ Insert Word Field ▾

McKenzie College
1694 Palm Street
Los Angeles, CA
90052

Mike Andrews
244 Kennedy St.
Atlanta, CA
30367

April 16, 1999

Dear Mr. Andrews:

Congratulations on your acceptance into the Visual Arts program at

Page 1   Sec 1   1/1   At 1.9"   Ln 6   Col 1

Start   McKenzie College Let...   12:00 PM

McKenzie College Letter - Microsoft Word

File Edit View Insert Format Tools Table Window Help

Insert Merge Field ▾ Insert Word Field ▾

FirstName
LastName
Address1
City
State
PostalCode
Greeting

McKenzie College
1694 Palm Street
Los Angeles, CA
90052

Mike Andrews
244 Kennedy St.
Atlanta, CA
30367

April 16, 1999

Dear Mr. Andrews:

Congratulations on your acceptance into the Visual Arts program at

Page 1   Sec 1   1/1   At 1.9"   Ln 6   Col 1

Start   McKenzie College Let...   12:00 PM

■ Before completing the main document, you must create a main document. To create a main document, see page 264.

1 Select an area of text that you want to change in each letter. Do not select any spaces before or after the text. To select text, see page 14.

2 Click **Insert Merge Field** to display a list of merge fields.

Note: The merge fields that appear depend on the field names you specified when you created the data source.

3 Click the merge field that corresponds to the text you selected in step **1**.

After I complete the main document, can I see an example of how my letters will look?

Yes. You can click ![] to temporarily replace the merge fields in the main document with the information for a person on your mailing list. To view the merge fields again, click ![].

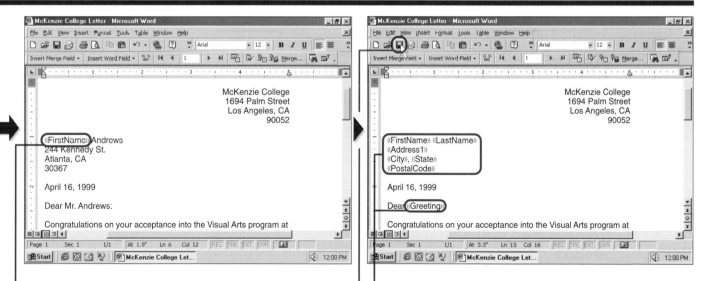

■ The merge field replaces the text you selected.

■ To delete a merge field you accidentally inserted, drag the mouse I over the merge field to select the field. Then press the Delete key.

4 Repeat steps **1** to **3** for each area of text you want to change in your letters.

5 Click ![] to save the document.

Note: If ![] is not displayed, click ![] on the Standard toolbar to display all the buttons.

■ To continue, you must merge the main document and the data source. To merge the main document and the data source, see page 276.

MERGE THE MAIN DOCUMENT AND DATA SOURCE

You can combine the
main document and
the data source to
create a personalized
letter for each person
on your mailing list.

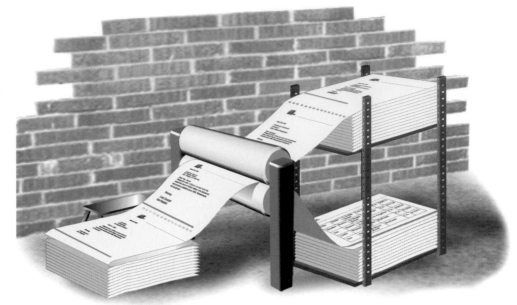

1 Click 🔳 to merge
the main document
and the data source.

■ A new document
appears, displaying a
personalized letter for
each person on your
mailing list.

■ Word replaces the
merge fields in the
main document with
the corresponding
information from the
data source.

Should I save the merged document?

To conserve hard disk space, do not save the merged document. You can easily recreate the merged document at any time by opening the main document and then performing step **1** on page 276. To open a document, see page 30.

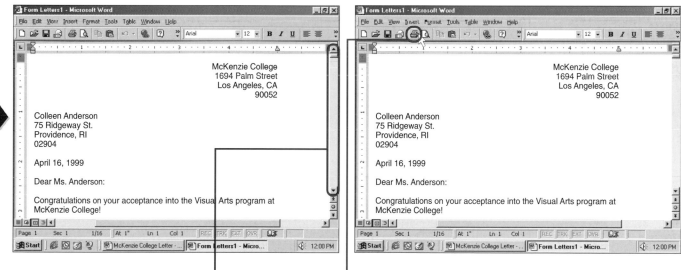

■ You can edit the letters as you would edit any document. You may want to add personalized comments to some letters.

■ You can use the scroll bar to browse through the letters.

PRINT MERGED DOCUMENT

1 When you finish reviewing the letters, click 🖨 to print the letters. To print only some of the letters, see page 184.

Note: If 🖨 is not displayed, click ⏩ on the Standard toolbar to display all the buttons.

USING MAIL MERGE TO PRINT LABELS

You can use the Mail Merge feature to print a personalized label for each person on your mailing list. This saves you from typing each label individually.

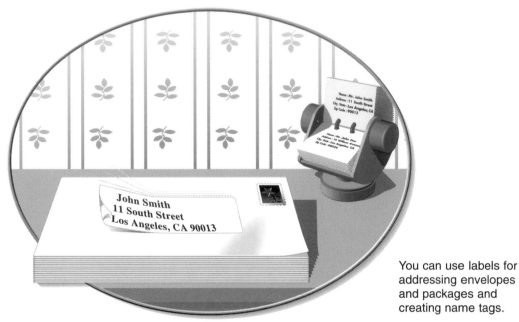

You can use labels for addressing envelopes and packages and creating name tags.

USING MAIL MERGE TO PRINT LABELS

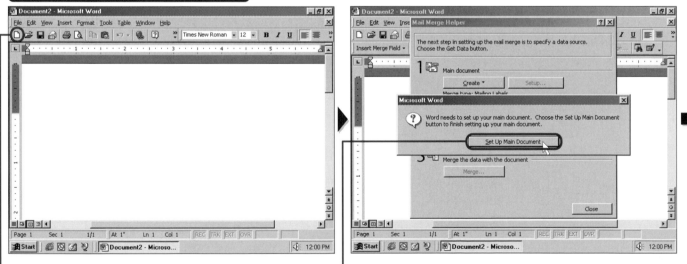

1 Click ▯ to create a new document.

Note: If ▯ is not displayed, click ▯ on the Standard toolbar to display all the buttons.

2 To tell Word that you want to create labels, perform steps **4** to **8** starting on page 264, except select **Mailing Labels** in step **7**.

3 To open an existing data source, perform steps **1** to **4** on page 272.

4 Click **Set Up Main Document** to set up the labels.

■ The Label Options dialog box appears.

Which label product and type should I choose?

You can check your label packaging to determine which label product and type you should choose.

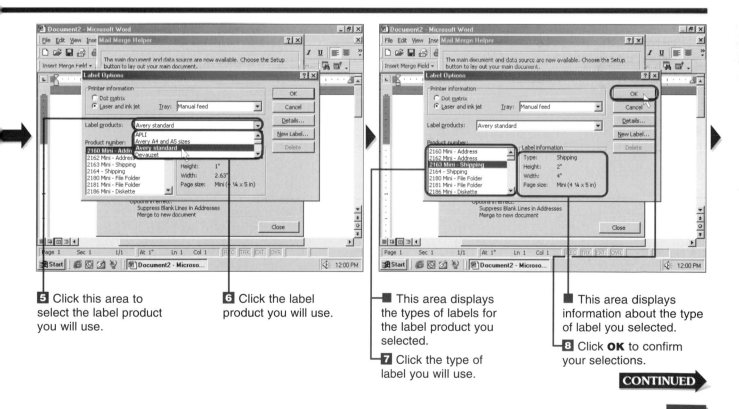

5 Click this area to select the label product you will use.

6 Click the label product you will use.

■ This area displays the types of labels for the label product you selected.

7 Click the type of label you will use.

■ This area displays information about the type of label you selected.

8 Click **OK** to confirm your selections.

CONTINUED ▶

USING MAIL MERGE TO PRINT LABELS

You must insert special instructions, called merge fields, to tell Word where to place the personalized information that will change in each label.

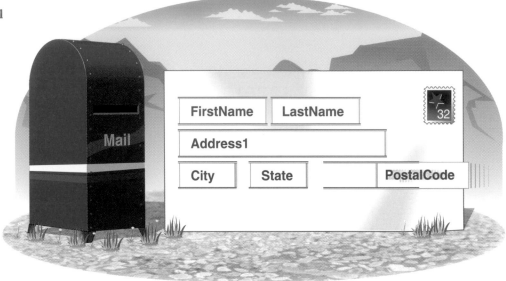

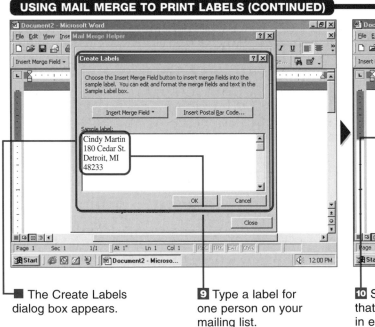

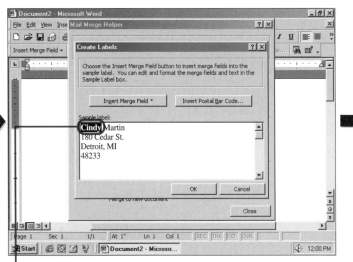

■ The Create Labels dialog box appears.

9 Type a label for one person on your mailing list.

10 Select an area of text that you want to change in each label. Do not select any spaces before or after the text. To select text, see page 14.

Can I create labels without using the Mail Merge feature?

Yes. You can type the text you want to appear on each label yourself. For information on printing labels without using the Mail Merge feature, see page 188.

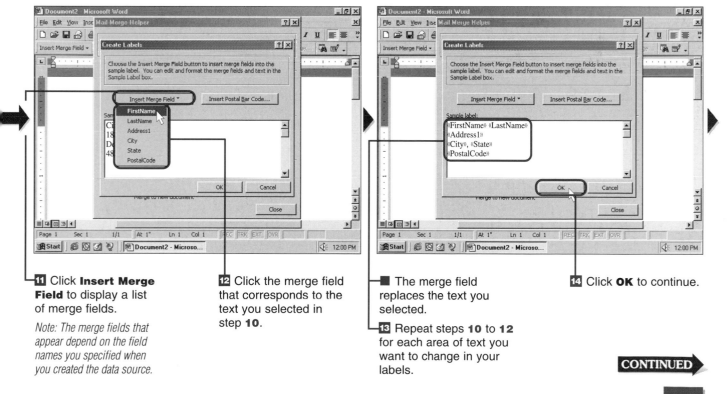

11 Click **Insert Merge Field** to display a list of merge fields.

Note: The merge fields that appear depend on the field names you specified when you created the data source.

12 Click the merge field that corresponds to the text you selected in step **10**.

■ The merge field replaces the text you selected.

13 Repeat steps **10** to **12** for each area of text you want to change in your labels.

14 Click **OK** to continue.

CONTINUED

USING MAIL MERGE TO PRINT LABELS

After you merge the labels and the data source, you can print the personalized labels Word created for each person on your mailing list.

USING MAIL MERGE TO PRINT LABELS (CONTINUED)

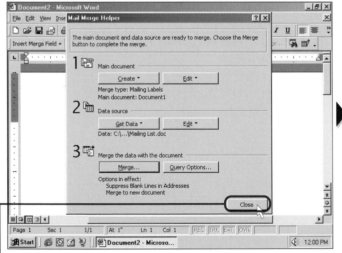

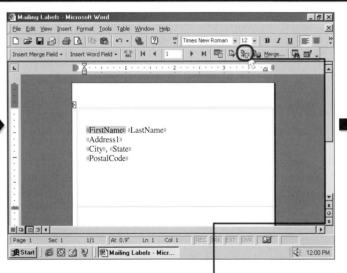

15 Click **Close** to close the Mail Merge Helper dialog box.

■ The labels appear, displaying the merge fields you selected.

16 Save the document. To save a document, see page 24.

17 Click 🖳 to merge the labels and the data source.

? Should I save the merged labels?

To conserve hard disk space, do not save the merged labels. You can easily recreate the merged labels at any time by opening the label document you saved in step **16** below and then performing step **17** below. To open a document, see page 30.

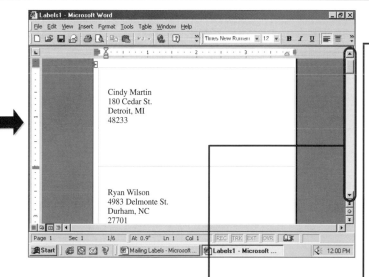

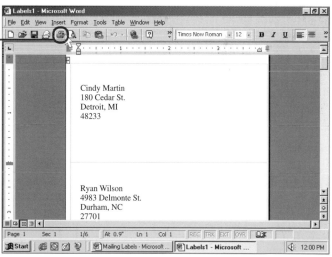

■ A new document appears, displaying a personalized label for each person on your mailing list.

■ You can edit the labels as you would edit any document.

■ You can use the scroll bar to browse through the labels.

PRINT MERGED LABELS

1 When you finish reviewing the labels, click 🖨 to print the labels. To print only some of the labels, see page 184.

Note: If 🖨 is not displayed, click 🔘 on the Standard toolbar to display all the buttons.

Boston Cycling Club

Welcome to the Boston Cycling Club Network. We have been riding and cycling in Boston for 15 years, and we are still going strong. To learn about the club, click one of the following connections.

Boston Cycling Club Newsletter

List of Upcoming Events Organized by the Club

History of the Boston Cycling Club

How to Become a Member

Contact Information

CHAPTER 14

Word and the Internet

Are you wondering how you can use Word to share information with other people on the Internet? In this chapter you will learn how to e-mail a document, save a document as a Web page and more.

E-MAIL A DOCUMENT

You can e-mail the document displayed on your screen to a friend, family member or colleague.

Before you can e-mail a document, Microsoft Outlook must be set up on your computer. Microsoft Outlook is a program that allows you to send and receive e-mail messages.

E-MAIL A DOCUMENT

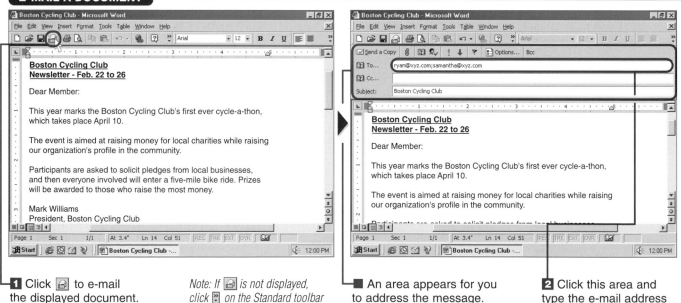

1 Click ▨ to e-mail the displayed document.

Note: If ▨ is not displayed, click ▸ on the Standard toolbar to display all the buttons.

■ An area appears for you to address the message.

2 Click this area and type the e-mail address of each person you want to receive the message. Separate each address with a semicolon (;).

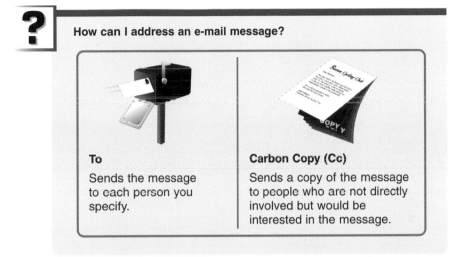

How can I address an e-mail message?

To

Sends the message to each person you specify.

Carbon Copy (Cc)

Sends a copy of the message to people who are not directly involved but would be interested in the message.

3 To send a copy of the message, click this area and type the e-mail address of each person you want to receive a copy. Separate each address with a semicolon (;).

4 Click this area and type a subject for the message.

Note: If a subject already exists, you can drag the mouse I over the existing subject and then type a new subject.

5 Click **Send a Copy** to send the message.

CREATE A HYPERLINK

You can create a hyperlink to connect a word or phrase in your document to another document on your computer, network, corporate intranet or the Internet.

An intranet is a small version of the Internet within a company or organization.

CREATE A HYPERLINK

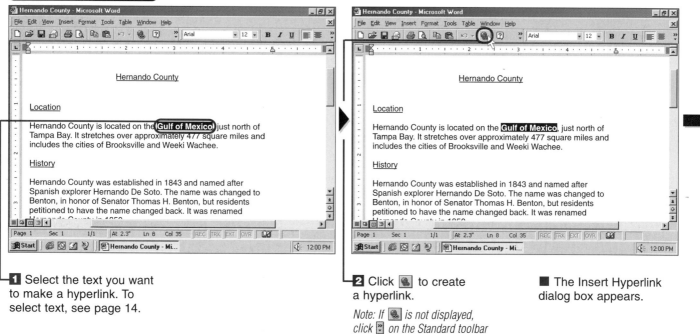

1 Select the text you want to make a hyperlink. To select text, see page 14.

2 Click 🔖 to create a hyperlink.

Note: If 🔖 is not displayed, click 📋 on the Standard toolbar to display all the buttons.

■ The Insert Hyperlink dialog box appears.

Can I make a graphic a hyperlink?

Yes. If your document contains a graphic, such as an AutoShape or clip art image, you can make the graphic a hyperlink. To make a graphic a hyperlink, click the graphic and then perform steps **2** to **7**, starting on page 288.

C:\My Documents\Astrology Report.doc

Hyperlink

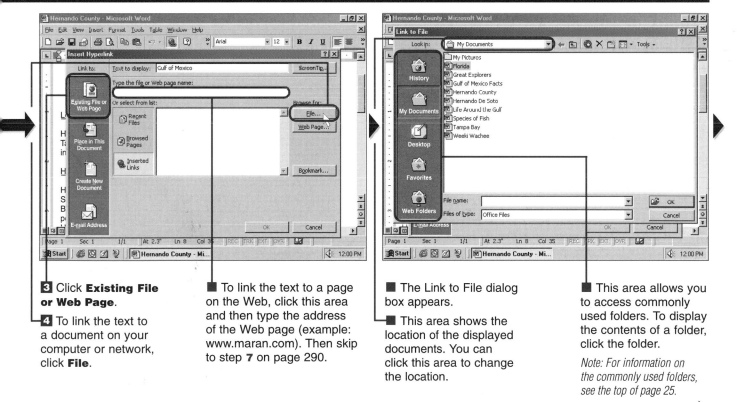

3 Click **Existing File or Web Page**.

4 To link the text to a document on your computer or network, click **File**.

■ To link the text to a page on the Web, click this area and then type the address of the Web page (example: www.maran.com). Then skip to step **7** on page 290.

■ The Link to File dialog box appears.

■ This area shows the location of the displayed documents. You can click this area to change the location.

■ This area allows you to access commonly used folders. To display the contents of a folder, click the folder.

Note: For information on the commonly used folders, see the top of page 25.

CONTINUED

CREATE A HYPERLINK

You can easily identify hyperlinks in your document. Hyperlinks appear underlined and in color.

EARTH WISE ENTERPRISES
We care about the environment.

All products created and marketed by Earth Wise Enterprises are designed to increase awareness of environmental issues around the world.

A list of our main types of products is presented below. To find out more about the products in any category, select the category name.

Tree planting kits

Recycle bins

Compost kits

CREATE A HYPERLINK (CONTINUED)

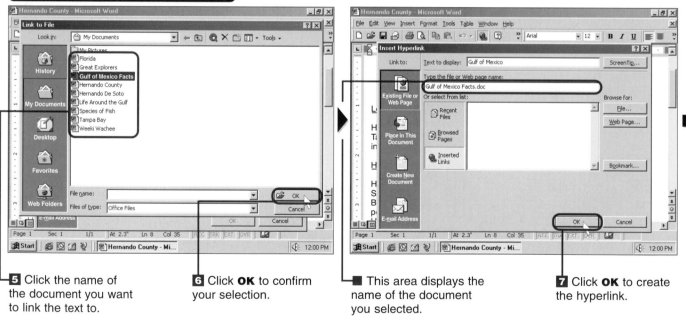

5 Click the name of the document you want to link the text to.

6 Click **OK** to confirm your selection.

■ This area displays the name of the document you selected.

7 Click **OK** to create the hyperlink.

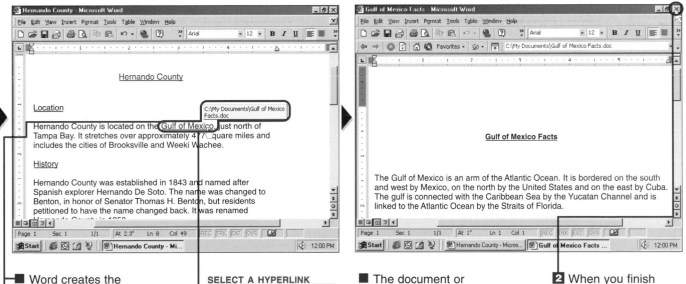

Can Word automatically create a hyperlink for me?

When you type the address of a document located on your network or the Internet, Word will automatically change the address to a hyperlink for you.

www.maran.com

■ Word creates the hyperlink. Hyperlinks appear underlined and in color.

■ When you position the mouse 🖑 over a hyperlink, a yellow box appears, displaying where the hyperlink will take you.

SELECT A HYPERLINK

1 Click a hyperlink to display the document or Web page connected to the hyperlink.

■ The document or Web page connected to the hyperlink appears.

■ If the hyperlink connects to a Web page, your Web browser will open and display the Web page.

2 When you finish reviewing the document or Web page, click ☒ to close the window.

SAVE A DOCUMENT AS A WEB PAGE

You can save a document as a Web page. This lets you place the document on the Internet or your company's intranet.

An intranet is a small version of the Internet within a company or organization.

SAVE A DOCUMENT AS A WEB PAGE

1 Open the document you want to save as a Web page. To open a document, see page 30.

2 Click **File**.

3 Click **Save as Web Page**.

■ The Save As dialog box appears.

4 Type a file name for the Web page.

■ This area shows the location where Word will store the Web page. You can click this area to change the location.

■ This area allows you to access commonly used folders. To display the contents of a folder, click the folder.

Note: For information on the commonly used folders, see the top of page 25.

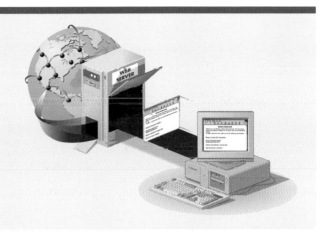

How do I make my Web page available for other people to view?

After you save a document as a Web page, you can transfer the page to a computer that stores Web pages, called a Web server. Once you publish a Web page on a Web server, the page will be available for other people to view. For more information on publishing a Web page, contact your network administrator or Internet service provider.

5 Click **Save** to save the document as a Web page.

■ Word saves the document as a Web page and displays the document in the Web Layout view. This view displays the document as it will appear on the Web.

Note: For more information on the views, see page 44.

INDEX

INDEX

INDEX

INDEX

INDEX

Read Less – Learn More™

Visual

Simply the Easiest Way to Learn

For visual learners who are brand-new to a topic and want to be shown, not told, how to solve a problem in a friendly, approachable way.

All *Simplified*® books feature friendly Disk characters who demonstrate and explain the purpose of each task.

Title	ISBN	U.S. Price
America Online® Simplified®, 2nd Ed.	0-7645-3433-5	$27.99
Computers Simplified®, 5th Ed.	0-7645-3524-2	$27.99
Creating Web Pages with HTML Simplified®, 2nd Ed.	0-7645-6067-0	$27.99
Excel 97 Simplified®	0-7645-6022-0	$27.99
Excel 2002 Simplified®	0-7645-3589-7	$27.99
FrontPage® 2000® Simplified®	0-7645-3450-5	$27.99
FrontPage® 2002® Simplified®	0-7645-3612-5	$27.99
Internet and World Wide Web Simplified®, 3rd Ed.	0-7645-3409-2	$27.99
Microsoft® Access 2000 Simplified®	0-7645-6058-1	$27.99
Microsoft® Excel 2000 Simplified®	0-7645-6053-0	$27.99
Microsoft® Office 2000 Simplified®	0-7645-6052-2	$29.99
Microsoft® Word 2000 Simplified®	0-7645-6054-9	$27.99
Microsoft® Word 2002 Simplified®	0-7645-3588-9	$27.99
More Windows® 95 Simplified®	1-56884-689-4	$27.99
More Windows® 98 Simplified®	0-7645-6037-9	$27.99
Office 97 Simplified®	0-7645-6009-3	$29.99
Office XP Simplified®	0-7645-0850-4	$29.99
PC Upgrade and Repair Simplified®, 2nd Ed.	0-7645-3560-9	$27.99
Windows® 95 Simplified®	1-56884-662-2	$27.99
Windows® 98 Simplified®	0-7645-6030-1	$27.99
Windows® 2000 Professional Simplified®	0-7645-3422-X	$27.99
Windows® Me Millennium Edition Simplified®	0-7645-3494-7	$27.99
Windows® XP Simplified®	0-7645-3618-4	$27.99
Word 97 Simplified®	0-7645-6011-5	$27.99

with these full-color Visual™ guides

The Fast and Easy Way to Learn

Teach Yourself VISUALLY™

Discover how to use what you learn with "Teach Yourself" tips.

Title	ISBN	U.S. Price
Teach Yourself Access 97 VISUALLY™	0-7645-6026-3	$29.99
Teach Yourself FrontPage® 2000 VISUALLY™	0-7645-3451-3	$29.99
Teach Yourself HTML VISUALLY™	0-7645-3423-8	$29.99
Teach Yourself the Internet and World Wide Web VISUALLY™, 2nd Ed.	0-7645-3410-6	$29.99
Teach Yourself Microsoft® Access 2000 VISUALLY™	0-7645-6059-X	$29.99
Teach Yourself Microsoft® Excel 97 VISUALLY™	0-7645-6063-8	$29.99
Teach Yourself Microsoft® Excel 2000 VISUALLY™	0-7645-6056-5	$29.99
Teach Yourself Microsoft® Office 2000 VISUALLY™	0-7645-6051-4	$29.99
Teach Yourself Microsoft® PowerPoint® 97 VISUALLY™	0-7645-6062-X	$29.99
Teach Yourself Microsoft® PowerPoint® 2000 VISUALLY™	0-7645-6060-3	$29.99
Teach Yourself Microsoft® Word 2000 VISUALLY™	0-7645-6055-7	$29.99
Teach Yourself Microsoft® Word 2002 VISUALLY™	0-7645-3587-0	$29.99
Teach Yourself More Windows® 98 VISUALLY™	0-7645-6044-1	$29.99
Teach Yourself Office 97 VISUALLY™	0-7645-6018-2	$29.99
Teach Yourself Red Hat® Linux® VISUALLY™	0-7645-3430-0	$29.99
Teach Yourself VISUALLY™ Computers, 3rd Ed.	0-7645-3525-0	$29.99
Teach Yourself VISUALLY™ Digital Photography	0-7645-3565-X	$29.99
Teach Yourself VISUALLY™ Dreamweaver® 3	0-7645-3470-X	$29.99
Teach Yourself VISUALLY™ Dreamweaver® 4	0-7645-0851-2	$29.99
Teach Yourself VISUALLY™ E-commerce With FrontPage®	0-7645-3579-X	$29.99
Teach Yourself VISUALLY™ Excel 2002	0-7645-3594-3	$29.99
Teach Yourself VISUALLY™ Fireworks® 4	0-7645-3566-8	$29.99
Teach Yourself VISUALLY™ Flash™ 5	0-7645-3540-4	$29.99
Teach Yourself VISUALLY™ FrontPage® 2002	0-7645-3590-0	$29.99
Teach Yourself VISUALLY™ iMac	0-7645-3453-X	$29.99
Teach Yourself VISUALLY™ Investing Online	0-7645-3459-9	$29.99
Teach Yourself VISUALLY™ Networking, 2nd Ed.	0-7645-3534-X	$29.99
Teach Yourself VISUALLY™ Office XP	0-7645-0854-7	$29.99
Teach Yourself VISUALLY™ Photoshop® 6	0-7645-3513-7	$29.99
Teach Yourself VISUALLY™ Quicken® 2001	0-7645-3526-9	$29.99
Teach Yourself VISUALLY™ Windows® 2000 Server	0-7645-3428-9	$29.99
Teach Yourself VISUALLY™ Windows® Me Millennium Edition	0-7645-3495-5	$29.99
Teach Yourself VISUALLY™ Windows® XP	0-7645-3619-2	$29.99
Teach Yourself Windows® 95 VISUALLY™	0-7645-6001-8	$29.99
Teach Yourself Windows® 98 VISUALLY™	0-7645-6025-5	$29.99
Teach Yourself Windows® 2000 Professional VISUALLY™	0-7645-6040-9	$29.99
Teach Yourself Windows NT® 4 VISUALLY™	0-7645-6061-1	$29.99
Teach Yourself Word 97 VISUALLY™	0-7645-6032-8	$29.99

For visual learners who want to guide themselves through the basics of any technology topic. *Teach Yourself VISUALLY* offers more expanded coverage than our best-selling *Simplified* series.

The Visual™ series is available wherever books are sold, or call 1-800-762-2974.

Outside the US, call 317-572-3993.

ORDER FORM

TRADE & INDIVIDUAL ORDERS

Phone: **(800) 762-2974**
or **(317) 572-3993**
(8 a.m. – 6 p.m., CST, weekdays)
FAX : **(800) 550-2747**
or **(317) 572-4002**

EDUCATIONAL ORDERS & DISCOUNTS

Phone: **(800) 434-2086**
(8:30 a.m.–5:00 p.m., CST, weekdays)
FAX : **(317) 572-4005**

CORPORATE ORDERS FOR VISUAL™ SERIES

Phone: **(800) 469-6616**
(8:30 a.m.–5 p.m., EST, weekdays)
FAX : **(905) 890-9434**

Qty	ISBN	Title	Price	Total

Shipping & Handling Charges

	Description	First book	Each add'l. book	Total
Domestic	Normal	$4.50	$1.50	$
	Two Day Air	$8.50	$2.50	$
	Overnight	$18.00	$3.00	$
International	Surface	$8.00	$8.00	$
	Airmail	$16.00	$16.00	$
	DHL Air	$17.00	$17.00	$

Subtotal _____

CA residents add applicable sales tax _____

IN, MA and MD residents add 5% sales tax _____

IL residents add 6.25% sales tax _____

RI residents add 7% sales tax _____

TX residents add 8.25% sales tax _____

Shipping _____

Total _____

Ship to:

Name_____

Address_____

Company_____

City/State/Zip_____

Daytime Phone_____

Payment: ☐ Check to Hungry Minds (US Funds Only)
☐ Visa ☐ Mastercard ☐ American Express

Card # _____ Exp. _____ Signature_____

Hungry Minds™

*maran*Graphics®